A Chinese Firm Goes Global:
The Gree Story

Chen Zonglin, Zhou Xibing

SPM
南方出版传媒
广东经济出版社

Pi Paths International Ltd

Contents

Preface

By Xu Haoran

The glorious title of Championship is always regarded as the highest honor in people's eyes from ancient times to the present.

During the Warring States period in China's ancient history, a great general named Song Yi, was conferred the honorable title of "Champion Qingzi"(Qingzi: Song Yi's courtesy name); subsequently, Huo Qubing , another famous general in the Western Han Dynasty in China, was bestowed the honor of "Champion Marquis" as well, which all meant that they were unrivaled in terms of bravery and fighting skills in their times. That is the origin of the word "Guan Jun (champion)" in China. From the Wei-Jin dynasties to the Southern and Northern Dynasties, the word "Guan Jun" became an official title of Great Generals in China. Now, the meaning of "Guan Jun" has expanded since then and is no longer just the name for the winner in a certain contest; but indicates some individual or organization achieving great success in his or its own field.

Championship is the dream that is worth everyone's expectation.

Our nation has won lots of praise and respect from the whole world with her glorious success after more than 20 years' experience and practice in her carrying out the policy of reform and opening-up.　China, the gaint in the eastern world, as an important resident of the global village, is actively putting herself onto the contest stage of global economy and cultural integration and is becoming one of the major activists as well as the backbone to push forward the vehicle of world economy. The "Made-in-China" products have occupied 6% of the global exports. Those products can be seen everywhere in the global markets: China's output of personal computer ranks No.1 in the world and far surpasses the output of Japan. The mechanical manufacturing output also occupies the first place worldwide and greatly exceeds Germany's production. Moreover, Chinese mainland, beating Taiwan Province, leads the world in the laptop production as well.... According to the prediction of "Organization for Economic Cooperation and Development "(OECD), the share of the "Made-in-China" products in world exports will rise to 10% by the year of 2010. At that time, she will be the world No.1 exporter and well ahead before America and Germany. In the 21st century, our world is entering a new era-- an era of China. The great dream of rejuvenating the Chinese nation is gradually becoming a reality to most Chinese people. The success factors attributing to the victory of Chinese economy are the daring pioneers and champion enterprises leading Chinese economy which are entering or have already entered the global arena.

Being a champion needs continually to rewrite the history.

There is an old saying in China "In the 360 trades, every trade has its master" , but in the post — industrial era and plural co-existence information age, this proverb must be changed into "In the 3600 trades, every trade has its champion." Whether China can crown the title of the world leader in the fierce global competition or not mainly depends on how many Chinese enterprises can outperform others and stand themselves out from the crowd in the future.Nevertheless, much to our relief, having struggled hard in the internationalization process, the King of air conditioners-- Gree, the King of microwave ovens-- Galanz, the King of color TV sets-- TCL and the king of sterilizers—Canbo etc, have all won the honor of world championship. Besides, the standard containers of China International Marine Containers (Group) Co., Ltd. dominate the global market with a 46% market share, BYD battery occupies 72% market share of world mobile phones and Shanghai Zhenhua Heavy Industries Co., Ltd. holds 35% share of global markets…These enterprises are becoming the important impetus for China's going global process. Meanwhile, there are also numerous "unknown champions" around us, who are always wholehearted and single-minded in work but modest in attitude; for example, the top performer in cabinet industry—Oppein, the first-class brand of nail clipper—Stallen, the No.1 manufacturer in piano key sector—TC Group and the world largest stationery manufacturer--Beifa Group, etc. All these Chinese champion enterprises that we should be proud of are just too numerous to count.

Champion is the reference for everyone in his or her work.

The emergence of champion enterprises actually represents the gradual rise of the "Made-in-China" products and the independent innovation of the products "created-by-China". It is said that the profits that those champion enterprises have made are usually three times higher than the average figure of the whole industry. Therefore, every enterprise is dreaming of becoming bigger and stronger in its own industry. But how those champion enterprises have been built and shaped? What are the opportunities and challenges they once had and met in their growth and development? What are the temptations and puzzles they once encountered when they become the champion enterprises? What can we learn from them? Hermann Simon, the famous management expert tells us that the success of champion enterprises lies in that "they go their own way" and the characteristics of their values are "sustained attention and continuous innovation" in their work. Their idea of being bigger and stronger is based on the precondition of being fully concentrating on what they are doing and engaging. They always tend to attach great importance to the market position of their enterprise and they are eager to become the policymakers and initiators of the market regulations and innovations ---"to be the spiritual leader of the markets"…It is true that one company's success cannot be copied by other firms in the context of a changeable market environment; however, the development path, inspiration, and revenues model of a company are not only its own treasure, but also the epitome of China's social economic development as well. To the thousands and hundreds of growing Chinese enterprises, the champion enterprises have the commercial model effect as well as the significance in social, historical, and cultural development.

Champion is the role example for every one of us who wants to be successful.

Enjoying the reputation of devoting itself in small projects of book publishing and communication, Beijing Nutalent Media has joined hands with China International Publishing Group and Guangdong Economic Publishing House as well as Peking University Press in taking the lead in the planning and releasing of the *Book Series on Marketing Cases of China's Top Enterprises*, which is a truly insightful move in the current book markets. As the editor-in-chief of the book series, I sincerely hope that our prudent and efficient work team can act in the spirit of "be responsible for the top enterprises and readers" in their work for the book series. Through the selection, investigation and analysis of thousands of top enterprises in our country and conducting a "systematic, scientific, theoretical and classic" study on the successful cases of those enterprises, we try our best to make the books easy and enjoyable to read in the light of the principles of "perceptiveness, effectiveness and readability". At the same time, we are also cooperating with those top enterprises or consulting agencies concerned to launch series of public lectures at a nationwide level and try to make the industrial value chain longer and maximize the values for enterprises, readers and ourselves.

To be a champion, is a great challenge for every pursuer in the world of competition.

By reviewing the list of "World Top 500 Corporations" by *Fortune* magazine, it is not difficult for us to find that in the time of 80's of the 20th century, about 230 enterprises disappeared from the list, and among the top 100 corporations in the 19th century , only 16 survived finally by the end of the 20th century. All the facts show us the truth: Perhaps it is not so hard to be the champion for a short period of time, but it is very difficult to be the champion forever. It is also the same with us that it is not very hard for us to release one good book at a time but it is a very tough task for us to ensure all the books released every time are good or excellent ones. However, we have every reason to believe that there will be more world champion enterprises coming out in China and we also have the reason to expect this *Book Series on Marketing Cases of China's Top Enterprises* will stand out to be a wonderful flower which will remain fresh and will never be fading in the sea of books. Hope it will be the nourishment for the readers' mind and the best vehicle for the promotion of the enterprises' corporate image. Let's applaud for those top enterprises, be proud of the struggling champions and give our best wishes to the rising of China.

(Xu Haoran: the editor-in-chief of *Book Series on Marketing Cases of China's Top Enterprises*, professor of Nanjing University of Aeronautics & Astronautics, senior editor of Jiangsu Broadcasting Cooperation, author of the books *Cultural Industry Management* and *Outstanding: Your Personal Brand*, etc.)

Foreword

By Yang Shulan

Gree's Two Bright Pearls: "Zhu" (Mr. Zhu Jianghong) and "Zhu" (Ms. Dong Mingzhu)--The Perfect Work Team in China's Business World

Speaking of the work team type of a gentleman and a lady in the political circle, the US president George W. Bush and the Secretary of State Condoleezza Rice will come into the picture. However, the type of work team "a gentleman and a lady" is often to be seen in the political circle, and now it seems to become quite common in China's business arena. From Zhang Ruiming and Yang Mianmian in Haier to Li Jinyuan and Bai Ping in Tiens Group, from Li Zhihao and Zhang Ping in Chigo to Zhu Jianghong and Dong Mingzhu in Gree Electric Appliances, they are all living illustrations of this type of work team. As China is not a country teeming with entrepreneurs, not to speak of women entrepreneurs, the work teams of the entrepreneurs are the rare of rarities, so the work teams of "a gentleman and a lady" are even much rarer. When the teams are winning one business triumph after another, their stories are gradually becoming the marvelous much-told tales in the business circle.

We Chinese often explain the scientificity of male and female employees working together with the idiomatic phase "It will make the work easier when a man and a woman are working together". This idea may sound very "tacky" today from the angle of biology and social psychology, but from the perspective of organizational behaviors and business management, there are some deep-seated reasons behind this phenomenon. That is to say, women's instinct and delicateness rightly provide a supplement for men's roughness and boldness. In regard to the differences in the thinking pattern, men tend to offer trains of thoughts, but women tend to control the workflow. Men tend to formulate macro strategies of maneuvers, while women tend to have micro strategies of meticulousness. Moreover, the awfulness of male supervisors can be eased and balanced by female's softness and kindness. The combination of men's firmness and persistence with women subordinates' peacefulness and gentleness can produce the effect of alternating kindness with severity in their work.

Nevertheless, not all the "a-lady-and-a-gentleman" work teams can be successful at every time. The success of "a-lady-and-a-gentleman" work teams is determined by many factors and their luck to meet each other at the right moment, which is merely by chance but not diligence in the work. The team of Zhu Jianghong and Dong Mingzhu in Gree Electric

Appliances Corporation offers us a conspicuous example. Miss. Dong Mingzhu is considered as an ironhanded person in Gree, but, on the contrary, Mr. Zhu Jianghong is calm and always tends to keep everything low profile. It is amazing that the team of the two different personalities become the golden partners in China's business world.

Miss. Dong Mingzhu has become the one in today's list of "The Top 50 Women in World Business" who once was an obscure saleswoman and Mr. Zhu Jianghong's small air-conditioner factory—Hai Li now has become the largest and professional air-conditioning company in China with the integration of research and development center, marketing department and customer-service department. The perfect work team's over ten years' efforts have ensured the brilliant achievement of Gree Electric Appliances Corporation today. So who is the lucky person of the two? Miss. Dong Mingzhu or Mr. Zhu Jianghong? Who helps the other to accomplish his/her success? It is said that some people in the industry of electrical appliances have already drawn this conclusion with admiration and mixed-feelings about them, that Mr. Zhu Jianghong was blessed when he met Miss. Dong Mingzhu and Miss. Dong Mingzhu was lucky to meet Mr. Zhu Jianghong. In Miss. Dong Mingzhu's own words: I think I have helped Mr. Zhu to accomplish his success; Mr. Zhu also has helped me to achieve that of mine at the same time. Both of us are working together to make Gree's brilliance.

Besides the reasons mentioned above, there are several other elements attributing to the success and steadiness of the"Zhu-Zhu"team.

The first element is that the two persons share similar personality and moral integrity.

People who are acquainted with Mr. Zhu Jianghong and Miss. Dong Mingzhu all know that the two have nothing in common in their characteristics: Mr. Zhu Jianghong is gentle and honest. He likes to be single-minded in making researches and is interested in the acquisition of air-conditioning intellectual property rights, but Miss. Dong Mingzhu who is forceful and vigorous loves playing game theory in the fierce market competition. Yet to people's surprise, the two always share tacit agreements on many things and no huge divergences have ever appeared between them in making the key guiding principles and policies inside the company.

It is reported that: the head of Gree Electric Appliances, Mr. Zhu Jianghong, always gives the President Miss. Dong Mingzhu his most unswerving support! From "asking for the financial help" when she started taking the office as the director of the Operation Department to the radical overhaul of the Operation Department, from creating the unique sales company model when she was the vice president of the Sales Department to the "cutting distributors" in Hunan and Anhui provinces,etc, as well as from the estrangement between Gree Electric Appliances and the King of electrical appliance retailers--GOME and the event of the Father-and-Son's fight between Gree Electric Appliances Corporation and

Gree Group, in the past dozens of years in Gree's history, behind every big move of Dong Mingzhu, there was always Zhu Jianghong's quiet and silent support. In the same way, if Zhu Jianghong was in trouble, he always had Dong's loyal and firm support.

Zhu Jianghong's magnanimity and generosity contrasting with Dong Mingzhu's simpleness and powerfulness, the big differences between the two people don't affect their trust in each other because they both share similar personality and moral integrity. According to Dong Mingzhu herself, she believes that they all hold fast to the idea of "company's interest comes first" so that they can always enjoy a tacit cooperation in the business affairs of the company. Dong Mingzhu clearly knows what to hate and what to love and when she makes a decision, she always takes action regardless of other people's personal feelings. Everything she did was for the good of her company and she never did anything for her own good and her own interests. She never trades the company's interest with others to conclude a deal during her game-playing with other dealers. It is because of her unswerving principle of "company's interest comes first" that when Dong Mingzhu was making the radical overhaul of the Sales Department, even she damaged the interests of Zhu's relatives, Zhu Jianghong never felt offended like other bosses. As a matter of fact, both Zhu Jianghong and Dong Mingzhu are practical, honest persons and always ready to take the responsibility. When it comes to the issue of choosing the right managerial personnel, Zhu Jianghong has a very clear requirement about it, that is, never to abuse power for his/her personal gains. Otherwise, he/she will be punished or fired for this reason. Many companies cannot do this, but in this respect, Dong Mingzhu and Zhu Jianghong always agree on it without any prior consultation. "If a person pays too much attention to his or her own interests, even a very loyal employee will come to no good end " said Dong Mingzhu, so, if there is any selfish motive existing in either of them, there will never be the harmony between the male boss and the female general manager.

Gree Electric Appliances is a genuine state-owned enterprise, but it has escaped the fate of many SOEs---- the management' corruption and erosion of state assets inside the company. In the past years, Gree Electric Appliances has experienced many troubles and undergone numerous frustrations, including, the father-and-son's style fight with Gree Group. Fortunately, every time, Gree could always overcome difficulties like a small boat passing through angry waves. In Dong Mingzhu's opinion, both Zhu Jianghong and she are all clean and they both are the committed guardians for the state-owned assets.

The similarity and complementarity in their moral integrity are the sound and profound basis for the Zhu-Zhu team. Both of the two want to make air-conditioners of high quality and try to break the vicious circle prevailing in the Chinese air conditioner market of "low price--to lower price for competition--trade frictions--export restriction--shortage of funds--product structure improvement constrained". Both of them are eager to make efforts for Gree's own core technology and market shares. The two are also complementary to each other in many ways: Zhu Jianghong is interested in technology researches and does not like getting too much publicity. Whereas Dong Mingzhu is known for her resoluteness and promptness in marketing in the industry; Zhu is busy with how to make better air-conditioners every day, but Dong Mingzhu has her own ways of selling all the air-conditioners of every design and type.

Some people said Dong Mingzhu and Zhu Jianghong are quite agreeable with each other, just like a talent meeting a good judge. The tacit cooperation between the two is beyond everyone's imagination. Perhaps it is not exaggerating to say that the cooperation between the two is just like they are singing the same tune every time. Zhu Jianghong trusts in Dong Mingzhu just like he trusts in himself, and vice versa. The high consistency in their ideas forms a wonderful work team, which is quite rare in the business world in China at present.

Furthermore, "the harmony between the male boss and the female general manager" would not have existed if there had been no tolerance and appreciation from the male boss.

When Dong Mingzhu was an ordinary salesperson, Zhu Jianghong had this insight to indentify her as a talent regardless of other people's objection. He has promoted her to the position of leadership and gave her important tasks gradually. Although Zhu Jianghong is supporting Dong Mingzhu all the way to make her a tough business woman from an obscure and common worker, he never boasts himself as a good talent hunter in front of Dong Mingzhu.

Some people in the industry criticized Dong Mingzhu for being a person who is very hard to deal with. Or they even have the comments of "Where sister Dong walks, no grass grows". (by one of Dong's competitors and widely quoted in Chinese media). On hearing those comments, Zhu Jianghong always answers with kindness and tolerance, "She is a good person actually and she just has a very sharp tongue". Because of the boss's magnanimity and trust, the female employee can do whatever she wants and is ready to face the consequences no matter how they turn out. Moreover, in a general sense, female subordinates tend to be touched and moved by everything done by the boss for them and they will bear the boss's every bit of care and appreciation deeply in their mind. For instance, Dong Mingzhu has often talked about the story of "Mr. Zhu's saving parking place for her". The other day, she and Mr. Zhu invited several distributors for dinner in a restaurant called "Shi Si Yan" in the city of Zhuhai. As there were so many diners in this restaurant, it was very difficult to find a parking place outside this restaurant. That day, Mr. Zhu Jianghong and other distributors arrived early, and he happened to find a parking place. Then, Mr. Zhu told his driver: "Save this parking place for Miss. Dong." He was afraid that other people would occupy this parking place, so he got out of the car to wait for Miss. Dong's arrival in the parking place. Afterwards, those distributors who came along with Mr. Zhu told Dong Mingzhu that Mr. Zhu had saved this parking place for her. Henceforth, Dong Mingzhu never forgets this small story and always feels grateful to Zhu Jianghong.

It may not be hard for a boss to provide his employees a stage to display their talents and abilities to the fullest extent, but it is so difficult for a boss to be generous and magnanimous to tolerate his subordinate's reputation and influence above him. Speaking of Gree Electric Appliances, Dong Mingzhu is always the first person to come into people's mind but not Zhu Jianghong who is always behind the scene. Take Dong Mingzhu's book publishing for example, from her first book *Check around the World* to the second one *Check without Regret*, instead of assuming that his subordinate overwhelming his authority and becoming jealous, Zhu Jianghong gave his sincere advice and full support to her in the book release.

Declining rewards for merits but taking the responsibilities, Zhu Jianghong makes himself and his enterprise blessed with his broad-mindedness and vision to have this "bright pearl" ---Dong Mingzhu.

October, 2007 in Guangzhou

(Yang Shulan: the Media Director of Eninfo Media, observer and researcher of Gree Electric Appliances, enterprise risk management expert and planner of Miss. Dong Mingzhu's first book *Check around the World*)

Introduction

Gree Electric Appliances, Inc. of Zhuhai (Gree Electric Appliances) is the world's largest specialized air conditioner company integrating R&D, manufacture, sales and customer service. Since the foundation of Gree Electric Appliances, it always has focused on the core development strategy of "specialization" and has grown in strength with the idea of "innovation". Winning the market and repaying the society with the business concept of "honest and practicality", Gree Electric Appliances keeps its steady and healthy development in the rather fierce competition and has yielded remarkable social and economic benefits.

In the year of 1991, Hai Li, a small air-conditioner factory merged with Guan Xiong Plastic Factory in Zhuhai, Guangdong province. In the year of 1992, the two merged factories were officially changed into the name of "Gree". In the development process of from a small company to a big company, the most praiseworthy factor is Gree's strong and powerful marketing channels. At the very beginning of its foundation, because of its weakness in competition, Gree Electric Appliances adopted the strategy of "capture the markets in cities by occupying the markets in rural areas first". The decision-makers in Gree focus their energy on developing those areas, like Anhui, Zhejiang, Jiangxi, Hunan, Guangxi, Hebei and Henan province, where those famous air conditioner brands like "Chun Lan" and "Hua Bao" have little influence in them. There Gree has built the image of its brand to consolidate its market share. During the implementation of the marketing strategy, the marketing channels for Gree are mostly special shops, in which Gree tries its best to ensure customers' interests via excellent after-sale services. From 1992 to 1994, the business of Gree rapidly expanded. In 1994, the production and sales volume of Gree air conditioners beat out other air conditioner brands to be No.2 in China.   In 1996, there was a huge war breaking out in air conditioning industry. The four top Gree sales distributors in Hubei province lowered their prices in order to seize more market share; under this circumstance, the market price system of Gree was flung into confusion. Subsequently, under the leadership of Gree head office, the four top sales distributors came together to set up "Hebei Xinxing Gree Electric Appliances Sales Limited Company" with the capital investment as the bond. Having founded this company, the four dealers integrated their dispersed markets and service networks, set a flat price for all the buyers and only sold air conditioners for Gree. That is the model of "positive sum game" advocated by Gree Electric Appliances, which is the mutual cooperation between manufacturers and sales dealers to expand the market share and makes the both sides reach a "win-win" situation. So in this way, after more than 10 years' successful operation, regional sales companies now are playing a significant and important role in regulating and stabilizing the market competition, protecting the interests of distributors and customers and safeguarding the health development of this industry. So far, Gree Electric Appliances has been promoting this original marketing model in over 30 provinces and cities in China and it has already become one of the important factors attributing to the Gree's leading position in the air-conditioner market.

Meanwhile, Gree also attaches great importance to its brand building stragety. As the spreading of the good reputation "good air-conditioners, Gree made", the brand of Gree air conditioner has laid the solid foundations for its pioneering position in China's air-conditioner market. Now, Gree Electric Appliances enjoys a great reputation within the industry. And it has repeatedly won the honors of "Famous Chinese Trademark", "Chinese Famous Brand Products", "State Inspection Exemption Product", the General Administration of Customs' "Red List of Import and Export Enterprises", BID's "WQC International Gold Star" and "Outstanding Achievements and Business Reputation of the Highest International Quality Award Well-known Honor". In October 2005, Gree Electric Appliances was also awarded the 2005 China's "Contribution to Energy-saving Prize" title and Gree Electric Appliances is the only company which received the top award in air-conditioning enterprises in Guangdong Province. In July, 2007, Gree was awarded the hononrary title "Symbolized Brand in Chinese Industry" by China Brand Research Institute. Then in September, Gree Electric Appliances was awarded "China's World Top Brand" by General Administration of Quality Supervision, Inspection and Quarantine; in November, Gree was honored with the title of "National Quality Award", which is the blue ribbon in China's quality field. Still in the same month, Gree became the holder of "Certificate for the Exemption from Export Inspection" granted by General Administration of Quality Supervision， Inspection and Quarantine of the People's Republic of China(AQSIQ) and Gree was the first enterprise to be the holder of this certificate in China air-conditioning industry.

In the stock market with various changeable situations, Gree's performance is still quite marvelous equally. It has been voted as "One of the Top 50 Chinese Listed Companies with the Greatest Development Potential" for 6 consecutive years and it is one of the blue chips of old brands as well. In September 2003, the famous global investment bank---Credit Suisse First Boston began to make an analysis on more than 1200 listed companies in China. Among them, Gree Electric Appliances was named "China's Most Investment Value of 12 Listed Companies".   It is also the only selected company in household electrical appliances industry, known as "the best listed company in Chinese household electrical appliance." In 2001-2006, Gree Electric Appliances was placed in the list of "100 Top Chinese Corporations" by *Forbes* China.

While actively advocates the strategy of fostering proprietary brand in the international markets, Gree Electric Appliances also tries hard in introducing China's brilliant culture to the world through the promotion of the Gree band. Presently, Gree has established sales and service networks in more than 100 countries and regions and is going to achieve greater market penetration in UK, France, Brazil, Russia, Australia, Philippine, Saudi Arabia and India, etc, over 70 countries and regions. Since the air-conditioners of Gree brand entered into the local markets of many countries and regions in 1998, in less than three years, in terms of market share, Gree has occupy the second place in air-conditioning industry. In 2001, Gree made huge investment and set up factories in Brazil, which created a precedent in the technological export of air conditioning enterprises in China. With many years' development, Gree's energy-saving technologies had received the most honorable commendations from Brazil government for two consecutive years. They are: "A-class Energy Label Certificate" and "Energy Star" trophy. In 2004, Gree's Brazil factories made a profit of RMB 25 million, which made Gree a role model of going global in China's enterprises... According to the Customs' statistics, the total exports and the export growth of Gree Electric Appliances are the highest among all its peers.

Innovation is the fundamental driving force for enhancing enterprises' competitiveness. Every year, Gree Electric Appliances will take more than 3% of its whole sales revenues to put into its technology research and development. This practice makes Gree the only company which puts the most money into air conditioning technology research. From the "king of air conditioners" with best price/performance ratio to the "king of cooling" with the great reputation of "cooler, quieter, more power-efficient", from unique "residential cabinet air conditioner" to the best product of "Digital 2000", Gree people are making arduous efforts with technique innovations to create the myth of the "air-conditioning king". Because the achievements that Gree has made, the vice chairman and president of Gree Electric Appliances, Dong Mingzhu was awarded "Top 10 Independent Innovation Figures of 2006". With great success in technology, marketing, services and administration, Gree is relating us affectionately a story of an enterprise shouldering the historical responsibility with a spirit of progress. The following is about the fruitful achievements that Gree Electric Appliances has made in its growth and development:

The first is its technology innovation.

So far, there are more than 20 categories, 400 series, 7000 varieties and specifications of air conditioning products in Gree Electric Appliances. Among them, 9 series and 1000 varieties for commercial use and 944 of them have applied foreign and domestic patents. Gree's research in developing multi-split air conditioning units and centrifugal in central air-conditioning system takes the lead in ultra-low temperature and heat pump in central air-conditioning units, which is the precedent in China, and broke the technological monopoly of US and Japanese air-conditioning giants to win the great reputation and influence in international refrigeration industry.

The second is the innovations in marketing.

In 1997, Gree has created the company model of regional sales company with capital investment as the bond, the brand as the banner and "three represents (represents the interests of manufactures, represents the interests of distributors and represents the interests of customers)" as the core policy. This company model has established Gree brand's leading position and it also has been hailed as "The brand-new innovation in Economy Field in the 21st century" by the economic and theory circles. The Gree model effectively promotes the healthy sustainable development of the air conditioning industry in China.

The third is the innovations in services.

On January 1st, 2005, Gree Electric Appliances was the first company to introduce the customer service policy of "6-year free warranty for a complete air conditioner unit", which completely eliminated the costumers' worries and helped to root out those illegal air conditioning maintenance factories in China. Gree's fulfilling its commitment gurantteed and protected the consumers' interests and make the air- conditioning industry stay away from those cutthroat and vicious competitions, such as "price war', so the all industry can enter into a new development phase.

The fourth is its innovations in management.

Gree Electric Appliances has set up a type of unique factory only for selecting and sifting air conditioning spare parts, in which there are more than 300 employees giving a full test on all the air-conditioning spare parts bought from other suppliers. This work does not produce any profits, but the cumbersome work ensures that every single spare part in Gree air-conditioner can stand the test of time.

The *Bible* tells us, "Enter through the narrow gate; for the gate is wide and the road is easy that leads to destruction, and there many to take it. For the gate is narrow and the road is hard that leads to life, and there are few who find it." Facing the choice of roads leading to the narrow gate and the wide gate, many people tend to choose the "wide gate", for they think the road to the wide gate easy and comfortable, even it leads to destruction. Only few people will choose the tough and bumpy road to enter the narrow gate and get into the heaven. In the face of the hard choice, Gree Electric Appliances has chosen a special way which looks easy on surface; in fact, it is quite bumpy and rough—to do the things that an enterprise with history of 100 years should do. Now, Gree is trying to bring their products into every corner of the world by fully and completely implementing the "quality strategy" and the strategy of "build the first class enterprise, make first class products and create the top class brand".

Chapter 1: Marketing Strategy Makes Gree a Winner

1. The Supremacy of Marketing Channels

It is Gree's marketing channels that facilitate Gree Electric Appliances from a small company to a large company and from a weak manufacturer to a strong manufacturer. Although the cost of raw materials for air conditioning industry is rising and soaring day by day and the process of industry reshuffling is speeding up greatly, Gree Electric Appliances still holds its leading position in this industry and its sales volume, sales revenues, profits and market share are still enjoying a sustabale growth. The production, sales and market occupancy of Gree air conditioners solidly rank the first place in the whole industry. From January to September in 2004, the accumulated sales income of Gree Electric Appliances was more than RMB 10.058 billion,rising 33.32% year-on-year and realized a net profit of RMB352 million, rising 18.02% year-on-year with all indices far surpassing the level of the year 2003. In the year 2005, Gree's sales volume hit RMB 18.2 billion and the sales revenues of residential air conditioners accumulated to a total number of 10 million sets, which leaped to the first place in the world. Continually from January to September in 2006, the accumulated sales income of Gree Electric Appliances amounted to over RMB18.1billion, equaling the level of last year and up 39.59% over the same period of last year. In the same year, Gree realized a net profit of RMB 497million, up 18.33% over the same period of last year. By the end of 2006, Gree's sales revenues exceeded RMB 23 billion. The reason for Gree's glorious achievements is its unique business layout and its powerful control of air-conditioning distribution channels, which become the key factor to Gree's success and makes Gree Electric Appliances crown the title of "individual championship" in the air conditioning industry.

1) The One Dominating the Distribution Channels Has The Biggest Market Share

At present, Gree's sales network spreads through over 100 countries and regions with more than 40 million users around the globe. And the Gree products of its proprietary brand have been sold in over 60 countries and regions and entered the major sales channels in many countries and regions. Growing from a small enterprise with the annual output of just 20,000 air conditioning units into a world famous enterprise with the production capacity of over 15 million units per year, in the past ten years, Gree Electric Appliances is getting closer and cloaser to its dream step by step with its vigorous strides and down-to-earth attitude.

If we consider that Mr. Zhu Jianghong (the chairman, corporate representative, President and Secretary of the Party Committee of Gree Electric Appliances) is a very important person in Gree Electric Appliances' development and brilliant achievements in the past ten years, we can say that Ms. Dong Mingzhu (the vice chairman and general manager of Gree Electric Appliances) is the key figure to the evolving process of sales model of Gree Electric Appliances. At the end of 1994, Dong Mingzhu, the director of Operation Department in Gree at that time, carried out drastic reforms inside the poorly managed Gree Electric Appliances and improved the sales management system. Before Dong's reform, there is no money in Gree's accounts receivable in 1995 and after that she created the miracle and all loans were recovered, which was unprecedented in China's air conditioning industry. Subsequently, the sale volume of Gree rose to RMB 2.8 billion in 1995 from RMB 450 million in 1994. In 1996, the sale revenues of Gree were increased by leaps and bounds from RMB3.2 billion , RMB 4.2 billion, RMB 5.5 billion, RMB 6 billion , and RMB7 billion to approximately RMB 23 billion in 2006. Those great achievements have made Gree occupy the first place in the following indexes of sale volume, market share and income tax in China air conditioning industry since 1997.

It is quite obvious to see that Dong Mingzhu has plenty of practical experience and advanced ideas in air conditioning marketing. Since 1994, Gree Electric Appliances launched the promotion policy of "off-season rebate" and "year-end rebate" to adapt itself to the development and changes of the air conditioning market and also laid a sound foundation for Gree's pioneering position in China's air conditioning industry by establishing the strategic cooperation with distributors in the form of integration of manufacturers and dealers.

At the end of 90's in the 20th century, especially in 1996—1997, there was a dramatic slump in global economy and domestic consumption demand. Many air conditioning enterprises showed deficits in their annual reports and many air conditioner distributors lost lots of money in the markets. Under this circumstance, the president of Gree Electric Appliances, Dong Mingzhu took the initiatives to make the reform of the tradition marketing pattern and to create a new model of channel distribution. At the end of 1997, in the area of Hubei province, Gree Electric Appliances and its distributors firstly set up a joint-stock sales company for the purpose of regulating and stabilizing the local marketing management and the pricing system. As a result, the distribution channels and service networks in that area were unified so that this sales company became Gree's governing body of the local markets, which protected the reasonable profits of distributors and made it easy for distributors to serve for consumers. This type of regional professional sales company model was formed by

Gree Electric Appliances and some big distributors in some areas (usually on a provincial level, e.g. the areas including: Zhuhai, Shenzhen, Guangzhou, Shantou/Yuedong, Zhanjiang/Yuexi, Shaoguan/Yuebei, etc). With the company share controlled by Gree Electric Appliances, the capital investment as the bond and the brand-building strategy as the guide line, this sales company works as an independent dealer responsible for the whole region's selling of Gree products. It turned out that this pattern effectively resolved the chaos existed in pricing and cross region sales—a difficult problem confronted by all air conditioning manufacturers at that time. This unique business model not only effectively helps Gree Electric Appliances have an ideal price matching for its brand image of high product quality. On top of that, this business model satisfactorily brings a profitable return to all the distributors.

The regional sales company model is the exclusive market model created by Gree Electric Appliances. It is exclusive because that Gree Electric Appliances has gathered all the biggest wholesalers in the provinces of the targeted local markets and made other air conditioning brands find it difficult to compete with Gree even though they are cooperating with other sales companies to grab the marketshare. After years' adjustment and development in marketing model and business operations, Gree Electric Appliances eventually has achieved a huge growth rate. Following 1998, there was a big increase of 40% in Gree's sales volume, the secondary dealers also made quite a lot of money and the market for Gree air conditioners came to be more complete and standardized.

When talking about the channel distribution, Mr. Zhu Jianghong, the chairman of Gree Electric Appliances emphasized that Gree's management conception is based on the idear of considering the distributors as the main factor. According to him, there are three major factors in the markets: manufacturer, distributor and costumer. Which one should come first in the manufacturer's priority order? Actually, different manufacturers have different ideas about it. In the air conditioning industry, some manufacturers regard the factor of consumer to be their first priority. They made every decision according to the consumers' requirements, which is not a too bad idea, for the consumers have the money in their pocket. But in China's air conditioning industry, it is probably better to put the factor of distributor in the first place, for it is more accordant with the situation and condition of our country. The reason is that currently consumers in China are easily influenced by the dealers and retailers in the markets; the immaturity of people's consumption psychology leads consumers to be confused about choosing the right products in the markets. When consumers are buying a product in a shopping mall, it is the distributors who are demonstrating the products to the consumers and it is also the distributors who are always trying to convince consumers to buy the products and the consumers are likely under the heel of distributors but not the one who made the products. Apparently, the distributor is like the bridge between manufacturers and consumers; if there is no distributor in the markets, the manufacturers cannot communicate effectively with consumers.

The industry experts' analysis shows that the idea of placing the distributor in the dominant place has penetrated in the whole process of Gree's business operation. In the early stage of its development, Gree Electric Appliances has gained an advantage in the marketplace with its regional marketing strategy and this advantage could not have been obtained without the loyalty to this brand and efforts from those distributors. Those big dealers, even now, are still the important factor for Gree's domination in the marketplace, especially for those large quantity orders from the group purchase. Over the past few years, Gree Electric Appliances' steady growth with only one type of products—air conditioner in its achievement could not have been made without the implementation of this business model. The benefits that this innovation of the manufacturer-distributor relationship brings are the following:

Firstly, the win-win co-operation between manufacturers and distributors is favorable to Gree Electric Appliances to acquire a bigger share of the market. The large air-con maker, Gree, is the pioneer in the domestic air conditioning industry and its production ranks No.5 in global air conditioning manufacturers. Its quality, product design and brand positioning are not inferior to old air conditioning brands in this industry. For Gree, choosing to cooperate with the strong and influential local distributors is certainly to make Gree enhance its competitive advantages in the local market place.

The second point is to effectively control the delivery channel. Having only one company in the local market responsible for the delivery channel, the sales company model helps Gree Electric Appliances to avoid the confusion posed by the multi-supplier system and maintains the healthy development of the local markets.

Thirdly, binding the interests of manufactures together in the form of stock ownership saves Gree from the game-playing between manufactures and dealers, meanwhile the sales company model keeps Gree away from the conflicts between distributors of equal strength, so the appropriate profits of the products can be assured.

The fourth is underlining the advantage of network sharing. At an earlier time, each distributor had had his/her own sales network and after they were in alliance with each other, all the scattered network resources could be pooled together to grab a bigger piece of the pie in the markets.

Fifthly, in order to save the distributors a lot of money and guarantee their commodity supply and pricing, Gree Electric Appliances adopted the policy of the "year-end rebate" to ensure the dealers' profits and reduce their business risks. The "year-end rebate" policy started in 1996, in that year there was fierce competition in the air conditioner market and those distributors tried to lower the price in various ways, but they still suffered a great loss in their business operation, which was the same for the distributors of Gree air conditioner at that time. However, after making researches on the markets, the decision-makers in Gree decided to take RMB 100 million from the coporate profits and offered all the dealers a rebate as a reward. In recent years, about RMB 50 million—100 million withdrawn from the profits has been used as the rebate for the distributors of Gree. The rebate policy has been gained great support from distributors; with the rebate policy they will not be having any risks in selling Gree products just like staying in a safe. As a result of the implemation of this policy, the dealers will put more efforts in promoting Gree products.

After decades of successful operations, the regional marketing model has been proved to be the best model dealing with the current situation that the industry competition is heating up and the price war is getting serious in China's air conditioning market. This unique and original new market model is an important factor contributing to Gree's leading position in China's air conditioning industry and has been hailed as "the brand-new marketing model in the 21st economic field" by the personages of all circles.

2) Channel Marketing is Distributor Marketing

On the heels of the global economic integration's deepening, enterprises' marketing has entered the era of "he who has the channel will be the king in the market". Some industry experts suggest that the local enterprises only have smooth marketing channels so that they can send their products to the consumers without any trouble. But in reality, the manufacturers have not enough energy in serving consumers directly, their marketing is just channel marketing and they only can serve the channels. Thus, the distributors are vital to the marketing and profit making of the product makers. To China's home appliance industry which took the open policy first and had the highest level of market orientation, after about twenty years' rapid development, it has already occupied an important position in global markets. In the meantime, in the context of the brutal market competition, the home appliance manufacturing industry is undergoing a series of reform and development in channel model. Especially in the air conditioning industry, the marketing of air conditioning products has its own characteristics. All the enterprises regard those big distributors very important and commonly adopt the measures of "year-end rebate". So it is the same with Gree Electric Appliances. Gree also adopts this practice but more than that, leaders in Gree place great importance on the principle of good faith when dealing with distributors and try to form a stable and long-term relationship with the distributors in many ways.

Having successfully overcome the downsides such as the rise of the price of raw materials and the bad weather, etc, in the refrigeration year, besides the high quality of its air-conditioners and the value of its brand, Gree Electric Appliances tried very hard in building its own marketing channel model and finally made it recognized by all the peers home and abroad. After about ten years' test in the market competition, with the unique marketing model, Gree has laid a firm and solid foundation for its overlord position in the markets of the 21st century. Although many air-conditioning enterprises still suffered great loss and had to be merged or went bankrupt at that time, in spite of so many adversities, Gree Electric Appliances still made profits and the profit making stability was comparatively high.

Some experts point out that channel marketing is distributor marketing. The relationship between Gree and the distributors is the critical factor in Gree marketing model. The so called "represents the distributors' interests", is to carry this policy out actively, not passively to safeguard the relationship between Gree and the distributors. So, Gree Electric Appliances has formed very strong cohesion with the distributors. "As to our attitude towards the distributors big or small, we all treat them equally with the same policy and sincerely cooperate with them on the principle of mutual benefits." Dong Mingzhu made the above comments when she was introducing Gree's marketing model. What's more, Gree also lays considerable emphasis on 'honesty' when dealing with its distributors. It never cheats its dealers and always keeps its promises, sometimes even brings surprises to the distributors.

Therefore, both of the two sides have formed a virtuous circle by the way that Gree greatly safeguards the interests of distributors and in turn, the distributors will promote Gree's products loyally. Just as the representative remarks made by Gao Dejun, the general manager of Sichuan Neijing Zhuoyue Electric: "The most attractive and appealing part for Gree Electric Appliances is that people in Gree never make a promise that they can't keep. The various policies of selling, rebate and rewards will immediately take effect as soon as the Gree's salespersons give the oral notice.

The first is honesty, the second is emotional attachment and the third is equality. The three are the very important keywords for Gree's winning the universal respect in channel marketing. In this way, it takes the initiative and leading position in the competition. From the year of 1995, Gree has got zero in Accounts Receivable and has not owed any money to any banks and distributors, which reflect the huge market value of Gree Electric Appliances. To an enterprise which has the ambition to be the world famous brand, this market value is far greater and more significant than any tangible assets.

The success of Gree's distributor marketing is also based on the sale policies made by Gree Electric Appliance. The success of sales policies lies on whether it is adaptable to the market or its operability in the market, not the completeness of the policy being made. When they are well-managed, the policies will make good results. Therefore, a well-managed policy could make the consumers enjoy the high quality products and services and it is also favorable for the manufacturer to have the recovery of the capital and use it in the extended reproduction. What's more, thanks to the well-managed sales policy, the distributors of Gree air conditioner will have a sense of trust and security when they are selling the products for the manufacturer. Eventually, considering that the distributors can establish a relationship of trust with consumers, Gree can build its brand image and then a beneficial economic cycle could be formed in the whole process of Gree's marketing and selling. In the light of this guiding principle, Gree's sales policy always remains consistent and only a slight adjustment will be made in the policy each year according to the conditions of the markets. This kind of "paperless" gentleman's agreement with its distributors reflecting Gree's responses to the changes of the markets has gained the recognition from them and the markets at large.

It is amazing that Gree's rapid response and adjustment to the changes of the markets help its huge productivity quickly turn into huge market potentials. Just within a few years, Gree Electric Appliances has occupied the leading position in China's air conditioning industry. If Gree's specialization in its production is the foundation for Gree to win the trust of the consumers, the channel marketing will be the key factor for Gree to be the winner in the market place. The chairman, Mr. Zhu Jianghong once said, "The good marketing channel is this kind of marketing channel through which the products can be sold well. Gree Electric Appliances is willing to take the risks and share the benefits together with any distributor. "

The spokesman of Gree Electric Appliances, Huang Fanghua further explained Gree's marketing channel strategy: "In future, we still stick to and try to improve Gree's exclusive marketing model, but what should be more specific here is that Gree does not exclude any sales channels based on the operating principles of sincerity, equality and mutual benefits. The chain-store channel is also a part of Gree's distribution and there are many distributors in the chain-store channel for Gree to choose to cooperate with. But right now in Gree's distribution channel, the franchise stores and exclusive shops still are the major ones, especially, the franchise stores. At present, there are over 2500 Gree franchise stores in China, which will be the prior development direction for Gree Electric Appliances in the future."

2. The Direct Sales Model

Although the people outside Gree Electric Appliances have different opinions about Gree's marketing channel, judging from Gree's practical situation in the markets, Gree's current sales channel model is still scientific, reasonable and healthy one. The franchise stores nationwide play a significant role in increasing Gree's market share. With Gree Electric Appliances' service philosophy for the direct sales stores of "appearing in one unified image, providing every customer with most professional services, situated in the nearest place to our customers, and offering every customer the convenient services", the franchise and direct sales stores help the Gree brand to become a household name in China.

1) The Franchise Stores Seize the Market Space

With the flexible operations, professional services and distinctive characteristics, Gree direct sales stores have enjoyed a favorable position in the marketplace and are very active in urban areas, countryside, and the big streets and small alleys of those communities. And now Gree has established a 3-level marketing network: with the city as the center, based on the sales network in regions and co

In regard to the existence of Gree's franchise stores, Zhu Jianghong believes that there are unties, supported by the network in villages and towns. The Industry experts indicated that, the reason for Gree's brilliant achievement is the importance of the franchise stores in constructing Gree's self-built channels. In building the franchise stores, people in Gree Electric Appliances have made great efforts in developing franchise stores and community stores. For example, the 5A community stores set up in the areas of Anhui provide service directly for the consumers around the community. Even in the market area mainly controlled by the two large retailers in China: Beijing GOME and Dazhong, Gree Electric Appliances still has set up dozens of stores to deepen its direct-sales channels and to compete with those chain retailers in those areas.

The aggressive expanding of Gree's franchise stores has seized the second and third tier city market space. At the closure of the 2006 refrigeration year and when Gree's Interim Report was made public, Zhu Jianghong accepted the interview from media reporters, and a reporter from the north press of China asked: "It is rumored that the direct sales model of Gree Electric Appliances has been threatened in the context of the home appliance channels with various changes and turbulence. What's your view on it?" Zhu Jianghong explained: "China has huge market potentials and great diversity of sales models in the market channels. The big retailer store is just one of many commercial channels and it neither can represent all the marketing channel patterns nor occupy the whole market share. There is still huge space for Gree's franchise stores' survival and development. If we can open stores in the communities of the cities, we can have stores in the markets of villages and towns as well".

several reasons for the survival of them:

Firstly, the air conditioners are semi-manufactured products and need professional installation service for its normal use. The direct-sales stores are the best marketing channels for air-conditioning products.

Secondly, Gree's direct-sales stores meet the essential requirements of the franchise stores' survival and development; that is, the high reputation, brand superiority, good word of mouth, high market occupancy, large sales volume and unified management, etc.

private enterprises; approximately 2000 private enterprises there and most of them are widel The third one is the variety of the marketing channels. It provides Gree direct-sales stores with a vast space for their survival and development.

Fourthly, Gree's direct-sales stores have their unique advantages, for example, their flexible operations, quick responses to the changes in the markets, good services, fast upgrade, and high efficiency. They can provide very professional installation and customer serive compared with other electrical appliance chain stores and they have no area restrictions but enjoy the obvious advantages in commercial and engineering air-conditioners.

The figures in the Gree's interim report in 2006 show that in the first half of the year that there was a strong growth, compared with the corresponding period of 2005 and the growth rate is up to 19.28%. Regarding this issue, Zhu Jianghong made the remarks that, in the current situation of the co-existence of many marketing channels, Gree's direct-sales stores still play a decisive role in the growth of Gree Electric Appliances' domestic sales.

Concerning that Gree's franchise stores are receiving more and more attention from the outside world under the circumstance that the integration among big retailer stores is increasingly deepening, The Gree Chairman, Zhu Jianghong said that the scale of Gree's franchise stores won't be smaller and smaller; on the contrary, they will become bigger and bigger. Perhaps, the increase in the sales volume of Gree air conditioners is not very obvious just in a single year, but judging from the growth rate in the recent years, there is a notable increase of sales volume in Gree products in every year, which sufficiently proves that the original marketing model and the strategy being carried out in developing the direct-sales stores is completely correct and proper.

Zhu Jianghong further stated that to exert great efforts in developing franchise stores is to require that those stores should regard Gree's standard rules as the guideline when they are providing services for the customers. Because Gree has established the concept of "Customer comes first", developing with high standards, those stores are gradually having better and better sales results each year.

According to Gree Electric Appliances' statistics, by July 25th, 2006, in Henan province, one of the important market places for Gree air conditioners, the sale volume there has accumulated to a total number of 700,000 units, which indicates that Gree air conditioner has captured a half of the market share in Henan province. It is really a miracle and a myth that Gree created so far in the air conditioning industry in China.

After years' of exploring and trying in this industry, Gree Electric Appliances finally become more confirmed in its faith of sticking to the direct-sales marketing channel. In order to manage and run the direct-sales stores well, the industry experts suggested that:

1. The adherence to specialization and standardization is a must to Gree. To have a good store, the first important point is specialization and to be wholehearted in the selling of Gree products, only in this way can the public awareness of direct-sales stores be raised. The next important one is standardization. The standardized store design, distribution channel and operation flow can guarantee the service quality and keep enhancing the brand reputation.

2. The unique marketing pattern distinguishing other stores is another essential factor. Due to the exclusiveness of Gree stores, Gree Electric Appliances must place great importance to the promotion of the brand, the development of the whole market and the planning of the marketing strategies based on the conditions of the whole sales market. Compared with retailer stores with many products of different brands, the direct-sales stores can better cater to residents' consumption needs. The flexibility of Gree stores is hard for big home appliances mall to achieve and in the respect, Gree stores need more support from the parent company.

3. To explore the marketing network in the four tier city markets. Gree Electric Appliances always persistently keeps developing the chain store model in third and fourth tier city markets. The sales net work in the third tier city markets has begun to take shape already, but there are hardly any Gree direct sales stores in villages and towns. For instance, Gongyi city of Henan province has been once the cradle of y distributed in towns and villages. In those areas, the residents' purchasing power is equal to those in urban areas, so there is vast development space for Gree direct-sales stores. For this reason, it is quite necessary for Gree Electric Appliances to set up Gree direct-sales stores in those towns, like Gongyi.

About the problems existing in managing the direct-sales stores, Zhu Jianghong once said in the interview from the newspaper *China Business*: "The direct-sales stores have undertaken the great sales tasks for Gree's sales. The increase in sale volumes every year comes from those stores. Certainly, it is quite common for some problems existing in some stores, but this does not affect the overall picture anyway. Meanwhile, even for those large chain stores, there are also some well-managed ones and ill-managed ones in their branch stores". About the question of "As the market saturation is appearing in the major cities and the hypermarkets are expanding their business scale, will Gree's marketing channel face the new challenges brough by them?" Zhu Jianghong answered: "The growth rate in our sales volume explains everything. In recent years, there is a very high growth rate about 20%

every year. Since Gree's base figure is too high, the rate of 20% will be more than 1 million air conditioner units per year and all the sales task of 1 million air conditioner units have been accomplished by Gree's franchise stores and special shops. It seems that there are still huge market potentials for Gree air conditioners; therefore, in the future, Gree only will open more and more direct-sales stores all over China and the business scale of Gree won't be smaller and smaller."

2) A 19.28% Surge in the Sales Volume

The president of Gree Electric Appliances, Dong Mingzhu once pointed out that, no matter what marketing channel an enterprise chooses, the first thing to consider is whether the technology of the products can take the leading position in the markets and the consumers can enjoy satisfied services or not. If an enterprise cannot do the both, there will never be an increase in sales. The reason for Gree's devoting great efforts to develop the direct-sales stores is not just only out of the competition between Gree Electric Appliances and other big chain stores. But for the reason that Gree's air conditioning products need the professional services provided by the franchise stores and only franchise stores can safeguard and proctect the consumers' interests. Gree stores always offer the customers excellent services, which is a very important reason for the success and rapid development of Gree direct-sales stores.

Having seen that Gree's winning the markets with its unique business model, quite a few air conditioning enterprises are imitating or copying the direct-sales model of Gree Electric Appliances. Regarding this phenomenon, Dong Mingzhu emphasized, perhaps the marketing methods can be copied, but the marketing innovation can never be copied. The advantage of Gree Electric Appliances is reflected in its accumulated experience for more than ten years' business operation, which is impossible to be copycatted by any enterprise in a very short time. Meanwhile, the different brands reflect different connotations and different corporate cultures. The enterprise culture of Gree is to guide the consumers' consumption idea. That is, one plus one is zero: the first one is the products of top class quality plus first class installation services, and there will be zero trouble both for customers and the enterprise, which is the modern industrial spirit advocated by Gree. The advanced idea and top class product quality of Gree are impossible for others to be the copycat; just like twins, although they look like the same, they still have many differences in their characters. As a matter of fact, in the past ten years, with this business operation pattern, the distributor team of Gree is getting bigger and bigger. And with this better and better virtuous circle in the cooperation between Gree and its distributors, the distributors are becoming more and more confident about what they are doing as Gree's partners.

To the industry experts' opinion, in the tough competition of the air conditioning market, if an enterprise wants to gain a firm foothold in the markets and to make great progress, the enterprise must have an active attitude in adopting marketing strategies. For Gree stores, besides strictly observing the rules and regulations stipulated by the parent company, they also keep deepening the marketing channels and constantly bringing forth new ideas in marketing channels based on the real conditions of the air conditioning market:

The first one that Gree stores did for selling Gree products is to intensify the brand awareness.

This slogan --"Good air conditioners, Gree Made" has been quite familiar to the public, but it still needs consumers' recognition and the stores in the third, fourth tier city markets make unremitting promotion activities based on the situation of the local markets and the consumers' preference. When the direct-sale stores have been set up, and after some distributors came to have the consent of Gree Electric Appliances, they constantly put commercial TV programs over TV or radio focusing on the brand promotion and raising the reputation of Gree stores. At the same time, the distributors also handed out leaflets widely to factories and mines, enterprises and public institutions, communities, shops and residential buildings. Moreover, they tried to cooperate with some the local news media and put exquisite billboards outside or inside their stores to help achieve very good advertising effect for Gree air conditioning products as well. During the product promotion days, the distributors paid more attention to the image of their stores by strengthening the publicity work and enhancing the grade of the advertising campaigns. In this way, the image of Gree band has been promoted too in the third and fourth tier city markets.

Secondly, to raise the reputation by providing good after-sale services.

Air conditioner is a product made up by selling accounting for 30% and installation for 70% for a normal use of an air conditioner. When an air conditioner is sold, it is just a semi-finished product and only high quality installation services can guarantee its normal use. So in such a way, the consumer can truly understand the idea of "Good air conditioners,

Gree made". For this purpose, Gree direct sales stores have trained the installation personnel and maintenance staff strictly according to every item stipulated in "Gree Air Conditioner's installation and maintenance manual" especially in the low business season. Moreover, all the workers have been required to do the field acceptance tests and to receive nonscheduled tests so as to make sure that everyone is qualified for providing high quality installation and maintenance services for the customers. The sale specialists in Gree stores have been also dispatched regularly to learn from their excellent counterparts and drew on the successful experience of their professional brothers, so that those successful marketing patterns and experience could be the useful references for them. In the meanwhile, the excellent workers have been asked to pay home visits and to do the maintenance work for customers as well, which win the good appraise from customers. Guaranteed by professional installation and excellent after sale services, Gree's sales achievement is climbing up year by year.

Thirdly, to implement the measures in direct sales marketing and to have new moves in off season promotion.

In recent years, during the off season of air conditioners, Gree has had new moves in product promotion, such as, special-price air conditioners, exquisite complimentary gifts for customers, and lots of special discounts, which all strongly promote the sales of the air conditioner in third and fourth tier city markets in off seasons. When all the favorable policies from Gree Electric Appliances are implemented, with the appropriate promotion activities based on the local conditions, the consumers' spending desire is immediately aroused. And there are also constant adjustments in the marketing strategy of Gree. The marketing strategies are like the following, e.g. all the sales persons are divided by area to collect the marketing information, try to cover all the market places for advertising and try to find every potential buyer to make sure that every possible deal will not be missed.

Thanks to the continuous innovations and efforts in Gree's marketing strategy, the miracle was finally made with a 19.28% surge in the sales volume of Gree air conditioners. When a high-level leader from Gree Electric Appliances was asked about this issue in interviews, he said that under the circumstance of the coexistence of many marketing channels, Gree direct sales stores do play an important role in the increase in domestic sales of Gree products and they will continue maintaining a stronger and stronger development momentum.

Zhu Jianghong, the Chairman of Gree Electric Appliances, believes that the big retailer store is just one of many commercial channels in China at present and it cannot replace all the marketing channels and models, because the marketing models in China's enterprises are various and diversified. It is also impossible for the big retailer stores to occupy the whole market share. Therefore, there is still huge market space for Gree direct sales stores' survival and development.

3. Keeping Creating Customers

To Gree Electric Appliances, "Creating customers" means having its eyes on the future development, effectively developing and making a full use all sorts of resources, providing high quality products and services and trying all the means to meet the customers' needs, so that Gree can continually expand the scale of its business operation. Only by keeping "creating customers" can "the satisfying profits and progressive increase reciprocated the business scale" and the sustainable development of Gree be realized and accelerated. The operating practice of Gree's "creating customers" is embodied in the following points: leading the development of air conditioning industry and creating the market demands.

1) Producing High Quality Products Should Always Be the First Place

In a complete marketing system, product quality always comes first. Without good products, there will be nothing at all for an enterprise. In this case, what kind of product is called a good product or a popular product? According to the President of Gree Electric Appliances, Dong Mingzhu, she thinks that the total product concept should include three levels: core product, tangible product and additional product. Core product is the interests pursued by consumers when they buy this product. It is what they really want; therefore, it is the most basic and important part in the total product concept.

Product is more important than marketing. Although many people still regard the marketing channel and the distributors are the top priority in the home appliance industry, Dong Mingzhu still strongly adheres to the idea of requiring the distributors' "payment first, delivery second." She once used the selling cost of 4 million RMB to create the sales figures of 10 billion RMB. As for the Gree's sale achievement and its slight dependence on the rising big chain stores in circulation field, Dong Mingzhu explained her own idea: "Speaking of sales, everyone thinks that marketing is the most important factor in an enterprise's development and many people even consider it as the top priority in an enterprise. Actually, it is people's misunderstanding about it. With the example of Gree's development course, the product is more important than marketing. If there is no high quality product as the backing, marketing is meaningless. Marketing is just a major part in the courses of an enterprises' development. If this enterprise wants to be successful, the more important for it is that technology innovation in its products and the advantages in its product's quality, plus combining manufacturing, research and development in technology, internal management control and all departments working together in harmony. Marketing should not be isolated and mystified; perhaps a good marketing model and an excellent sales team can make an enterprise to be crowned with success for a very short period of time, but an enterprise should not overestimate the power of its marketing team. There are also some salespersons getting very good sale results thanks to the brand of their products with good reputation, then they think very highly about themselves by overestimating their ability in the whole business operations and then they begin to have arrogant attitude towards the company. Sometimes the group job-hopping event even happens in those sales staff. In fact, compared with marketing, the contributions made by brands are far greater than the contributions made by certain salespersons."

No doubt, the high quality product is the precondition and guarantee for the marketing strategy to be carried on normally. For this reason, Gree Electric Appliances always places the quality of products in the first place and always stands on the product strategy of "providing the quality product is the best service." Here, we can see its product strategy reflected in the following points:

First, when making the products, Gree removed all those unnecessary and redundant functions in the products. In this way, the manufacturing cost of the product is lowered and the consumers are benefited from it. (They will not get confused in numerous concepts any more) and the market share is increased. "Air conditioner" as implied by the name, is "a machine used to condition the air"; its main functions should be freshening, cooling and heating the air and the air conditioner manufacturers should not hype the various concepts of the superfluous functions in air conditioner products.

Second, the high quality products escort Gree to dominate the market. What the air conditioning users are really concerned about is the quality of the products. No one is willing to suffer any sudden failure in the air conditioners when they are using it in a very hot summer day. Therefore, in order to avoid the quality problems and failures in its products, Gree Electric Appliances unswervingly sticks to adopting the technology suited to conditions in China and tries to produce the products of highly reliable quality. Considering the instability of China's electric power, Gree was the first manufacturer to launch the new products of convertible frequency air-conditioners. The year of 2003 witnessed a power test in over 60 foreign and domestic air conditioner brands in China. The result showed that among all the brands home and abroad, only 5 brands measured up to the national standards, but only two domestic air conditioner brands passed the test and Gree was one of the two domestic brands in this test.

Third, in order to guarantee the quality of the products and provide customers convenient after-sales services, most Gree products only have been changed in the product design and the electric cabinet section of every product remains the same. That is to say, all the electric cabinet sections in Gree air conditioner are interchangeable and universal. So consumers can feel easy and reassured to use Gree products; even there is a breakdown occurring and Gree's service personnel will make a quick replacement of the electronic control part in the air conditioning unit.

Fourth, strive for perfection and seek the "simpler" ways. In order to make the products more convenient for customers, Gree Electric Appliances is formulating the plan of simplifying its products. The policy-makers in Gree begin to have the idea of putting the accessory case (an air conditioner includes three parts: an indoor unit, an outdoor unit and accessories, which are all put in a paper case) into the packing case of indoor unit to further simplify the package of the products.

Dong Mingzhu deeply believes that, the perfect marketing system should have a corresponding product system so that the marketing system can take the initiative in the competition of the market-oriented economy. The tangible product is the form realized by the core product and the core product provides product entity and service image through the form of tangible products. If the tangible product is physical goods, it is generally manifested as the quality of the product, appearance characteristics, design, brand name and packaging. When consumers buy a certain product, they are not for the purpose of taking the possession of the tangible product, but for acquiring the effectiveness or interests of this tangible product; that is the core product. Thus, marketers firstly should focus on the interests pursued by consumers when they are buying the products, so that the marketers can manage to meet the consumers' demand successfully; then to design the products according to the above views. Only in this way, will consumers be guaranteed for the certain need when they have this product and all their needs relevant to the products be fulfilled.

2) 100% Customer Satisfaction

When Dong Mingzhu was an ordinary saleswoman in Gree, she had widely read some successful stories about those original marketing strategies of foreign enterprises. When she was interviewed by the media, she told a story of "two salesmen selling shoes" which has impressed her most:

The story is about two shoes companies dispatching two salespersons to expand the shoes market and tap new customers for their own company, one named John Jackson, other James Elson.

On the same day, both of them arrived in an island country in the south of the Pacific Ocean. To their surprise, from the King to the paupers, from the monks and priests to the noble ladies in this country, no one was wearing any shoes.

At that night, John Jackson sent a telegram to the head office of his company: "Oh, my god! Nobody wears shoes there. Who wants to buy shoes? I am going back tomorrow." In the same manner, James Elson sent a telegram the home office: "It's great! The people here don't wear shoes. It is a good opportunity for us to open up the market and dominate the footwear market in this country. I suggest that our company should send all our stocks to me. Moreover, I have decided to move my home here and settle down in this country for good".

Two years later, all people on that island had shoes on their feet...

In this story, Dong Mingzhu thinks highly of the second shoes salesman very much. In her opinion, the second salesman is the one who is really farsighted and insightful. His business philosophy is: First, to create the product which seems nobody really needs, and then create the needs for the product; although this kind of need is a latent demand, it is still the real need for customers.

Therefore, if an enterprise wants to realize 100% customer satisfaction; firstly, it should know the consumers' practical needs. In Gree home appliance sales achievement, once appeared a scene like this: Many people queued for the chance to snap up Gree air conditioners and 24,000 air conditioner units had been sold in just 4 days. With all the products out of stock and asking the airfreight to help the restocking, an unprecedented grand occasion was created. In that month, the sales revenues of Gree Electric Appliances notched up RMB 160 million... How did Gree accomplish such great achievements? The industry experts think the reason for the "queuing buy" phenomenon of Gree air conditioners is that they know very clearly what the consumers really want. Certainly, to know the real needs of consumers is not just a catch phrase, but should truly provide the products of excellent quality and reasonable price for consumers.

Today, the enterprises have already entered the era of stiving for 100% customer satisfaction, which is a yardstick to measure the services and products provided by all the enterprises. Hence, Gree Electric Appliances has put forward the conception of "Gree air conditioner--100% customer satisfaction project"; that is, to make the customers the real God satisfied by creating 100% satisfaction services and products. The project theme has been chosen as "Creating 100% customer satisfaction is the forever pursuit of all the employees in Gree Electric Appliances". In order to promote the new concept in air conditioning industry without any practice of commercial speculations, the Beijing office of Gree Electric Appliances decided to pay home visits of inquiring the customers who have used Gree products for more than 10 years about the experience of using Gree products. What's more, it also launched the campaign for selecting "Ambassadors of Witnessing the Quality of Gree Air Conditioners" and set up the club of "Ten Years' Club". Then, the organizers took the "Ambassadors" to have a tour in Zhuhai air conditioning production base so that they could have a close look at the producing and manufacturing of Gree air conditioning products and know more about Gree air conditioners.

The concept of "100% customer satisfaction" has become a very important factor for

Gree to forge high quality air conditioning products successfully. Zhang Bo, the Deputy General Manager of Gree Beijing Branch Office once said: "To be Frank, there is no secret in Gree's air conditioning product promotion. Gree air conditioner rarely has played any commercial speculations and there is no new marketing hype of concepts either this year. But so far to the development of the air conditioning industry, we think that it is necessary to lead the competition of this industry to be back on the right track. It will be a healthy development direction that all the air-con enterprises should fight for the product quality and the service life of their products." As some air conditioning industry experts pointed out, among the top 100 China's electronic & information enterprises, the average industry profitability is only 0.61% and the overall situation of the air conditioning industry is not higher than that figure. The root cause for it lies in the enterprises' irrational competition in price and concept. In fact, compared with the peak-season of air conditioning industry in 2005, the year of 2006 saw a slack business in the air conditioning industry. No moves in reducing price by 10%-30% frequently were seen in 2006 at the very beginning of the peak season compared with 2005 and usually there were many bargains for consumers every year but there was nothing in 2006. In the year of 2006, every air-conditioning enterprise learned more about the serious difficulty in the whole industry.

Zhang Bo also stressed that: "Under this circumstance, if Gree launched the wars of pricing and concept at the cost of its profits, there would be a bigger number in the sales results, but it is a meaningless move. Gree Electric Appliances is an enterprise which always attaches great importance to the profits. If people have the opportunity to take a look at the financial statements of those enterprises which tend to be in the wars of concept speculation and price, people will see the poor performance in their finance report, which is quite self-evident. Regarding this aspect, Gree Electric Appliances always tries to put more resources into its management and R&D and its other spending is quite low. In the meantime, the higher the product quality is, the lower the service cost will be. As a result, the customers will use Gree's products smoothly and the cost is also lowered as well. Because of the deep understanding of the relationship between product quality, price, concept and services, Gree fully supports the establishment of the "Ten Years' Club". The profound meaning of the "Ten Years' Club" is to make the service time of every air conditioner over ten years under an ordinary usage. The "Ten Years' Club" is an embodiment of the product quality, also a reflection of an enterprise strength. "Any brand to compete with us in this respect in any form is welcomed. But we won't enter any contest of pure conceptual speculations to fool our consumers," Just as Dong Mingzhu, the vice chairwoman of Gree Electric Appliances, pointed out.

Therefore, if want to realize 100% customer satisfaction, enterprises should know what consumers really need, know what is going on in their inner world and hear their voice.

Sticking to this guiding principle, Gree Electric Appliances hopes to know what consumers need, to further understand their needs and take the analysis based on consumers' needs as the guideline to enhance the internal work of Gree, and then comprehensively promote the idea of "Gree's 100% customer satisfaction project".

Review: Why Marketing Strategies Can Make Gree a Winner?

Peter F. Drucker, the widely influential writer and thinker on the management theory and practice and management consultant, once had the statement in his book *The Practice of Management*: "Because the purpose of business is to create a customer, the business enterprise has two--and only two--basic functions: marketing and innovation." These philosophical words tell us, the purpose of business is nothing but to keep creating customers; marketing and innovation are the two basic means to achieve that goal. If a business wants to be a successful one, it must have a group of loyal customers and it should have the ability to make this group larger and larger. How to achieve this goal? According to Peter F. Drucker, there are two basic means: one is marketing, the other is innovation. So we can say that marketing is the key factor for a business to succeed and to win in the market competition. The case of Gree Electric Appliances in practice once again has proved Mr. Drucker's theoretical point of view. That is to say, Gree made great efforts in innovation and marketing, which is perfectly to accomplish the basic functions of an enterprise. Consequently, it has realized the value of this enterprise.

The key point in the success of Gree's marketing is to appropriately handle the relationship between manufacturer, dealer and consumer. It did represent the interests of dealers, the benefits of consumers and the profits of manufacturers. The embodiment of the "three represents" is called as the marketing system of "Gree model", especially the combination of regional sales company, direct-sales store and customer service system. The pre-investment in Gree's marketing system is the significant factor in nurturing the enterprise's organizational capacity.

About this point, it reminds of me the conclusion in the book *Scale and Scope* written by Mr. Alfred Dupont Chandler Jr., a professor of business history at Harvard Business School and Johns Hopkins University, who wrote extensively about the scale and the management structures of modern corporations during his life time and has passed away recently. In this book, the author's case study on 200 great enterprises in US, UK and early Germany indicates that: The first step is to invest in and manage those production facilities to make them big enough to realize the economies of scale and economies of scope; the second step is to invest in and manage the wholesale, distribution outlets and purchasing network; the third step is to recruit and organize necessary management personnel as well as to establish a management team of integration hierarchy according to the various functions of the company. The combination of three factors constructs the core of industrial capitalism motive power--organizational capacity; among them, managing officers' capacity is the very critical factor. In the past twenty years and in the respect of basic principles, the formation of Chinese enterprises is in conformity with the development of early foreign enterprises, but now, they have essential differences from the conditions of foreign businesses. Therefore, if Chinese enterprises want to take foreign businesses as the role model, they should learn something from the experiences in the early course of the development of the foreign businesses.

Marketing channel is one of the key factors in a marketing system. In China's home appliance industry, Gree's marketing system is out of the ordinary. What is the point in the view of "He who controls the marketing channels will have the whole market"? We all know that in the planned economy era in the past, all the commodities in China had a relatively complete marketing system, e.g. all sorts of wholesale companies, supply and marketing cooperatives and Xinhua bookstores, but after the reform and opening up since the year 1978, these national marketing channels had gradually been disintegrated and disappeared from the market. In the case of delivering the products to the consumers, Chinese enterprises must build their own marketing channels or employ market-based distribution system to help them to send their products to the consumers. The innovation of Gree's marketing channels lies in its integration of the above two elements organically.

As to this problem, Chen Chunhua, the famous Professor, entrepreneur and writer on corporate culture and strategy in China, made a thorough study in her book of *The Leading Way* (*Ling Xian Zhi Dao* in Chinese), in which she samples China's pioneering enterprises and probes into their leading ways in the market place. Her research indicates that the marketing channel is the critical external motivation for those pioneering enterprises, and there is a close connection between the recognition of products and the building of the marketing channels. Each enterprise has its products of different features and the marketing strategy designed is quite different from others. In the view of this idea, Gree's unique marketing model is based on the characteristics that the air conditioning products are the semi-finished products. When the consumers are buying them and the products need professional installation services provided by the direct-sales stores, which is quite reasonable for the existence of Gree's direct sales stores. Talking about this marketing channel model in the future, along with the fact that the circulation system in the markets is becoming complete day by day and the channel intermediaries are becoming more and more rational, concerning the question--what value lies in Gree marketing model, we still need more observations on it.

Chapter 2: Top Priority for Brand Building

1. The Made-in-China Brand Becoming World Famous

Staying in the global home appliance industry of fiercest competition, especially in the air conditioning industry with the industry giants from US, Japan, South Korea and strong rivals back home, in term of development history, Gree Electric Appliances is not the one with a long history; in term of financial strength, compared with those international big names, Gree is facing an unequal contest in this tough competition. But why did Gree which is the latecomer has surpassed all the early starters in just about ten years' time and become the world champion in the area of household air-conditioning?

In reviewing the development history of Gree Electric Appliances, it has been awarded the title of "China Top Brands" by AQSIQ, "Symbolized Brand in Chinese Industry" by China Top Brand Strategy Promotion Committee and "100 Top Chinese Corporations" by *Forbes*. What kind of magic power to make Gree a myth and to support this large battle ship to brave the raging wind and wild waves in the generally acknowledged industry of fiercest competition? Here, we are going to reveal the "genetic code" that make Gree become the world famous brand.

1) The Big Brand from a Small Workshop

The year 2006 witnessed Gree's global sales volume hitting RMB 23 billion, which is the largest sales figure so far in the global air conditioning industry. According to the list of "China's 500 Most Valuable Brands" issued jointly by World Brand Lab and *World Executive Weekly* in 2006, the brand value of "Gree" is worth RMB 7.648 billion, jumped by RMB 429 million, compared with the number RMB 7.219 billion in 2005. In 2006, Gree Electric Appliances is No. 64 in the list, with the ranking up by 5 compared with the ranking of No. 69 in 2005. Here we can't help thinking that what the reason is for Gree from a struggling small air conditioning brand to be a very influential world famous brand? How did it create its astonishing and brilliant achievement in the world air conditioning industry? Here, let's have a review of the rising of Gree Electric Appliances, the largest air-con maker in China.

The first stage: the start-up stage (focusing on the quantity of the products)

From 1991 to 1993, the newly established Gree Electric Appliances was an unknown small factory. Its simple and crude production line only had a yearly output of 20,000 window air conditioners. Under the leadership of Zhu Jianghong, all the employees in Gree worked their way through the difficult time and tried their best to overcome the various difficulties in the entrepreneurial stage. Finally, they mananged to develop a series of marketable products and seized the opportunity of taking the market share to initially establish the image of Gree brand and lay a solid foundation for its future development. As a "late starter" and a small business in the air conditioning industry, what Gree lacks is not just the yield capacity but also the understanding of air conditioners, not to mention the core air conditioning technology.

The present senior researcher, Li Jiangyun from the Refrigeration Institute of Gree Electric Appliances, still can clearly recall the stories at the early stage of Gree: "At that time, every day after work, all the cadres from Guanxiong Plastics Factory would meet with each other in a small room and learn the basic air conditioning principles. Then bit by bit, they came to be familiar with the air conditioning design, manufacturing process and workflow. Meanwhile, the workers from Guanxiong also studied the practical operations in the workshop. Soon many of them had been trained to be the experts of making air conditioners and some of them become the vice president of the Technology Department or the vice-president of the Manufacturing Department later. In those days, the supply was inadequate to meet the demand in the air conditioning market; Gree seized the historical opportunity to open up its market quickly. After that, it was on the way to expand its production scale: in the riverside of Qianshan, Zhuhai city and next to Nanping bridge, the first, second, third, fourth, fifth and sixth phase of Gree expansion projects had been put into construction: subsequently, 500,000 units, 1million units, 2.5 million units, 6 million units, 8 million units, 10 million units, 15 million units, the production capacity was multiplied geometrically.

The second stage: the development stage (focusing on the quality of the products)

From 1994 to 1996, Gree Electric Appliances began to take the quality of imporving product quality as its core task and formulated the policy of "make the first class products, establish the famous brand, increase productivity and aim at achieving the world top-grade level". At the same time, it announced the "14 prohibition rules issued by the President" and began to implement the "zero defects project". Having made great efforts in improving the product quality, Gree Electric Appliances had undergone a qualitative change in its product quality, which laid a sound foundation for the quality advantage of Gree products and facilitated forging "Gree"—the famous brand and establishing a good reputation among consumers since then.

The third stage: the expansion stage (focusing on marketing, lowering production cost and expanding production scale)

From 1997 to 2001, in the context of Gree Electric Appliances paying close attention to the market development, Dong Mingzhu created the regional sales company model, which was praised as "the brand new market model in the economic field in the 21st century". The sales company finally turned out a magic weapon to help Gree to be the winner in the markets. In 1998, the third phase of Gree expansion projects was completed. In 2001, Chongqing branch of Gree Electric Appliances was put in to construction and the Brazil production base was also under construction at the same year. After the series of expanding production scale, Gree's production capacity was enhanced steadily and its economy of scale was achieved to a large extent; at the same time, the practice of strengthening cost control helped Gree to realize the profit maximization. Since then, Gree's production, sales volume, sales revenues and market occupancy had been the No.1 in domestic air-conditioning industry. And the economic benefits of Gree Electric Appliances have been growing steadily for successive years; all these above factors contributed Gree's staying on solid footing both in domestic and foreign markets.

The fourth phase: the internationalization phase (striving for being the world No.1 brand)

From 2001 to 2005, Gree Electric Appliances set a goal of striving for world No.1. In order to achieve this goal: all the employees in Gree made continuous innovations in management: introduced Sigma Management, carried out the achievement evaluation management model, beefed up their efforts to strengthen the development of international markets and try every means to make Gree an international air-con maker. The year 2005 aw that the sales volume of Gree home air conditioner amounted to 10 million units, which realized the goal of world No.1 in sales achievements and made Gree the top one in selling home air conditioners in the world. The industry experts pointed out, the era of "Gree air conditioner leading the world" is coming.

The fifth phase: the phase of creating the world famous brand

After Gree had successfully realized its goal of being the "world champion", in 2006, Gree Electric Appliances announced its growth strategy of "building the first class enterprise, making the first class products and creating the first class brand" and worked very hard for accomplishing the lofty mission of "promoting the industrial spirit, pursuing the perfect product quality, providing professional services, and creating a comfortable environment for customers" as well as advanced bravely toward the vision of "building the leading enterprise in global air conditioning industry and perfecting the century-old Gree brand".

Having experienced violent rain and storm, Gree air conditioner finally saw the sunshine that has been long awaited. Since 1995, Gree has been the leading position in sales volume, sales profit, and market occupancy for more than ten consecutive years. As the statistics show that, Gree all ranked No.1 in the following indexes: sales volume, sales revenues, export figures, funds in research and development and eventually, it was selected as the "Symbolic Brand in Chinese Air Conditioner Industry" with most votes.

2) Gree Brand Going Global

air conditioner is the first world famous brand in Chinese air conditioning industry Gree. Depending on its strong technical strength and pursuing the spirit of devotion, professionalism and absorption, people in Gree persistently have been making great efforts to build the professional standard of the industry and provide the first class air conditioners with a combination of human diligence and wisdom. "Good air conditioner, Gree made" is not only a slogan and tagline, but a declaration and determination; "for good quality, choose Gree" is not a bragging, but a benchmark in this trade. With the eminent technological strength and quality advantages, in the arduous journey of "building a century-old enterprise and creating the global brand", Gree finally has won the affirmation and high recognition from its 40 million users worldwide. Since 1995, its proformace in production and sales volumes had occupied the top place in the industry for eleven consecutive years; in the year of 2006, it became the world No.1 air conditioner maker in the global air conditioning industry and finally, it earned the real championship in the whole world.

Ever since 1997, shouldering the responsibilities of promoting national brands and leading the global air conditioning industry, Gree Electric Appliances has won one triumph after another in its field. The following lists show Gree's glorious achievements in the past years:

Awards	Issuance Organization	Awarded Date
Most Competitive Brand	Ministry of Commerce and CCTV	2007.2
Exemption from Export inspection	General Administration of Quality Supervision, inspection and Quarantine	2006.11
China Quality Management Award	China Association for Quality	2006.11
Commercial Contribution in BAHIA State in 2006	Salvador in BAHIA State in Brazil	2006.09
China World Brand	General Administration of Quality Supervision, Inspection and Quarantine, and China Promotion Committee Top Brand Strategy	2006.09
Symbolic Brand in Chinese Air Conditioner Industry	China Brand Institute	2006.07
Top 100 Tax Payers	the State Administration of Taxation	2001-2006

The first place of China Top 50 Listed Companies for technology	*China Internet Weekly*	2006
20 Most Valuable Chinese Brands	*Business Week*(US)	2006.09
No.10 of China 100 Top Companies for Technology	*Business Times*	2006.08
Red List for General Administration of Customs	General Administration of Customs	2004-2006
4 awards of First Guangdong Enterprise Innovation Record	Guangdong Enterprise Innovation Record Authorized Committee	2006.08
China Top Enterprises	*Forbes China*	2006.08
100 New Global Challengers	Boston Consulting Group	2006.08
Green Advertisement	China Central Television Advertising Center	2006.07
Top 100 Chinese Listed Companies	*Forbes China*	2006.07
"Top 10 Companies" in Key Industries in China	China Industrial Information Issuing Center	2006.07
World Top 500 Chinese Enterprises	World Eminence Chinese Business Association and China General Chamber of Commerce	2006
Top 200 Exporters in China	*China Customs and Business Watch Magazine*	2006.06
Investor Relations --Top 50	*Securities Market Weekly* and School of Management and Engineering, Nanjing University	2006.06
Guangdong IPR Model Enterprises	Guangdong Intellectual Property office	2006.06
2006 Annual Users Assured Air-conditioning Brand	China National Household Electrical Appliances Service Association	2006.06
Top 100 listed Companies	*China Securities Journal*	2006.06
The Best Brand Enterprise Award (Guangdong & Hong Kong)	Hong Kong Productivity Council	2006.06
First Prize of Guangdong Foreign Trade	People's Government of Guangdong Province	2006.01
Top 100 Tax Payers of China Listed Companies	the State Administration of Taxation	2001-2005
Top Chinese 100 Listed Companies	*Forbes* (USA)	2001-2005
100 Export State-owned Companies	General Administration of Customs	2005.12
China Top Brands on Exporting	Ministry of Commerce	2005.12

Energy Saving Contribution Award	China Certification Center for Energy Conservation Product	2005.10
Excellent Enterprise on Quality Management	China Association for Quality, All China Federation of Trade Unions, the Central Committee of Communist Youth League, and China Association for Science and Technology	2005.10
Excellent Company on Quality Benefit in Foreign Trade in 2004	China Shippers' Association	2005.10
Guangdong Most Satisfying Companies by Chinese Users	Guangdong Quality Association and Guangdong Customer Committee	2005.09
Guangdong Advanced Company on Implementing Performance Excellence Model	Guangdong Quality Association	2005.09
Advanced Company on Implementing Performance Excellence Model	China Association for Quality	2005.09
Most Satisfying Companies by Chinese Users	China Association for Quality	2005.09
Quality Summit International Award for Excellence and Business Prestige	BID(Bussiness Initiative Directions)	2005.06
Outstanding Enterprise of Guangdong Province	Guangdong Provincial Enterprises Confederation and Guangdong Provincial Association of Entrepreneurs	2005.4
Special Prize of Excellent Company on Quality Benefit in Light Industry in (2001-2004)	China National Light Industry Council	2005.04

In 2006, under the situation of a weak demand and oversupply in air conditioning markets, Gree still kept its leading position of selling 13 million air conditioner units. With its high brand reputation and effective business operations, the year 2006 saw Gree's main business revenues and net profit reaching RMB 18.12 billion and RMB 490 million respectively in three quarters, up 39.6% and 18.4% respectively. To find out the reasons for Gree's success, it is not hard for us to find that Gree's outstanding brand is the key factor for attracting consumers' demand and its products and customer services of high quality are the decisive factors in consumers' choice of Gree air conditioners.

According to the statistics issued by the State Information Center of China, during 2003-2005, 150 air conditioner brands were reduced to the number of 69. It is expected in

2007 that about one third of the air conditioning enterprises would disappear from the markets. On the contrary, instead of a sharp decline in business, Gree Electric Appliances enjoyed a rising reputation, for it has been the first air conditioning enterprise in China to promise the consumers the after sales services of "6-year free warranty for a complete air conditioner unit", while the policy of "a three-year guarantee" stipulated by Chinese government is universally implemented in all the air conditioning enterprises at that time. This new move fully reflects Gree's excellent product quality and it has effectively enhanced Gree's brand reputation all over China.

To sum it up, seeing the production and scale ranking No.1 in the world, the well-known and widely praised product quality, the good reputation in home and abroad and the great contributions to China's internal and external trade, we will find that all the remarkable achievements that Gree has made are by no means accidental.

2. Core Technology to Build the World Famous Brand

In order to build a world class brand, an enterprise must have its core technology for making products. As to that point, the President of Gree Electric Appliances, Dong Mingzhu once said: "The exporters of home appliances in China currently are mostly Original Equipment Manufacturers (manufacture products or components that are purchased by a company and retailed under that purchasing company's brand name). A majority of those companies do not have their own brands and some enterprises never have a brand name for their own products. They just depend on processing and making the products under a foreign brand to keep the status quo of their company, which obviously is not a reliable or permanent solution for an enterprise. As a home appliance enterprise, many years ago, we realized that if we want to build a world class brand, we must have our own core technology."

1)   What Are the Advantages of the Brand?

As early as in 2001, the capital input in Gree's technological transformation and new product development reached RMB 150 million; the sales revenues of new products accounted for 48% in the whole sales revenues of all products. Taking Gree Electric Appliances as an example, its developing system, manufacturing system and quality assurance system all have reached the advanced level in the world and in the research fields of frequency conversion, intelligence and power saving. Gree Electric Appliances also has been the key global player in the air conditioning industry. Now, Gree launches about 200 new types of products every year, some of the new products can catch up with or even surpass the international standards. Furthermore, Gree's large scale production plan has always been accomplished on the condition that its technology innovation and product quality are assured.

In 2005, facing many strong competitors from home and abroad, Gree's multi-connected central air conditioner defeated its so many rivals including Japan's Daikin and triumphantly won the bid to supply the central air conditioners for the General Building of China Unicom Jieyang Branch. Just three years ago, Japanese brands had occupied most of the market share of multi-connected central air conditioners. However, since 2002, Gree had begun to be engaged in the independent research and development of the core technology in making multi-connected central air conditioners; then after that Gree appeared itself as a dark horse to grab the lion's share of the multi-connected central air conditioner markets rapidly with an overwhelming victory over Japanese brands.

At present, the multi-connected central air conditioner is a product combined highly sophisticated technology with the integration of "multi-splits", intelligent control, power-saving and network control. At the beginning of 2001, a large foreign enterprise in Chongqing intended to call for a bid of 50 units of "4-splits" multi-connected central air conditioners nationwide. The minute when the news was spread among the air-con makers in China, all the air conditioning big brand names including Gree entered the bidding war. "In fact, at that time neither any enterprise nor Gree had the technology and capacity to make this multi-connected central air conditioner." Zhu Jianghong confessed, but "As one of the national brands, we have the responsibility to break the monopoly, create China's own first class brand and embark the road of independent innovation."

Having mastered the technology of manufacturing multi-connected central air conditioners, Gree Electric Appliances didn't have to rely on other air conditioning manufacturers in the aspect of core technology eventually. From that moment, Gree was on the same starting line with those Japanese air conditioning enterprises which possessed the international leading technology. Because of Gree' entry into the markets, there was a huge fall in the price of Japanese multi-connected central air conditioners, e.g. the price of 10 plus horse power of multi-connected central air conditioners fell dramatically from over 200,000 RMB per unit to less than 70,000 RMB per unit. The date of August, 2008 was so important and unforgettable for Gree Electric Appliances: the first batch of water-cooled centrifugal chillers in possession of intellectual property was put on market; the entry of those chillers in the markets successfully broke America's technology monopoly in centrifuge researching and filled in the gap in Chinese technology field. In November of the same year, as the first batch of ultra-low temperature multi-connected central air conditioners made by Gree Electric Appliances emerged on the markets, they were evaluated to reach "the advanced level" by the experts invited by the Ministry of Construction in China. Thanks to this new product innovation, the worldwide difficult problem was smoothly solved--that Chinese air conditioners not only can bring warmth to the cold area of 25 degrees (77 Fahrenheit degree) below zero, but also can highly and effectively save power and heat for thousands of homes.

Through the continuous technology innovations, Gree Electric Appliances has presented itself as a strong and powerful image in the global air conditioning industry.

2)   The Precondition for Keeping a Foothold in the International Markets

To build a world class brand definitely needs core technology. Dong Mingzhu has been always wide-awake about it and once she said that to have a big budget in advertisement is not enough for building a brand to be a world class one; it should depend more on advanced technologies. Currently, Gree has more than 700 domestic and foreign patents and it has fully mastered the world advanced core technologies ranging from residential air conditioners to commercial air conditioners. Although Gree earned so many honors and credits, it never rests on its laurels; instead, it has set many higher, and more demanding goals for itself hoping there will be more breakthroughs in more projects.

"An enterprise without innovation is the one without soul; the enterprise without core technology is the one without backbone; when one has no backbone, he can never stand up." The chairman of Gree Eletric Appliances, Zhu Jianghong once said. He also told Gree people that: "What Gree wants to be is not a copycat of other air conditioning companies, but the world brand of 'Gree Made'." For the news that Gree has been voted as the "World Famous Brand", Zhu Jianghong keeps a very cool head about it. He told his employees, if we could not be selected as the "World Famous Brand", the pressure that we are having is for a short period of time; if we are voted as the "World Famous Brand", the pressure that we are having will be for good, for we must hold this title for all our life. In order to make us deserve this title, we need to put enormous efforts and conquer many hardships. It is hard to imagine an enterprise without core technology can gain a foothold in the competitive international markets and make substantial progresses; it is even harder to imagine a brand without the core technology can be a world famous brand.

If Gree wants to stay on solid footing in the international market, the core technology is the prerequisite. Zhu Jianghong emphasized that: "As a specialized air conditioning industry, not only should Gree be better than its competitors in technology, but also should be in a leading position in sales volume and sales revenues. Only if it has its own core technology, Gree can take the initiative in the competition."

December, 7th, 2005 is an unforgettable and proud day for Gree Electric Appliances. In the morning of that day, in the conference of Science and Technology Achievement

Evaluation held by the experts from some related state departments in China such as, Ministry of Construction, Development and Reform Commission and some authority organizations, e.g. Chinese Association of Refrigeration (CAR) and China Refrigeration and Air-conditioning Industry Association, Gree's newly developed ultra-low temperature multi-connected central air conditioner passed the experts' appraisal, and was evaluated to reach "the advanced level" in the international arena.

In reviewing the hundred-year development history of air conditioners, the companies of USA and Japan had monopolized most of the air conditioning core technologies. The first air conditioner in the world was invented and produced by USA; after World War II, Japanese enterprises made technology innovations in split air-conditioning units and surpassed the technology of USA, but USA always has the absolute superiority in the field of making central air conditioners. Zhu Jianghong thinks that, if China wants to surpass USA and Japan, she must rely on her own efforts and should not count on the technology 'largesse' from USA and Japan. From so many years of dealing with the air conditioning giants from USA and Japan, their attitude towards China has been the inclination of blockading Chinese enterprises in the respect of core technologies and trying to strangle their competitor in cradle.

Zhu Jianghong repeatedly stressed that, "We must have our own core technology in making our own air conditioners". In August, 2005, the first large central air conditioner--water-cooled centrifugal chiller in possession of intellectual property was put on market and broke the technological monopoly of American "four enterprises" in the field of making centrifugal chillers. This time, Gree Electric Appliances defeated American enterprises by winning hundreds of projects of supplying the air conditioners for the big hotels in Huang Shan, Huizhou of Anhui province, Zhuhai Hua Run Wan Jia shopping mall and Qu Fu World Trade Center of Shandong Province in the bidding wars.... American enterprises were astonished at Gree's victory. Just three years ago, the market of multi-connected central air conditioners in China was still dominated by Japanese brands, now, the major markets in East China, North China and South China have been presented as "The market share has been divided into three major parts and Gree is occupying one of them". Not this merely, in overseas markets, the Japanese enterprises also feel the threat from Gree. They felt as astonished as its American counterparts too when they were competing with Gree for the market share.

The Gree Vice chairwoman, Dong Mingzhu said, in the road of building the world famous brand, there is no finishing point for Gree. "As a great nation, rising along with the family of nations in the core technologies of various industries, we cannot blindly follow suit." Looking into the future, Gree Electric Appliances will continue to devote itself to becoming the Chinese enterprise to lead the world air conditioning industry.

3. Promote the Industrial Spirit, Power the Self-owned Brands

In the 2006 National People's Congress, the president of Gree Electric Appliances, Dong Mingzhu, from Zhuhai, Guangdong province, advanced two proposals: one is about setting up the "Chinese industrialist award" by the state related departments, so as to support that manufacturers should develop their "industrial spirit" from a long term perspective, not just seek short term profits; and reward those role model enterprises who have created long term interests for the development of their enterprises through their technological innovations. The second proposal is suggesting amending the current export (tax) rebate policy to provide more support for China's own brands. At present, the figure of OEM exports is quite big in many enterprises, but they lack core technologies; on the contrary, some enterprises with their own brand face many difficulties in exporting their products in the international trade. The export policy should be more favorable to this kind of enterprises, because they need to make more investment in exporting and nurturing their own brand.

1) The Industrial Spirit Is Essential to Enterprises

Dong Mingzhu pointed out: "We advocate the spirit of dedication in Gree Electric Appliances, an industrial spirit, being practical without the thought of playing speculations. What we are doing now must be responsible for the future of our own, and every employee should bear it in their mind. Only with this spirit, can we build quality products and will our internal management be more precise. So our team can overcome various difficulties. " Being a loyal and staunch supporter of the "industrial spirit", She believes, it is no doubt that to initiate dependent innovation is important, because "innovation" is the "fruit"; therefore, if Gree people want to promote innovation in the company, the "industrial spirit" is the determinant factor. In order to promote the industrial spirit, on the one hand, people in Gree should talk less, practice more and be well-prepared for a long-term war in research, development and independent innovation; on the other hand, Gree people should not only pay attention to the current consumer demand, but also should attach great importance to the basic needs of consumers; actively shoulder social responsibilities, propel the society forward with corporate power, and be responsible for the future with today's actions. That is to say, promoting the "industrial spirit" is promoting the spirit of dedication.

Now, it is well-known that, China is regarded as "the big manufacturing nation" by the all world but it is not a "world powerful manufacturing nation" yet. According to statistics issued by the State Statistics Bureau, the Added Value Ratio of China's manufacturing industry is only 26.2%.   With regard to this situation, Dong Mingzhu frankly gave her opinion on it, in the advantages of cheap labor, land and other resources, many enterprises formulate their development ideas purely from the perspective of commercialism and short term profits.

Her analysis shows that there are three reasons for the lack of independent innovation ability in Chinese enterprises:

Firstly, the domestic and foreign enterprises enjoy different policies, which makes some industrialists seek quick success and instant benefits with those favorable policies. And they are not willing to make researches in their business operation and technology innovation. Secondly, relevant state policies have no different treatments in the exports of national brands and OEM products, which causes the enterprises with their own brands to be less competitive. The third reason is that quite a few industrialists in air conditioning industry cannot bear the hardships and easily succumbed to the temptations from other industries, so they gave up their business in making air conditioners halfway.

The president of Gree, Dong Mingzhu continues analyzing the situation and she believed that: "Promoting the 'industrial spirit' in China can attract people's strength and wisdom from the simple commercial exchange of goods into the innovation field to the greatest degree, thus the 'industrial spirit' could help Chinese enterprises break the vicious circle of "products of low price --lower the price for competition--trade frictions--export restriction--shortage of funds--product structure improvement constrained" in China's air-conditioning industry and lay a solid technological foundation for China's building national brands to lead the world."

The facts has proved that, in air conditioning and refrigeration industry, Dong Mingzhu always regards the "industrial spirit" --work steadfastly as one of the mottoes for Gree's development. But, how many people really understand the meaning of it?

(1) Henry Ford's "Industrial Spirit"

In the times of Henry Ford, many people got to know the "automatic generator" in magazines, but it just aroused their interests not enthusiasm about it. Nobody made any researches or experiments on it, but Henry Ford was different from others. He firstly tried to understand the basic principles of automatic generator; then formed the conception of making twin cylinder engines. After that, in 1892, he successfully made the first car in the world.

About a hundred years ago, Henry Ford was successful owing to his persistence in carrying out the "industrial spirit". A hundred years later, today, people still need the same industrial spirit in running enterprises and doing other things. Industry is quite different from commerce. Industry is a huge building made up of ideas, sweat and every spare part. The height of the building is determined by the solidness of the groundwork. Fluke mind and speculation do not work here. Only pursuant to the "industrial spirit" step by step can people have the bright future.

After Gree has experienced so many years of development, Dong Mingzhu deeply understands that the growing of an enterprise not only depends on its competitiveness, but also needs a spiritual support to enrich the spiritual culture of the enterprise. From Dong Mingzhu's own experience, it is an urgent task for an enterprise to transform the "business spirit" to the "industrial spirit" in the respect of spirit drive for an enterprise.

(2)The Interpretation of the "Industrial Spirit"

Eever since the opening up in China, most of the Chinese enterprises succumbed to the "business spirit" in the growth of the enterprises and their marketing development. They will do whatever is profitable and the profit is everything to weigh up the gains and losses for their enterprise, which makes them swamped by pursuing profits, price war, product homogeneity and overcapacity. Consequently, the business spirit brought all these unavoidable after effects to Chinese manufacturing industries.

By surveying the history of all the countries in our world, it is not hard for us to find that those leading corporations are outwardly pursuing their development under the guidance of "business spirit". In reality, the core power for their development is still their "stubbornness" and "never-giving-thought-to-one's –gain- or- loss" spirit. If Henry Ford had not had the "stubbornness" in only making automobiles but in financial speculations, there would never have today's Ford motor company; if Bill Gates had not made great efforts in software industry but interested in the windfall profits from investing in the real estate, "Microsoft" would never have been existed either. Therefore, to push forward an enterprise's stepping to the future is not just only technology innovation, but also the spirit, the "industrial spirit".

The "industrial spirit" to Dong Mingzhu is to talk less, practice more, to pay a full attention to the consumers' needs, to promote the social development with corporate power and to be responsible for the future with today's actions. In simple terms, it is the "never-giving-thought-to-one's –gain- or- loss" spirit. This "industrial spirit" can bring human's power and wisdom together infinitely to realize the autonomous innovation, to build national brands, to enhance the development of China's manufacturing industry and economy and to meet the international standard and achieve an advanced level in the world.

In the eyes of Dong Mingzhu, the real industrialist is the practicer of the "industrial spirit" and the one with lofty ideals, high aspiration and social responsibilities, is always willing to give up the immediate interests and to be the real industrialist. The real industrialist is the one who regards promoting social responsibilities as his/her lifework not just only for the sake of making profits. They want to gain profits, but profit-making is not their only single goal. Their profits come from the core technology development realized by the independent innovation of their businesses. To Dong Mingzhu, the direction of Gree Electric Appliances is the direction of Chinese air conditioning industry; that is to say, to make the best air conditioners in China even in the whole world. Dong hopes that Gree can be the well-known world first class brand and the brand that every Chinese air conditioning enterprise is proud of and all the foreign peers have to admire. In order to strive to achieve this goal, Gree only makes air conditioners and leave itself no other choices; for this goal, Gree has built the largest air conditioning lab in the world…Dong Mingzhu does not know how many things Gree should give up and how much effort Gree should make to accomplish the dream, but she clearly knows that only by persevering in practicing the "industrial spirit" can Gree reach the brilliant destination of success.

2) Never Make Experiments on Consumers

As the competition of air conditioning industry is becoming tougher and tougher, the price war, concept war and service war launched by the air-con makers for grabbing the market shares are all confusing and misleading consumers. When the convertible frequency air-conditioner was launched, many manufacturers, for fear of failing to keep up with their competitors, hurriedly and hastily placed those immature products on the markets one after another. As a result, many "breakdowns" occurred in those products; even those imported famous brands were no exception.

But Gree Electric Appliances did exactly the opposite. As Gree advocates the idea of "Never make experiments on consumers" and it always practices what it preaches, before the quality of products is good enough, it never puts them on the market hastily only for catching the market share. According to Gree people, Gree will not launch the new products until all the problems in the new products are completely solved.

"Never make experiments on consumers" is the crucial point for Gree to win the markets. On 28th December, 2005, the investigation part of the CCTV program --Oriental Horizon announced the findings of an investigation "home appliance brands of highest consumer recognition" from *sina.com*. Gree Electric Appliances is the only one air conditioning brands winning the highest consumer recognition. In this investigation conducted by Oriental Horizon of CCTVE, there were 1449 consumers taking part in it. The result showed, among the four major home appliances--- color TV, refrigerator, washing machine and air conditioner, 80-90% consumers chose to buy products of national brands, and the ratio is the highest for consumers to purchase the air conditioners of national brands, which was up to 91%. In the air conditioner field, Gree air conditioner gained the most votes.

According to experts' analysis, on the one hand the reason for Gree to win in this voting is the good quality of Gree's products, on the other hand the factor contributing to Gree's most votes is its high performance/price ratio on the whole. This investigation centered on the independent innovation capacity of developing countries' home appliance industry. The experts suggest that to see whether an enterprise has the ability of independent innovation or not, for one thing, this could be manifested in its share of the hard numbers for technology, brand, patent and industry technological standard; on the other hand, the second important index is its performance in the fields of soft power, such as regulations, management and marketing. Perhaps the reputation in markets and the products and innovation capacity of an enterprise are not the same thing, but if a home appliance enterprise cannot win the recognition of the consumers, not to mention its independent innovation capacity.

"Never make experiments on consumers", is a sword for Gree to win customers' loyalty, is the principle that Dong Mingzhu has remained constant to, and is the navigation mark for Dong Mingzhu to lead her team to make the best air conditioning products with determination and practical manner. It was in the year 2005 that there was a hardest competition for the central air conditioner industry. The number of central air conditioning enterprises dropped sharply from the original 130 to about 50, which aroused a huge increase in brand concentration. According to the explanation given by some industry experts, at that time, the ones who had higher sales volumes were mostly foreign brands, but the national brands led by Gree rose abruptly based on their accumulated strength and rapid development. They began to lead the world in core technology and keep taking the market shares from foreign famous brands with fine quality, professionalism and advantages in localization service. In 2006, *Business China, Journal of HV&AC, Central AC Business Information, aircon.com.cn*, etc, dozens of authoritative medias joined hands to launch the campaign of "2006 Top 20 China Famous Residential Central Air Conditioner Brands": the well-known national and foreign air conditioner brands, including Gree, York, McQuay, Trane, Tsinghua Tongfang were successful selected in the "Top 20" list.

The experts pointed out, this selection activity was launched unprecedentedly in the history of China's residential central air conditioner by the authoritative organizations. With self-evident authoritativeness, this activity was designed to promote the healthy development of the air conditioning industry in China. The selection criteria, including: product quality, performance, after-sales services, survey of public opinions, and market price. And this activity is conducted among all the well-known national and foreign air conditioner brands.

In view of the existing situation that some manufacturers hurriedly place the immature products on the markets for the purpose of occupying the mark share, Dong Mingzhu believes that the standard set by the consumers and the market is Gree's only standard. In 2006, *Business Week* (US) presented a highest award of affirmation to Gree--

"20 Most Valuable Chinese Brands" issued jointly by *Business Week* (US) and global leading branding consultancy Interbrand. Gree, China mobile and China Unicom, etc, were included in this list. In this list, Gree Electric Appliances was selected in the list and ranked No.18 with its excellent performance, brand value of $140 million and net profit of $ 60 million. What attracts most people's attention is that Gree was the only one in the list from China's home appliance industry, but also was the only one of the brands in the few competitive industries.

"Never make experiments on consumers" is Gree's responsible attitude towards consumers. Although, today in the society full of commercialism, Dong Mingzhu still holds fast to the belief of devotion—"the industrial spirit" and never make experiments on consumers. But it is a pity that many consumers misunderstand the price war and they think that they have picked up the bargains in those price wars. Actually, those price wars have harmed the interests of consumers. While the prices are getting lower and lower even under the price of 1,000 RMB, are the quality of the spare parts in air conditioners still can be assured? The fact is that, no enterprise will fight with rivals at the cost of its own profits. Behind those price wars, there must be shoddy work and inferior materials used in the products for the purpose of lowering the production cost and the retail price, or some immature products which was hurriedly placed on the market for grabbing the market shares.

Review: Branding Is to Form Customers' Mindset

What is brand?

According to the definition in many text books: "brand is the identity, logo, slogan, design and service of a specific product, and the consumers' recognition of a product is fully reflected in their use of this product and enjoying its service. Their use of the product is influenced by its advertisements and the product design. Brand is the motive power for an enterprise's development."

In the writer's opinion, branding is to form the consumers' mindset. In the process of consumers purchasing a product, their shopping behavior is mostly controlled by the decision-making function in the brain. Generally speaking, there are three types of decision-making in consumers' shopping behaviors: the first type is to collect enough information about the product, make comparison with its peers; then to make analysis on it and consider other people's opinions about this product; and the last step is to buy the product. The second type is to buy a product on the shelf instantly without much thinking and analysis on it. The third type is that the consumers have a very high degree of dependence on a certain brand; when they have the need for this kind of products, they will buy the products of their desired brand without any hesitation because they have already formed the mindset for using this product of this brand. This type is the combination of the first and the second consumer type, that is to say, when the consumers have made enough analysis and have their recognition for some brand and once they have formed the consumer mindset in them, they don't have need any decision-making analysis for their next shopping behaviors.

Why is the slogan of "good air conditioner, Gree made" a success? Because the slogan "good air conditioner" is closely associated with the brand name of Gree, which arises consumers the association of Gree when they are thinking about "good air conditioner", just as the same for "Benz" and "luxury", "BMW" and "driving", "Volvo" and "safety". When a certain product represents a certain concept, this concept will be another name for the products of this brand.

This is the brand positioning theory put forward by American marketing professional, Al Ries. According to him: "Positioning is not what you do to a product, it is what you do the prospect's mind to condition how he/she thinks about the product... That is, your position (place) the product in the mind of the potential buyer... What you do to 'get heard': the process of coping with the mental position that a larger, more established competitor occupies. A tool to cope with overloaded information (and anxiety)." Well then, how to form this kind of brand positioning? One of the approaches is to find a certain and specific name for the product. The book of *Positioning: the Battle for Your Mind* written by Al Ries and Jack Trout told us, human being is in an age of information overload. The best way for an firm to solve the problem of information overload is to oversimplify the message and information of its products. What is the most simplified message? The easy way to get into a person's mind is to be the first one in its field, the best one in the trade, that is to say, the consumers' first choice when they want to buy this kind of products. In every year's so many sports games, each game has its champion, runner-up and third winner, but in most cases, at last, people only remember the champions, and forget the runner-ups and the third winners... If your enterprise is the champion in the industry, your enterprise should have the "name" in the mind of the potential buyers, an illustration for this industry. Gree Electric Appliances is just like this way. It is not only the champion enterprise in China's air conditioning industry, but also the champion in the global air conditioning industry; naturally, it occupies the name of "good air conditioner".

If there is other enterprise leading the industry, the possible strategy for a firm is to narrow down its business scope, to be the No. 1 in some subsector of this in industry. Under the premise of Gree leading the Chinese air conditioning industry, if other enterprises want to find a "name" for themselves, they must narrow down the product scope, e.g. to be No.1 in of cabinet air conditioners, commercial air conditioners or special purpose air conditioners, etc. Then, to be the best one in the markets and shape the consumers' mindset: When they see certain products, they immediately think about the brand name and when they see the brand, they quickly associate it with the products represented by the brand.

Chapter 3: No Limits in Management

1. Zero- Defect Quality Management

Gree Electric Appliances always regards product quality as the life stream. Therefore, Gree is implementing the idea of "quality is the life stream of Gree" in its practical production process. When talking about quality issues, Dong Mingzhu held that, "Gree's products should be the ones which do not need any after sales services", which means the consumers will not have to worry about the product quality the moment when they purchase the high quality Gree products. Under the guiding principle of "pursuing top class product quality, building an international brand, forging the century-old enterprise", Gree is continuously pursuing the perfect quality control management in its business operations. In the past dozens of years, Gree Electric Appliances has established a unique branch factory for selecting and sifting spare parts, enacted strict rules and regulations--"14 Prohibitions Issued by the President" and implemented the "Quality Strategy", "Zero Defect Project" and "Six Sigma Management" successively. Meanwhile, it has established a scientific and complete supply and purchase system inside the company.

1) Consumers and the Market Demand Are the Only Standard for Gree

This is an era of focusing on product quality. Product quality is the life stream and is the foundation for an enterprise. Zhu Jinghong believed, "When talking of improving the product quality, we should be 'relentless'. In China, many domestic products have no differences with foreign ones when in a small serial production, but when in mass production, the quality would become worse compared with foreign products. Why? The main reason is that many workers in China do not form good operating habits; they don't strictly enforce the process operation rules and regulations and they are apt to have a very relaxed manner when they are in work and the quality inspection and control tends to be less rigorous and strict." Dong Mingzhu also agrees with Zhu on this point, she thinks that technology and quality is the bottom line for a top class brand. If there is no high quality product, there will be neither the high-end market share nor the first class brand.

Gree Electric Appliances' quality standard has been established on the basis of wholly beyond the national standard, and Gree is always persistent in carrying out its own enterprise standard oriented by consumers and the market demand. For instance, according to the state standard, if the capacitor surface temperature of an air conditioner reaches 70 degree (158 Fahrenheit degree), the normal operation hours of an air conditioner reaching 600 is acceptable. But to Gree Electric Appliances, that the normal operation hours must be 1000 hours under the same condition can be acceptable. Indeed, to an enterprise, facing strong competitors is not the most terrible thing but the most terrible thing is the quality problems in its own products which will ruin its own reputation. Therefore, Gree always has the belief in the concept "make products with excellent quality and the best will come". In this manner, Gree Electric Appliances has gradually left its every footprint in the history of air conditioning quality management:

In 1994, Gree put forward the strategy slogan of "making first class products, having bigger productivity, building the top class brand".

In 1995, Gree formulated a series of strict management systems including "14 Prohibition Rules Issued by the President" to assure the product quality. From a very small working procedure, e.g. pasting sponges, Gree began to implement the "Quality Strategy" on a large scale.

In 1995, a "selecting branch factory" made up of 500 hundred workers was set up in Gree Electric Appliances. It is chiefly responsible for 100% quality inspection of all the purchased spare products from other suppliers so as to ensure the quality of the whole air conditioner units.

In March, 1995, Gree passed the ISO9001 quality system certification, which marked a great step forward in the quality of Gree air conditioners and established Gree's good quality image in the domestic and international markets.

From 1996, in every peak season, there would be many activities about every business operation designed for the "quality month". And all the staff members were motivated to participate in it.

In 1997, Gree proclaimed its slogan of "good air conditioner, Gree made" and aroused the awareness of quality among all the employees.

In 1998, this year was defined as "the year of reducing production costs" by Gree, with the slogan of "enhance quality and lower cost". In this year, Gree achieved its success in the both aspects of enhancing the product quality and lowering the production cost.

From July, 1998, a quality complaint card issued by *China's Long March to Quality Campaign* magazine was added to every packing list of Gree air conditioner. From then, Gree Electric Appliances was become the first company in China which dared to actively let consumers voice their complaints about Gree products to *China's Long March to Quality Campaign*.

From the end of 1998 to the beginning of 1999, Gree became the first enterprise to set up a long term air conditioning research lab and it started to put all the new products and finished products in bad working conditions for a long term testing in the lab, which is a facilitator for enhancing the reliability, stability and consistency of Gree air conditioners.

In 1999, Gree began to promote the "zero-defect" project and started a 1 million special-purpose fund to reward those staff members who made great contributions to the promotion of the "zero-defect" project for the company.

In February, 2001, approved by General Administration of Quality Supervision, Inspection and Quarantine of the People's Republic of China (AQSIQ), Gree was given the title of "National Products Exemption from Quality Surveillance Inspection".

In March, 2001, the campaign of "see the key parts clearly, buy air conditioner without worries" was launched in Beijing. There was an "anatomical demonstration" of Gree air conditioners, which made Gree the first air-con maker in China bravely to show the key product spare parts to the media and consumers.

In September, 2001, Gree won the honorary title of "China Famous Brand" from AQSIQ and China Top Brand Strategy Promotion Committee.

......

In terms of secleting and chosing raw materials for Gree products, the chairman of Gree Electric Appliances, Zhu Jianghong, addressed, "A good air conditioner should be made of good materials. In order to guarantee the quality of Gree air conditioner, Gree Electric Appliances would rather be more 'conservative'" in choosing and purchasing the raw materials for the air conditioning products. Considering that many domestic air conditioning manufacturers all purchase materials from the domestic suppliers, Gree is very 'conservative' in choosing the raw materials from the domestic suppliers. For instance, in the using of copper pipes, Gree always adheres to purchasing the copper pipes made by the largest copper pipe manufacturer in the world; for its quality is regarded as the best in industry, though its price is 5% higher than other copper pipe manufacturers. And there is also a big difference in the price between cold-rolled sheets and rustless galvanized sheets. As many air conditioner manufacturers tend to use ordinary cold-rolled sheets in their products, the differences in the two materials, to Zhu Jianghong, the story about the differences between the two materials still remain fresh in his memory:

Before 1995, Gree also used the cold-rolled sheets in its air conditioners and once there appeared a very award situation in the products. It took place during Zhu Jianghong's tour of observation in Italy. An Italian hotel purchased more than 30 units of Gree air conditioners, but in less than three months' time, some corrosion spots began to appear on the shells of the outdoor units. In fact, this hotel was a seaside hotel in Italy and the air was of high humidity and very salty there, so the cold-rolled sheets were quite easy to get rusted. Actually, this situation was not accounted to be a problem back in China, but the Italian owner of this hotel didn't agree on it. He said he had intended to use those air conditioners for at least ten years or longer, but to his disappointment that those air conditioners began to rust in less than 3 months. He asked Zhu Jianghong that what they would be like in another three months? Or three years later, could the orgrinal look of the shells of those air conditioners still be seen? He thought this quality problem was quite unreasonable. Later on, Zhu Jianghong agreed that all the air conditioners should be returned to Gree and he would change the rusty products for the owner of this hotel.

This quality problem had great impact on Zhu Jianghong. When he was back from Italy, he decided to carry out a sweeping reform of the product quality of Gree products. In view of preventing the shells of air conditioners from rusting again in humid weather and atmosphere, Gree finally decided to replace the cold-rolled sheets with galvanized sheets and employed spraying technology on the surface of the galvanized sheets in Gree air conditioners, which was the first one in the industry. As a result, the air conditioners will not become rusty in 5 years or even 10 years' time. Although this change would lead a higher production cost, the production cost would be RMB 1500 higher in galvanized sheets per ton than the former material and the total cost would be increased to more than RMB 70 million for every year. However, the above embarrassing quality problem has never happened to Gree products any longer.

To Gree people, they firmly believe that the consumers and the market are the only standard and yardstick for Gree's work and performance. Here, let's take a look at how the employee in Gree Electric Appliances, Yu Sisheng, from No.1 subsidiary factory handled the quality problem which once occurred in their working procedure:

"I clear remember that it was in the busy season of that year, after we had finished the packing of KFR45W/F split outdoor units and we were surprising to find that there was one extra circuit diagram, which probably meant one of the workers missed sticking on one of the air conditioning units or the quality control department gave us an extra one. Then, the team leader ran to the quality control department to enquire whether they gave us an extra circuit diagram or not, the answer was "No"; then he asked the coworkers who were responsible for sticking the diagrams on the air conditioning uints and they all promised that they did not miss any one. Perhaps in the eyes of common people, it is not a big deal whether there is one extra circuit diagram or not. It is even not worth mentioning and they probably will think that it won't bring great harm to the product quality or the image of the company, but we don't think it that way. We believe everything we are doing now will be important to our users later.

Finally, the group leader ordered: all of us must redo the packing. So we did not have a rest at the noon. All the 1000 units that already had been finished packing should be checked again and remade. If we couldn't finish the work in the afternoon, we would go on with the packing after the work time until the problem was solved.

The 1000 air conditioning units was not a small number, and we could only do after our work time for we must finish the original task for that day first. Nevertheless, when we received the assignment, no one complained about it. What we cared most was the assignment, not time; in the process of redoing the packing, what we asked each other about was "how much work is left" not "what time is it". Until all the work had been done, we knew that we had already worked for 16 continuous hours. What we were proud of was: the result showed that we did not miss pasting any circuit diagram on any unit after our redoing and checking the 1000 units."

From this small accident, we can see that every employee in Gree maintains a high sense of responsibility towards the users. The idea of "everything we are doing today will be important to our users later" is deeply rooted in every worker's heart. "We shall try our best in whatever we are doing, if we cannot do our best, never do it" is the common consensus for all the employees in Gree Electric Appliances. The consciousness for doing one's best is reflected in every working procedure in Gree. From production to marketing, from pre-sales services to after sales services, people in Gree always try their best to pursue the perfection of their work and build their superior brand with high quality products.

2) To Enhance the Product Quality Is Like To Cultivate their Life

In 2003, in order to improve the product quality management, Gree Electric Appliances officially employed the most advanced quality management method—Six Sigma Management to prompt Gree's product quality control so it can reach the international advanced level.

The Six Sigma management seeks to improve the quality of process outputs by identifying and removing the causes of defects or errors and minimizing the variability in manufacturing and business process. A six sigma process is one in which 99.99966% of the products manufactured are statistically expected to be free of defects (3.4 defects per million). It was originally developed in by Motorola, USA in 1986 and then was put into practice. Now it is the very important strategic tool for businesses to pursue excellence in their management. Today, it has been widely adopted by many enterprises from all over the world. The Six Sigma management has helped the enterprises to achieve noticeable results and laid a solid and sound foundation for those companies to remain their unconquerable position in the age of globalization and informationalization. Presently, almost all the 500 global top corporations have begun to implement the strategy of Six Sigma management.

As the largest and most comprehensive air conditioner maker in China, Gree

Electric Appliances has adopted a strict quality control as well as promoted its "quality strategy" and "zero-defect project". After the series of measures were brought into effect, Gree's product quality has been greatly improved. In the indexes of measuring air conditioner quality, the reliability and stability of Gree products have surpassed all the domestic peers. The repair rate of Gree has sharply dropped to in parts per million; in reality, the repair rate of some advanced enterprises is still in permillage, so that even some Japanese enterprises cannot help praising Gree's very low repair rate.

But even so, Gree still sets a higher goal for itself. "Product quality is the life blood of Gree Electric Appliances". In Zhu Jianghong's (the chairman of Gree Electric Appliances) opinion, China's air conditioning enterprises should make greater efforts in "going global" to face the bigger challenges from those multi-national corporations with strong financing background and technical strength. Now the gap between the domestic air conditioning enterprises and the foreign air conditioning barons does not only lie in technology feild, performance or exterior designs of products, but also in the reliability and stability of their air conditioners. Considering this situation, China's air conditioning industry must work harder to enhance the quality and reliability of the air conditioning products. And if Gree wants to be the top class air conditioner brand in the world, it must learn from the world famous multi-national corporations and adopt more advanced and more scientific quality control methods—like Six Sigma management to make Gree Electric Appliances more adaptable to the pressure from globalization and the omni-directional competition.

Since 1995, the staff members in Gree have begun to enhance the product quality just like cultivating their life. When Zhu Jianghong had his tour of observation in Italy, he found that one of the costumers complained about the noise of the air conditioners and asked for a refund. Then he opened the air conditioner to find the cause for the noise and Zhu found that it was because that the sponge inside the shell was not stuck on the right place. This is caused by the workers' carelessness in work, which made Zhu Jianghong feel awfully and terribly "shameful". Despite the fact that the Gree products were quite popular in the markets, he immediately gave the order to carry out a sweeping reform of the product quality control. It was because the "burning shame" brought by the small sponge that aroused all the employees in Gree the idea of "ensuring the quality, building top class products".

It was quite common for an enterprise to pay great attention to its quality assurance, but it was really rare for the president of a company to formulate the prohibition rules on the quality control of the company. As to this issue, the vice president of Gree Electric Appliances, Huang Hui said, "To ensure the quality of Gree air conditioners, the key point is to control the important steps in the work flow. Regarding this aspect, Gree made very strict rules on those working procedures in which errors tend to happen. According to the related rule and regulations, any worker who violates one of the rules and regulations will be dismissed or fired on spot. There is no bargaining or green light on quality control issue--this 'high-tension line' "inside the company.

In order to control the quality of all the spare parts purchased from other suppliers, Gree Electric Appliances has set up a unique branch factory for checking every single spare part purchased from other suppliers even including capacitors --the smallest spare part in air conditioner units. And Gree also has a special team for quality inspection team, with Zhu Jianghong as the head of this special team, which has been set up only for supervising and inspecting the quality problems in working procedures. The chairman of Gree, Zhu Jianghong, demanded that once any air conditioner of poor quality is found, the quality control department should smash and destroy the air conditioners of inferior quality with the sledge hammer right away. He has hung a sledge hammer on the door of the quality control department, so as to keep the employees vigilant on this aspect and show his determination in enhancing the product quality of Gree air conditioners. "Let our customers feel rest assured in purchasing and using our products and make sure that our users feel 100% satisfaction with the products that we provide. We should never make experiments on consumers." Zhu Jianghong often addresses the employees with this remark.

In 2003, under the circumstance of huge stock, a dramatic jump in the price of raw materials and a sudden epidemic of SARS, many air conditioning enterprises encountered serious difficulties in selling products that year. In spite of the difficult situation, Gree still achieved wonderful results in selling their products with its advantages in professionalization, good reputation in consumers and unique sales model. Meanwhile, Gree continued to keep on intensifying its internal and quality management and rely on the strength of management to maintain the steady growth in its corporate scale and profits.

The series of strategic moves in Gree including: the implementation of Six Sigma, improving the production capacity and strengthening the management measures, all facilitate Gree's achieving its steady growth in sales volume and revenues. In 2001, Gree saw its sales revenues up to RMB 6.588 billion , which was higher than the brand in the second place about 8 million RMB; in 2002, Gree's sales revenues reached RMB7.030 billion , which was higher than the second place brand about RMB1.4 billion and the corporate profits hitting RMB 296 million compared with RMB 273 million in 2001, which was in a sharp contrast with the considerable reduction in the sales and profits of quite a few competitive brands in China's air conditioning industry that year. During the business slump of the air conditioning industry in 2006, contrarily, the sales revenues of Gree hit RMB 23 billion. Just as the iron lady of Gree, Dong Mingzhu stressed that, "Profits come from the good management"—is a goal so important which needs time of generations to realize. In the future, Gree people should use every means to ensure the good quality in our products."

2. Based on Proprietary Intellectual Property Rights

The chairman of Gree, Zhu Jianghong has reiterated that: "Only has the core technology, can Gree take initiatives in competition. The core technology neither cannot be "brought" nor be "given" by others. Gree should not only get ahead of opponents in sales volume and sales revenues but also should take a lead in technology research and development." Dong Mingzhu also pointed out emphatically that in order to gain a strong foothold in the international markets, Gree must possess its own intellectual property rights.

1) The Key Technology Is Not Given by No Means

Our country is generally known as the "world major manufacturing country", but it does not mean that we are the "powerful manufacturing country", for the absence of our own brand names becomes the "worry" of manufacturing enterprises and the lack of independent innovation capability is no doubt to become the biggest obstacle for the domestic enterprises' branding strategy.

If a manufacturing enterprise wants to achieve its independent innovation, Dong Mingzhu thinks that it must carry forward the "industrial spirit" with wholehearted devotion and should talk less and practice more. Moreover, it should be well-prepared for a long time battle in research, development and independent innovation. Additionally, it also should pay attention to the current consumer demand and attach great importance to the basic needs of consumers as well as actively shoulder the social responsibilities, propel the society forward with the corporate power, and should be responsible for the future with today's actions. Dong Mingzhu believes, promoting the 'industrial spirit' in China can attract people's strength and wisdom from the simple commercial exchange of goods into the innovation field to the greatest degree and lay a solid technological foundation for China's building national brands to lead the world.

To gain a foothold among the arena of the competition full of world famous brands, China's enterprises must possess their own intellectual property rights. Presently, many businesses all boast that they have very big production capacity of thousand units per year, but the key points are: Firstly, whether the output of thousand air conditioning units can be sold or not; secondly, is there any technical content in the products? The third point is that the research and development capacity of the enterprise is strong or not. In view of the above important points, Gree always invests much money in technology and advocates its independent research and development.

Gree Electric Appliances now owns over 1000 patents with more than 40 international patents. At present, Gree's research and development is the most advanced among its international counterparts and now it is gradually forming its strong competitiveness. After more than ten consecutive years' innovation in technology, management and marketing, Gree finally could top other competitors in the sales volume of air conditioners.

The president of Gree, Dong Mingzhu further stressed that: "To build Gree a real world class brand is my pressure and motive power, because it is not only the company's own need for its own development and it is also the need for the development of the whole society. I wish more Chinese self-owned brands to become the world famous brands to share the dream of transforming China from a large manufacturer to a powerful manufacturer in international community."

The vice chairman of Gree Electric Appliances, Dong Mingzhu also mentioned, the technology of centrifugal central air conditioner in the air conditioning industry was monopolized by four US companies in the past. For the purpose of monopolizing the markets, the four companies only sold the whole air conditioning units and never sold spare parts. But it only took Gree Electric Appliances about one year's time to break the monopoly of the American companies in this technical field. In August, 2005, the first batch of centrifugal central air conditioners with Gree's own independent intellectual property rights left the assembly line, which marked Gree's initiative to break through the American companies' long time monopoly in this area. And not long ago, the company once again has successfully developed the world's first ultra-low temperature digital scroll multi-couple unit and made its inroads in the field of central air conditioners.

Just as Dong Mingzhu believed that although the international peers were not willing to share a little bit of the core technology for making good airconditioners, they even monopolized the markets with their advantages in core technology, Gree as one of the national brands in China has the responsibility to smash up the monopoly and establish the image of Chinese top brands. It is also the very reason why Gree Electric Appliances must take the road of independent innovation in its development direction.

In the hundred year history of air conditioners, the core technology in this industry was always dominated by US and Japanese companies. Regarding the situation, the chairman of Gree Electric Appliances, Zhu Jianghong thinks that the advanced technology is never the largesse given by other companies. In order to keep improving the capacity of independent innovation, Gree has invested a large fund in its technology research and development with 3% of its sales revenues every year, which is the biggest fund among the companies in Chinese air conditioning industry. So far, Gree Electric Appliances has about 1200 research staff members including the experts in air conditioning field from home and abroad. Among them, 90% of the personnel are the bachelor degree holders or above, and at the same time, Gree set up the award "prize for progress in science and technology" to reward those staff members who made great contributions in the scientific researches. Besides, for those employees who have made great contributions in science and technology will obtain the bonus from Gree Corporation. And the bonus for a single award is usually as high as RMB1million. Through the series of effective measures taken in its research and development, Gree Electric Appliances gradually has built a very good environment for making scientific researches and respecting knowledge and talented people.

With the purpose of keeping close pace with the most advanced technologies in the world air conditioner manufacturing, Gree Electric Appliances has built the world largest R&D center with more than 220 professional experiment labs, such as the labs for testing the thermal equilibrium, noise and reliability of Gree air conditioners. These labs all maintain a leading status in the world in the aspects of numbers, sizes or levels of technology. Moreover, there has been a biggest institute of Refrigeration Technology in Gree; so far, it has already applied for more than 1000 patents with the most product specifications and types in the international markets.

2) Foster the Correct Patent Awareness

The competition between enterprises now is chiefly the competition of their patented technology, Dong Mingzhu once said. The secretary general of the Patent Protection Association in China, Mr. Hu Zuochao quite agrees with Dong Mingzhu on this point. He thinks that Chinese enterprises should know very clearly about that to apply for patents is the requirement and demand of the market competition currently. To any enterprise, a patent is not necessarily an invention made by the enterprise. As long as anything produced by the enterprise which is popular in the markets and has its commercial value, it can be called as a useful patent.

In our age, as the new high-tech achievements are continually emerging and the competition in science and technology is growing increasingly tougher and tougher, the advancement and innovation in science and technology have become the leading force in influencing and driving forward the global economy and political pattern. In this process, the multi-national corporations with strong innovation capacity are playing one of the leading roles in global economy and science activities. In this context, Gree is constantly placing great stress on applying patents. The activity of the "Establishment of Intellectual Property Rights Exemplary Enterprises in State Enterprises and Public Institutions" organized and launched by the State Intellectual Property Office were received close attention from the whole national intellectual property system. In this event, Gree was honorably selected into the first batch companies of the list. This campaign aimed at giving credit to and awarding the vanguard enterprises or public institutions with strong innovation capacity. It also tried to encourage the establishment of intellectual property rights exemplary enterprises as well as raise the level of the work of intellectual property rights of enterprises in an all-round way by setting up typical examples, summarizing the experience, and spreading the demonstrations.

For so many years, Gree Electric Appliances has been persistent in carrying out its independent innovations and promoting its quality strategy and now it has made significant progress in the work of intellectual property rights. So far, Gree owns more than 1000 foreign and domestic patents; among them, the patents from its invention are over 100, which shows Gree's very important role in leading, guiding and demonstrating for the intellectual property right protection in our national home appliance industry.

To uphold the independent innovation, an enterprise must foster its correct patent awareness. From the perspective of technology research and development, our nation needs to stress the ability of invention and creation, which is also the need for promoting our country's scientific development. Moreover, a patent is also a demonstration of the development of an enterprise's scientific technology, that is to say, the industrialization of its scientific technology development. The most important factors for an enterprise are the market share and commercial value. It does not matter what the patent or the invention is, as long as it has commercial value for the enterprise.

But in the understanding of patent awareness, there is a big difference between Chinese enterprises and foreign enterprises. Some Chinese enterprises either have no patent awareness at all or have wrong understandings about it. Some Chinese enterprises even do not know why they are applying for patents and a few enterprises parade themselves as successful businesses just because they have their own patents. In comparison, those foreign enterprises are very clearly about that the patent war is for pursuing market profits. and those so called core patents can demonstrate this point. However, as to the scientific technology itself, core patent can be a big puzzle in science. But from the angle of market value, to enterprises, the core patent should be the product which is made from the core patent as well as both popular and valuable in the markets.

At the early stage of Gree's development, Zhu Jianghong once hoped to import Japanese advanced technology of manufacturing multi-connected central air conditioners, but out of Zhu Jianghong's expectation, the Japanese enterprise which once had a very good cooperation with Gree for many years flatly refused Zhu's request. The representatives from that firm explicitly stated that they had spent 16 years to develop this core technology and they would not give this technology to any Chinese enterprise in any circumstances. As there was no ready-made core technology for Gree to use, it had to make a fresh start in its core technology research and development. In the face of setbacks, Zhu Jianghong didn't give up easily instead he immediately set up a research team and determined to spare no efforts to master the core technology of making multi-connected central air conditioners. "What a professional large air conditioner manufacturer will be like if it has not its own core technology? God only helps those who help themselves." Zhu Jianghong once said to the staff in Gree. In order to develop the core technology of making multi-connected central air conditioner, about 20 engineers in Gree made their home in the lab and did experiments around the clock: collected first-hand data, applied new technology of intelligent control and digital control to solve the difficult problems of capacity calculation, accurate distribution of refrigerant consumption, and oil return in digital multi-connected central air conditioning unit. Eventually, by the end of 2002, China's first digital multi-connected central air conditioner successfully came into being. The birth of this air conditioner proclaimed that Chinese enterprises broke up Japanese enterprise's technological monopoly in the production of multi-connected central air conditioner field and finally Gree had its own intellectual property right.

In terms of enterprises' patent strategy, Gree Electric Appliances has provided a reference sample for those Chinese enterprises which are trying to enter the global markets.

3) Take the Highroad of Innovation

If we say that channel marketing innovation is a sharp weapon in marketing strategy, the innovation mechanism based on technology and management is the solid foundation for supporting Gree to become a bigger and stronger enterprise. Talking about today's achievement, Zhu Jianghong gave all the credits to technological innovations without the least hesitation. He expressed this view to the media more than once: "China's air conditioning industry is a late starter in the international arena compared with other countries. Our technology is much weaker than those long-established firms in developed countries. Under the situation of the global air conditioning industry mainly dominated by US and Japanese enterprises, if we want to catch up with them or surpass the world level, we must be innovative."

For a long time, quite a few businesses took the business management as the core task in their business operation and they were always keen on pursuing the increase of product quantity as well as the expansion of their company size, but there were few changes in their products and most of their products were of slight differences. As a result, many enterprises began to wage "price wars" and fighting with their competitors in the price wars , in the end both the the enterprises and their competitors suffered great loss, and it seems that the customers always "profited" from the wars.

Taking the long view of the sustainable development of air conditioning industry and the air-con makers, it is not really a good solution for the raise of production capacity at a low technical level. Once this production capacity exceeds the demand of the markets, the economic development of air conditioning industry will be stuck in trouble. The best way to solve the deep-rooted problems in the air conditioning economic development is to develop manpower resources with strong innovation capacity and impel technical innovations. The so called technical innovation is a process from the birth of new ideas, to product design, trial-manufacture, manufacture, marketing and marketization, which is also the whole process of the creation, circulation and application of scientific knowledge. It is safe to say that technical innovation has already been regarded as the driving force for the economic growth and become the new religion in industry in the western world.

Innovation is the trump card for Gree Electric Appliances to win the market share. Gree keeps investing heavily in the self-innovation technology by putting 3% of its whole sales revenues into technology research and development every year, which makes Gree – the first company putting the most money into air conditioning technology research among all the air-con makers in China and even the whole world. Meanwhile, Gree also has set up the institute of Refrigeration Technology to keep close pace with the medium and long-term development technology and sophisticated technology in the field of air conditioner making.

Looking back on the history of Gree, it rose from a small air conditioner factory with the annual output 20,000 air conditioner units per year to become a large enterprise with output totaling 10 million air conditioner units in 2005 and occupy the No.1 place in China's air conditioning industry. Its dream of surpassing LG and becoming No.1 in air conditioning industry finally came true. So, how was Gree's myth created? The mystery of Gree's rapid development perhaps lies in its continuous pursuing technology innovation and dependence on technology innovation for its growth.

(1) To Occupy the Commanding Position with Technical Innovation

In order to foster technology innovation and to occupy the commanding position of building core technology, Gree has invested RMB 30 million—RMB 50 million in the research and development of new products annually, so there will be more than 10 new products every year going into markets. Zhu Jianghong has given the personnel and financial power to the deputy general managers and he only focuses on the core task of technology innovation. In Gree's achievement of new products and patents, Zhu Jianghong's contribution is said to account for 30% of it.

(2) Only "Specialization" Can Guarantee Top Class Product Quality

Specialization is the most distinctive character in Gree's business operation and also the key point for Gree to realize technology innovation and hold the commanding position in markets as well. Specialization is for making the first class products, only specialization can ensure high quality and top class products.

The modern production is socialized mass production; the division of work has fallen into many detailed category. Instead of setting foot in all fields, an enterprise should focus its all resources and energy on specializing in a certain field or several fields. Gree Electric Appliances has set its market positioning strategy of specialization and gathered its all man power, finances to focus on one field. Thus, it can greatly shorten the development cycle of new products. So the products could be directly put into manufacturing from product designing and small serial production to mass production. And lastly the effective and convenient installation and maintenance services assure that the products are deeply favored by consumers. Specialization provides a firm basis and reliable guarantee for Gree's technology innovation. Surely, specialization will put pressure on the manufacturer and bring the risks to it as well. "Put all eggs in one basket" is undoubtedly increasing the exposure to market risks. If any error happens, Gree could lose everything that it owns now, and there is no turning back absolutely. However, the risks could turn into the pressure and motive power. Gree people deeply knew it, so they cut off all the means of retreat and tried all their best to accomplish their goal. It turned out that the Gree's pressure finally became the strong power and motive for its technology innovation.

(3) To Meet the Market Demands and Exploit the New Markets with Technology Innovation

In consideration of technical and product innovation, people in Gree Electric Appliances always cling to their own principle: "Care for the interest of the consumers, address the consumer's concern", which is fully demonstrated in the whole process of their technical innovation. "Care for the interest of the consumers, address the consumer's concern", means putting all efforts to meet the consumers' need. Zhu Jianghong found that what consumers need is a high efficient, lower noise, cooler and more power-saving air conditioner. To Gree, the consumers' needs are the starting point and the desired end for the technical innovation. In 1992, when the markets of air conditioner supply was falling short of demand, Gree began to make researches in energy-saving split type air conditioners---"air conditioner king": the new goal for Gree's product innovation is to make the air conditioners with the best cooling effect in the world and Gree wants the Energy Efficiency Ratio to be higher than 3.3, despite the fact that the national standard is 2.8. After trying so hard and making numerous arduous efforts, finally, the "air conditioner king" has been successfully made. When it was put into the markets, it created a public sensation in air conditioner markets and immediately caused a buying rush among consumers.

However, the success of "air conditioner king" did not slowdown Gree's advancing steps in its technical innovation. Immediately, subsequent to the "air conditioner king", the "cooling king" developed by Gree appeared on the home appliances stores' shelves in November, 1996, with two key indexes leading in the world, the Energy Efficiency Ration raising to 3.35 and noise lowering to only 34.2 decibels. Since the success launch of "cooling king" into the markets, it was very popular and always in the short supply and it was not only sold well in the domestic markets but also entered the global markets.

In accordance with the market demand for residential air conditioners in China's big cities, Gree kept working hard on another new type of products --"residential cabinet air conditioner", which was highly praised by the consumers as the "residential central air conditioner". The new product is small and exquisite in its size and exterior design with extremely low noise. It is amazing that a family only need one air conditioner unit can meet the needs for cooling three bedrooms and a living room. Considering that the commercial stores in some prime locations in cities need high-power air conditioners but they do not have enough place for it, Gree specially designed 3 hp wall mounted air conditioner, ceiling air conditioner with a split system and wind pipe patio type air conditioner to satisfy all the consumers' various needs.

3. Characterization of ERP: the Turning Point of Strategic Transformation

The implementing and practicing of ERP System (Enterprise Resource Planning) facilitates Gree Electric Appliances reaching a new level from management concepts to management model in its internal management control. The use of ERP System not only has enhanced Gree's competitive strength but also has built an information platform for the enterprise's long term development. In today's information era, Gree Electric Appliances fully understands the importance that it should grasp every new opportunity, timely adopt reform plan and promptly convert information into the enterprise resources to gear up the business operation activities. As early as in the 90's of the 20th century, most enterprises still adopted the manual accounting system, whereas Gree was the pioneer to use the computer in its financial management, which greatly increased the financial personnel's work efficiency and made it convenient for the company to make a quick query and analysis on the financial data at any time.

1) Rationalization First, Institutionalization Second
Gree's success comes with its corporate culture of innovation and its vigor and

vitality make Gree a creative and innovative firm compared with its peers. At present, Gree Electric Appliances has an air conditioning manufacturing base with the largest production scale and strongest technology strength. Currently the original value of fixed assets of Gree Electric Appliances reaches RMB 800 million and the annual production output has climbed up to 15 million units. So far it has developed air conditioning products of 7 series, more than 50 types and 1200 specifications and it topped the whole industry with so many products of different types and specifications. All the achievements of Gree Electric Appliance are closely related to its full use of information means.

Since the application of computer network in management in 1991, Gree constantly has been keeping advancing towards one direction--to serve the goal of business operation, to improve the response capability and to raise the operational efficiency of Gree. According to the chairman, Zhu Jianghong, he said that the informatization of Gree Electric Appliances started with a management operating system. At that time, Gree was in the enterprise transformation featuring enterprise reformation, reshuffling and restructuring under the context of from the extensive production management produced by socialism planned economy to the modern business operational pattern which is better compliance with the requirements of the market development. With the purpose of adapting to this reform and meeting the business operational requirements, the computer center of Gree Electric Appliances developed an information management system covering all the aspects of its business operation activities. As expected, this system played a huge role in Gree's miraculous rise. From 1991 to 1996, in just five years' time, the production capacity grew from 28,000 units to 920,000 units with the output value from RMB 120, 000 million jumping to RMB 2.9 billion. But along with the development of Gree, its formerly existed modular information system gradually couldn't meet the demands continually emerging from Gree's growth and because the different modular programs were developed by different people in different time, therefore, the fomer information system appeared to be lacking an overall design and posing some problems in practical operation, such as low degree of information sharing and bad integration of all the modules.

Therefore, in 1997, Zhu Jianghong resolutely decided to bring ERP system into practice. Before the implementation of ERP system, Zhu Jianghong invited the experts from 863 Program (State High-Tech Development Plan) to conduct several trainings for high, middle-level cadres and technicians in Gree, so as to well popularize and promote the implementation of EPR system. Subsequently, it took Gree half a year to make investigations and researches in dozens of software providers, such as the domestic software providers: Riamb Software and ICAX, as well as foreign software companies: SAP, Oracle, SSA, Baan, and QAD. Then, Zhu Jianghong realized that there is no good software, bad software, or perfect software. When choosing the right software for the company, instead of considering that the product is produced by a domestic or foreign company or the software company is big or small, the key point is to see which company's software is the most suitable for Gree's conditions and can solve the key problems in the business operation. After going through many procedures of business optimization, demand analysis, software demo and comprehensive evaluation, Gree eventually chose the ERP system provided by Baan.

About the effectiveness brought by using ERP system, Zhu Jianghong believed, ERP system not merely enhanced the efficiency of the company's overall management, also helped Gree to produce good economic benefits and to solve the following problems:

Firstly, the implementation of ERP system has standardized the administration in Gree Electric Appliances. After the EPR Implementation, Gree got to know very clearly about its current situation and the development direction for its future development. Furthermore, the software assisted Gree in standardizing management and operation model and helped Gree to build a scientific management system and a quick response managerial mechanism. In the process of EPR Implementation, according to the specific requirements of the system, all the material resources in Gree has been given unified codes and uniformed names, so they can be well managed through the management system. And all the suppliers and distributors, warehouses and transit warehouses in other areas have been given unified codes and category accordingly. Thus, it solved the problems of the enterprise's not clearly knowing the situation of its all material resources, the lack of standardization in managing suppliers and distributors and the confusion in managing and classifying the material resources in warehouses.

Secondly, the implementation of ERP system has provided a practical basis for the company to make decisions. The business reengineering process of Gree Electric Appliances has optimized its workflow and helped the enterprise further complete the basic management, greatly enhanced the work efficiency, intensified the administrative work and improved its market competitiveness and coping capacity in market competition. During the implementation and operation of EPR system, because of the information sharing, timely and reliable data, the enterprise leaders can be perfectly clear about what is going on in the company. Hence, the system provides a basis for them to make decisions. For example, if the decision-makers get fully acquainted with the inventory status, they will get to know the relevant information about how to reduce the inventory; if they clearly know about the product sales status, they will have the basis for strengthening the sales and marketing of the company; if they completely understand the procurement status, they will know how to improve and solve the problems of the procurement bottlenecks in management based on the information; if they know the production status very well, they will know how to fully exploit the present production capacity to produce more products which are more suitable for the markets.

Thirdly, after the implementation of the ERP system, the enterprise's economic benefits have been increased significantly. And the direct economic benefits are increased as well. It helps to shorten the development cycle of the products; the quality of products is also obviously enhanced with a very quick market response. In normal conditions, a new product only needs 90 days from the conception of new products to the steps of leaving the product line and the cross-examination pass rate reached 99.8% in 2001 from 98.5% in 1998. Moreover, it also affects the indirect economic benefits. In the whole process of EPR system implementation and operation, via the inventory management system, the enterprise is completely clear about the stockpile in the warehouses of factories and transit warehouses in other areas, which helps the management staff members to make a detailed plan for reducing the production of overstocked products and intensifying sales efforts in selling overstocked products and helps to lower the production cost and holding cost for the company as well. In the meantime, it also has greatly ensured the quick capital return of sales financing for Gree. Since Gree peole effieicently took the material requirement data calculated by ERP system into their analysis and work plans, the procurement management of Gree Electric Appliances has been greatly strengthened, the exactitude of Gree's material purchase has been improved and the inventory status of Gree's warehouses has been upgraded too.

Fourthly, the implementation of the EPR system has enhanced the accuracy and feasibility of working plans. According to the management thought and logic of the application software, people in Gree have redesigned the production plan by optimizing the production management process and increasing Gree's production. Facing every year's price war, Gree still managed to realize the growth rate of 20% each year in its main business. Because of the full use of ERP system, the accuracy and promptness of the enterprise's decision support have been raised and the company has established the basic data, such as the enterprise's internal basic data and the supplier and distributor basic data, which greatly has raised the accuracy of Gree's marketing, manufacturing and purchasing plans. With the repeated job scheduling provided by ERP system, the feasibility of the plans made by the company can be sufficiently reflected.

Fifthly, the implementation of the EPR system has solved the problems of poor data management in the enterprise finance management. For a long time, the inconsistency in the business fund account and the real account as well as the poor data management in finance management have long vexed the company. Since the use of ERP system, the timely collecting and processing of data in the account receivable and payable have solved the above problems that have existed for a long time.

According to the person in charge of this project and from the analysis of the system operation and enterprise management in Gree, we can see that ERP system not only has solved many problems in Gree's enterprise management, but also has assisted Gree in raising management level and economic benefits. On the whole, it has helped the largest air conditioner maker in the world to achieve the desired results. However, if enterprises want the implementation of this system to be very smooth, the industry experts think there are some aspects which need to pay attention to:

First, the preparation of the product basic data is the key to the success of the project. The complete and accurate data preparation in a project is just like "a good beginning is half done".

Second, in the phrase of the project implementation, the responsibility in every stage of the project should be clear determined: timely summary, clear planning, complete and accurate documents.

Third, strengthen the communication and publicity with the assistance of a tight training plan to ensure the smooth operation of the project. Try to avoid the situation that some departments and branch factories' taking their heavy tasks in production as the excuse to give insufficient and inadequate support to the implementation of the project and show insufficient cooperation in the operation of the project.

Fourthly, should pay more attention to the stability of the consulting team and project team. In the early period of the project of implementing ERP system, Gree once made very slow progress in the implementation of the EPR project because of the internal problems and chaos in Baan during the time when it was about to be acquired by a company. When Baan was finally purchased by another company, the project of Gree's ERP system implementation was eventually put on the right track and could be developed along the right lines.

2) The Startup of ERP System Management

The popularization of ERP system management is not just a movement, but an inevitable course for the company to lead to informationalization. In this process, only the mature products which provide sweeping and professional service assurance can meet the users' actual needs. The goal of the ERP system implementation is to let the users obtain the real value in employing ERP system, instead of making them experience difficulties without seeing the accomplishment. Therefore, a good use of ERP system is the foundation of its popularization.

The smooth application of ERP system is a milestone for Gree's qualitative leap in its business management level. During the product designing and manufacturing, Gree Electric Appliances introduced the software systems, such as CAD, CAM, CAPP to improve the design and level of product processing. The introduction of the systems has boosted Gree's product design and level of product processing, which facilitate Gree's launching hundreds of high quality new products every year. The product sales of Gree is all over the country, connected by Gree's remote communication system; with it, Gree head office could timely and easily know everyday's sales volume in detail, so that it could effectively make adjustments in its marketing strategy and reasonable arrangements of manufacturing through the data transmitted from the branch offices nationwhide. With the assistance of informationization construction, Gree has effectively lowered its production cost, greatly enhanced its work efficiency, highly improved its product quality and dramaticly promoted its sales volumes. It is easily to see that the informationization construction's huge role in Gree's production and operation management. Additionally, Gree has been actively engaged in promoting the application of internet inside the company. In recent years, many large enterprises like Gree began to acquire relevant information on Internet and send emails to strengthen the ties with their clients. Moreover, as early as in 1996, Gree Electric Appliances already registered its domain name and built the wed site of "gree.com".

Currently, most small and medium-size enterprises can afford a set of ERP system products for the price of ERP system is not so high to them, but they find it quite hard to accept that ERP system is a long term investment. Using the ERP system like buying insurance, they have to continuously spend money for the maintenance service. Many SME users think having the ERP system is like having a car; they have the money to buy the car but they haven't enough money for tending and maintaining the car. The follow-up investment in the ERP system becomes a formidable obstacle in the way of promoting this system, which makes it impossible for the popularization of ERP in a short time. Nonetheless, to Gree Electric Appliances, to decide to purchase an ERP system is a relatively easy job, but the implementation of the EPR system is a task full of challenges. Only a strong and powerful leading team can ensure the success of the project. Leaders in Gree Electric Appliances deeply knew this situation and then they decided to let the Total Quality Management Office which has the power to evaluate the performance quality of all departments and monitor the business work flow in the company act as the lead in the project team made up by the key personnel and employees from the information center. After the project is finished, the Total Quality Management Office's task in supervising the implementation of the ERP system will be transferred to the Information Center of Gree Electric Appliances. The project team can demand that other departments change their management process according to the requirement of ERP standardization, which created the favorable conditions for the ERP implementation. In March 3, 1999, the startup of ERP implementation in Gree Electric Appliances officially kicked off. Thereby, the curtain of the project ERP system implementation was finally raised in Gree.

In the whole process of the ERP system implementation, Gree Electric Appliances has purchased all ERP modules from Baan. When the ERP implementation was successfully done, Gree could handle all the business activities ranging from financial management to sales forecasting, procurement, inventory management, production control, project management, service and repair, distribution and transportation.

(1) Gree Electric Appliances Enterprise Module

Gree has utilized the combination of the optimized workflow through consulting and software process of Baan to establish the Gree Module and set different menus and user permissions for every employee. It has efficiently helped Gree to put more energy in the series of advanced features instead of being confused by complicated application software configuration or endless product setups.

(2) The Implementation of Distribution Subsystem

On 1st January, 2000, this system was started to put into use in parallel with the old system. On 26th August, 2000, it was officially put into the practical business operation. The Distribution Subsystem of the software includes the following modules: distribution demanding planning, marketing contract, electronic data interchange and marketing control.

(3) The Implementation of Production Subsystem

The Production Subsystem Module began to have its test run on 26th October, 2000 and in January, 2001, it was officially bought into service. The old and former production system was finally replaced by the new system on 26th July, 2001. The new system mainly includes the modules in Baan production system, namely, capacity requirement plan, production control, engineering change control, master production schedule and engineering data management.

(4) The Implementation of Financial Subsystem

The financial subsystem was brought into use in January, 2001, with the constant improvement in the features of the modules. On 26th October, 2001, the old system was replaced by the new Financial Subsystem and the brand new system was begun to put into service. The new modules in the Financial Subsystem are mostly the Baan ERP financial subsystem modules including, account receivable, account payable, cash management and budgeting system.

4. Specialization Forging Gree's Competitive Strength

"Shall we expand the company by means of diversification or specialization?" This is the trickiest and most controversial dilemma faced by many Chinese enterprises after they become the powerful and large enterprises in the world. The relevant data show that through the sample analysis and case study on 412 enterprises in China, in the rate of return on capital, the business operation of specialization is much higher than the way of diversification. In the road of China's enterprise diversification, many Chinese tycoons have failed in their business operations. From the bankruptcy of Leveno's 365FM to Haier Biological Pharmacy's unsuccessful campaign, the Start Group (Fujian Start Group Co.Ltd) stock reduced into Special Treatment stock, the shutdown of AUX automobile and the collapse of Delong Firm (the revenues model of a big family business in China), some scholars even made the comments: "Including Haier, no Chinese enterprises have been successful yet in diversification expansion." In China's home appliance industry, Gree Electric Appliances is a large enterprise only specializing in producing air conditioning products. Since the founding of this company, it has considered making air conditioner as its main business, and only focused on manufacturing residential air conditioners and central air conditioners. When many companies in home appliance industry are engaged in their multiple-line operations by the reasons of spreading risks and rapid expansion, Gree still adheres to its specialized operation of making air conditioners.

1) The Road of Specialization

Gree Electric Appliances always persists in its own operating characteristics and unswervingly sticks to its business policy of specialization in China's home appliance industry and finally came to be the successful example in domestic home appliance industry.

Since the founding of this company, it has decided to take making air conditioner as its main business, and only focus on manufacturing residential air conditioners and central air conditioners. The year 1995 witnessed Gree with slight advantages surpassing Chunlan air conditioner, the pilot enterprise in China's air conditioning industry in the former days, to be the No.1 in sale volume of this industry. Soon afterwards, Gree was facing the problem of expanding the company by the choice of specialization or diversification. At last, after much thought, Zhu Jianghong, the chairman of Gree, made a critical decision concerning the future development of Gree Electric Appliances—to take the road of specialization as Gree's long term development strategy.

Generally speaking, there are usually two developing roads for expanding an enterprise: one development path is through specialization, the other is through diversification. Under normal circumstances, if an enterprise doesn't have overwhelming advantages and superiority to be No.1 in a field, generally it would not easily to take the path of diversification. According to the statistics provided by *Fortune* magazine, among the world top 500 corporations, there are 140 companies in which the sales volume of their single product accounts for more than 95% in the total sales revenues. There are 194 enterprises in which the sales volume of the predominant products takes 70%--95% in the total sales revenues. As to enterprises, they should formulate an appropriate development strategy for themselves based on their own advantages, disadvantages and external factors. Unquestionably, Gree chose a right development path for itself in that very year. The subsequent achievement of Gree also has proved Zhu Jianghong's foresight and sagacity.

The reasons for Gree's persistence in specialized operation strategy lie in the broad space for development of the air conditioning industry and high probability of success. In our country, the products of TV set, refrigerator, and washing machine entered Chinese common families in 80's of the 20th century, but the growth of air conditioner market was comparatively lagging behind the above home appliances out of various factors and reasons. In 90's of the 20th century, came the growth phase of the air conditioning industry with a rapid increase in marketing demand. Some relevant data show that in 1985, the demand of for residential air conditioners in China is about 80,000 units; in 1995, the booming demand of the city residents for air conditioner products was increased by 33.4 times, up to 2.7 million units. In 1997, the sales volume of the country's air conditioner was raised by 2.15 times, totaling 8.51202 million air conditioner units. At the beginning of the new century, the ownership rate of China's residents for air conditioners is 16.29%, that is to say, there is still huge potential in the markets for the development of air conditioning enterprises. All these offered Gree a great opportunity for specialized operation strategy. The industry experts suggest that Gree Electric Appliance's specialized operation strategy has been realized via its internal model of development, that is, intensive growth strategy.

(1) Market Development Strategy

At the very beginning of the foundation of the company, Gree Electric Appliances chiefly adopted the strategy of "encircle the cities from rural areas". It primarily focused on capturing the markets which are the weak marketing areas for the famous air conditioning enterprises such as "Chunlan", "Huabao" etc. Gree established its brand image in the following provinces, namely, Anhui, Zhejiang, Jiangxi, Hunan, Guangxi, Henan and Hebei, and it built its market foothold in those areas. In the process of actualizing the strategy, Gree emphasized building the direct-sales stores and guaranteeing the interests of the consumers through excellent after-sale services. In the middle of 90's, while consolidating the existing market share, Gree turned its focus from the existing markets to the major and influential cities, like Beijing, Shanghai, Nanjing in China. At the same time, it is also heading off to the overseas markets.

(2) Product Development Strategy

Everything that an enterprise is doing now should be market-oriented, and should meet the market demand. To create the market based on the future trend is one of the standards for Gree's product development. In the aspect of adjusting its products to the market requirements, Gree Electric Appliances has successively developed the series of products: "air conditioner king"—the air conditioner with best cooling effects; "king of lowest noise" --- the air conditioner with lowest noise; 3 hp window air conditioner—the air conditioner with the lowest price compared with the prices of Gree's competitors at that time. In the market development, Gree made cabinet air conditioners with colorful light box best suitable for pubs and bars, residential cabinet air conditioners best for family use, as well as 3 hp wall mounted air conditioner, ceiling air conditioner with split system and wind pipe patio type air conditioner, etc. These products with their distinctive characteristics formed a comparatively a complete product system, which fully reflects the superiority in Gree's specialized operation strategy.

(3) Market Penetration Strategy

In terms of market penetration strategy, Gree has adopted a series of measures to penetrate the market by expanding production and reducing its production cost, as well as lowering the price for a bigger of the market. In the meantime, Gree intensified the efforts of publicity: "Good air conditioner, Gree made", this slogan highlighting Gree's brand superiority of excellent quality and services which make Gree brand enjoy popular support with consumers. What's more, Gree Electric Appliances has built marketing channels based on direct-sales stores and electrical installation companies to build its all-in-one service package of selling, installing and repair.

Specialization is the most distinctive operation characteristic in Gree's business activities. It is also the key point for Gree to realize technology innovation and occupy the commanding position in the markets. Specialization is for achieving good product quality; only specialization could guarantee the first and top class products. In modern mass production, the division of labor based on specialization is becoming more and more detailed; only concentrate human, material and financial resources and specialize in one field, can shorten the product development cycle and hold the commanding position in technology field. In the case of Gree Electric Appliances, specialization in business operation has laid the solid groundwork and provided a reliable assurance for its technology innovation. Due to Gree's sheer persistence in specialization strategy, in the end the road of specialization has built Gree a successful example in China's manufacturing industry. In taking the path of specialization, Gree, the late starter in this industry has surpassed the early starters and rapidly became a formidable rival competing against the famous brands in China, such as, Chunlan, Haier, Kelong etc.

2) An Enterprise Needs Specialization

As Zhu Jianghong firmly believes the ancient Chinese idiom, "One can be the master only in his own special field". Therefore, when other air conditioning factories began to take the diversification strategy by making color TV sets, washing machines, micro ovens even mobile phones, Zhu Jianghong still strongly clings to the field of manufacturing air conditioners, concentrates on taking specialization road with all its available resources. Thus eventually Gree people have built the only professional and specialized manufacturer of air conditioner with strong competitiveness in China, even in the world.

Dong Mingzhu said Gree will not stop making air conditioners until the air conditioner product is replaced by some more advanced products. "We don't think 'When one door shuts, another opens' is workable in the manufacturing industry." Dong emphasized. The energy for an enterprise is quite limited, if it wants to have diversification expansion, it not only needs to take its financial strength into consideration and it also must have more considerations about whether it has the management system corresponding to the diversification expansion strategy. Every industry needs to be supported by professional talents and relevant expertise. The enterprise will pay an enormous price, if it blindly expands its business scope without the accumulation of professional talents and technology.

The facts show that specialization strategy is the in-depth business development strategy of the products and markets, which can help the enterprise obtain value-added benefits and avoid misplacing priorities in its business plan. The specialization in the business development strategy is to take the competitive and overall situation into consideration. The train of thought for specialization requires concentrating the limited human, financial, material resources, leaders' attention and the potential of an enterprise on a certain area. And the enterprise should strive for penetrating and making a breakthrough in a field, a profession or an industry to form and highlight the local priorities of the products and then to win the initiative position and favorable conditions with the accumulated energy and in-depth development of local priorities.

To carry out the implementation of specialization business strategy needs firmness and perseverance. If Gree attains great achievement in its business operation, it should give all the credit to its development strategy. The fruitful results are not only produced by the development strategy but also achieved by the leaders in Gree Electric Appliances whose profound understanding, firm implementation and precise practice of specialization strategy. As a matter of fact, to an enterprise, there is no wall of partition between specialization and diversification. In the process of implementing specialization strategy, the enterprise has been tempted by diversification all the time; especially, it will be lured by the new market opportunities and profits that the diversifaction strategy brings. Hence, in most cases, the enterprises easily succumb to embark on the road of diversification especially in the light of the present market situation.

Certainly, specialization strategy does not equal to disordering and chaos in the business operation. When many enterprises are implementing the specialization strategy, the dispersed strength and focus of the work as well as the messy work pace began to show in their work. This situation is caused by the absence of specific and careful planning in the strategy overall design.

According to Dong Mingzhu: once there were many other manufacturers (of refrigerator, color TV set, washing machine, etc) inquiring Gree about using its brand on the products, but Gree all turned them down considering its specific conditions, such as human and material resources. As a result, Gree decided only to make air conditioners, from residential air conditioners to central air conditioners. It constantly firmly has this belief that there is always the market share for air conditioners, in which the market potential is infinite. Specialization can let an enterprise always under pressure to keep working hard and making progress. "To be better and far exceed the rivals on the road of specialization." On this point, Gree's firmness and clear-headedness is rare and commendable. Especially it is still "steadfast and unmoved in its stand" facing criticisms from those "trouble-makers or war mongers" outside of Gree and even outside the industry, which rightly reflects Gree's wisdom in making strategies and skills in implementing its specialization strategy.

"Specialization forging the competitiveness", the reasons for Gree Electric Appliances from an obscure brand to China's well-known world famous brand with huge turnover every year are its perseverance and persistence in independent technology innovation and building its self-owned brand. The global market once was the world of foreign brands in the past, because Chinese air conditioner brands lacked popularity in the markets, and the OEM export becomes the short cut for Chinese enterprises going global. At that time, Gree exploited its competitive advantages in lower its manufacturing cost to obtain many OEM orders from multi-national corporations, namely, Panasonic, DAIKIN, Whirlpool and Siemens. With the surge in export volumes, Gree improved itself greatly in its production process and management ability through the process of making the products under foreign brand names. After a thorough understanding of the actual situation in the markets, Gree came to realize that OEM is just the inevitable course that an enterprise has to choose in its growth phase. If an enterprise really wants to go global, it must have its own brand and take the road of specialization.

Having overcome the various temptations from diversification expansion and keeping a cool head in concept wars and price wars, Gree still decided to put all its limited resources of human, material, financial into air conditioning industry, and strove for the perfection in product quality and technology. Just as expected, in the first half of the year 2006, Gree's overseas market revenues totaled about RMB 4 billion and enjoyed a 76.67% surge year-on-year. The brand advantages of Gree Electric Appliance have become the highlights in the international competition.

Review: Specialization Forging the Global Champion Enterprise

In the book *Focus* written by Al Ries, he provides us with the analogy of the sun and laser light to illustrate the power of focus "The sun is a powerful source of energy. Every hour the sun washes the earth with billions of kilowatts of energy. Yet with a hat and some sunscreen you can bathe in the light of the sun for hours at a time with few ill effects. A laser is a weak source of energy. A laser takes a few watts of energy and focuses them in a coherent stream of light. But with a laser you can drill a hole in a diamond or wipe out cancer. When you focus a company, you create the same effect. You create a powerful, laser like ability to dominate a market." Obviously, the magic and strong power of business concentration or specialization can be easily understood through Al Ries's analogy in his book.

Gree Electric Appliances is just one of successful cases of focusing the company in its business operations.

From China's air conditioning industry to the whole global home appliance industry, Gree's focusing on air conditioner specialization strategy is a very special case among so many companies. Another Chinese company, Galanz originally also focused themselves on making micro ovens then after long time's struggle, it has become famous for making micro ovens in China's home appliance industry, but in 2000, it began to expand its product line to make other products. Different with Galanz's diversification strategy, Gree's clinging to specialization strategy helps itself win the championship in today's global market. According to the writer, there are few points needed to pay attention to in adopting the specialization strategy:

Firstly, the first principle of the weak enterprises' strategy should be focusing all its resources. If the small businesses want to manage a diverse collection of unrelated products under limited conditions, they will spread their resources thinly like a sun dissipating its energy over too many products and too many markets. The enterprises which adopted the way of diversifying its products, in today's increasingly competitive world, they will reach a point of diminishing returns, even go out of business, go bankrupt or to be taken over. Only focus their resources, can the small and weak enterprises have their bright future. When Gree entered the market at the very beginning, it was a typical small company. Later on, it adopted the strategy most suitable to itself—focusing on the specialization strategy of making air conditioners.

Secondly, adopting focusing strategy for a short time is not difficult, but the most difficult is to carry out this strategy persistently. Quite a few enterprises can focus their all resources when they entered the market at the very begining, but when they have occupied the leading position in the markets, they will assume they are very powerful and begin to be engaged themselves in expanding their product lines. Fortunately, so far, there is no sign of diversification of products in Gree Electric Appliances. However, its spirit of perseverance is quite precious.

Thirdly, only employing specialization strategy can promote the managerial skills and capability. The wideness and narrowness of an enterprise's business scope decides the complexity and difficulty in its management. When this enterprise focuses on a certain field, the complexity and difficulty in the management will be lower than the unfocused company which has many product lines. Gree's focusing on air conditioning industry ensures its energy in keeping promoting the management level inside its company. The failure of many Chinese enterprises' product diversification is not resulted from the factors of external markets, but the managerial ability inside the enterprise. American GE is one of the most successful enterprises in employing diversification expansion in the world. In China, many companies take GE as their role model to follow, but the result is less satisfactory, e.g. the 999 Group (a group with its main business in life and heath and it failed in its diversification expansion strategy) in China. What is the reason for their waterloo? The foundation of GE's success in diversification strategy is—its mature leadership skills and its strong managerial capacity for the overall operation, which can not be found in today's Chinese enterprises right yet.

In the 21st century, the development strategy for Chinese enterprises should start from focusing on certain fields and win favorable positions for themselves. In the mean time, they should pay more attention to improve their managerial capacity for the overall management of the enterprise, and then, they can begin to make plans for entering the new field suitable for themselves.

Chapter 4: Customer-oriented Services

1. Pre-Sale Services and In-Progress Services Are More Important

To many people's understanding, customer service only means after-sale services which only represent maintenance & repair services. On this point, Gree Electric Appliances' views and ways of doing things are always quite different from others'. They consistently regard product quality as the top priority in the overall work. For eight consecutive years since 1999, Gree conducted a large campaign of paying visits to its customers throughout the whole country. In Dong Mingzhu's view: "customer service should be reflected in all the parts of product manufacturing and marketing. Compared with after-sale services, pre-sale services and in-progress services are far more important." Gree's sincere customer service is to fulfill the promise made to them with practical actions.

(1) Without Good Product Quality, All the Forms of Services Are Meaningless.

The market share of a company is mainly decided by consumers who have their money in their pockets. Dong Mingzhu, the president of Gree Electric Appliances, firmly believes that to do a good job in marketing, a manufacturer must win consumers' hearts. Human heart cannot be bought with sweet words and honeyed phrases or empty promises. Gree's belief is to bring practical benefits to consumers with quality products and sincere services. The founder of Panasonic and famous Japanese industrialist, Konosuke Matsushita, also known as "the god of management" once said: "Service is first and foremost in terms of production and sales." That is to say, service is the first important factor both in the process of manufacturing and marketing. The plain truth always remains true for all the time.

When the 21st century is ushered in, how should a famous brand do to stay competent in the global market? Stepping into the service economy era, the customer service process must be stressed in marketing activities in the 21st century. And quality service is not only the sharpened weapon for enterprises in market competition, but also the living skills which decide the life and death of enterprises. In the narrow space for pricing products, it is hard for all the businesses to gain market share with low prices in the price war. Considering the real situations in today's market, the phenomenon of products' homogenization is growing gradually conspicuous. If an enterprise wants to stand out from so many competitors, it must have excellent, unique and creative services to continuously satisfy its consumers' needs and to win their hearts. After China's entry into WTO, the service industry in China began to feel the full impact of global competition as customers are asking for higher requirements. In the wake of China's entry into WTO, the competition will be more diversified, the service content should be deepening and consumers will have higher standards for judging the service provided by companies in the international arena. So, how to prepare to meet the challenges is a big issue for China's home appliance industry and relevant stakeholders.

Talking about customer services, Dong Mingzhu has placed a great deal of importance on it. She thinks that without good product quality, all forms of services are meaningless and insignificant. In most consumers' hearts, Gree Electric Appliances always enjoys the favorable reputation as the saying goes "buy quality products, choose Gree brand". In Chinese air conditioning industry, Gree home appliance is usually known for its high product quality. Without Gree's arduous efforts in improving quality and services, the brilliant achievements would never have been attained. From the concept of "every little thing you are doing is the big thing for Gree in the future" to "never make experiments on consumers", from "heighten quality awareness and go beyond after-sale services" to "top class product + top class installation service = zero maintenance and repair", every leap Gree made in its concepts, and every innovation it brought out are the contributing factors for Gree's leading position in the air conditioning industry today.

Dong Mingzhu continues to point out, "Product quality is vital to an enterprise. To make stable and reliable products is the basic respect for consumers." Gree carries out its customer-oriented services through the whole process of its production and marketing and builds a product service system and a series of unique standard manuals for customer service including before-sale, in -progress and after-sale services.

The leaders of Gree repeatedly emphasized that if they want to assure the high quality of air conditioning products, they must pay full attention to the raw materials—the very source of a product. "Before you buy our products, we already have provided you a sufficient guarantee" is the goal that Gree has tried all means to realize by making great efforts in enhancing product quality. Usually, an ordinary air conditioner at least needs about 1500 spare parts; the quality of any spare part will have an impact on the quality of the finished air conditioner. In order to solve the problem which is encountered by all the air conditioner manufacturers, Gree adopts a very "clumsy" method to solve the problem by setting up a special inspection team for checking the quality of all the spare parts purchased from suppliers --a branch selection factory. There are approximately 500 hundred workers in this factory checking and sifting all the spare parts strictly and their task is to make sure there is no defect in products along the production line; if there is any defect in a spare part, it is prohibited from putting on the production line.

In Gree's envision for making air conditioning products, they always stick to the principle of "never make experiments on consumers" and never put immature products into the markets. Gree Electric Appliances now owns a permanent air conditioning lab equipped with the most advanced technologies and the most complete facilities. Before any product is officially launched in the market, it must have about three to twelve months' test run or even a longer period for testing its reliability in poor working conditions, such as in the conditions of ultra-low temperature, high temperature and high humidity. The research fellows in Gree try their best to find all the problems that will probably appear in actual use and fix them all before the product is officially sold the markets. For ensuring the reliability and durability of air conditioners, Gree has invested heavily in introducing foreign advanced equipments and built about 170 "Nationally Recognized Testing Laboratories", which are the largest and most advanced air conditioning laboratories in the world so far.

A few years ago, Dong Mingzhu addressed: "When the air conditioner is sold, it is better for us not to see our users visit us for repair or maintenance in the following eight years." Then Gree created a precedent for quality guarantee in the air conditioner sector. This idear not only comes from Gree's own confidence in its products, but also raises a higher requirement for itself—should not be satisfied with what Gree people have already achieved and should work harder for making air conditioners which do not need any maintenance & repair service.

In 2006, the whole air conditioning industry was being confronted by the price of raw materials soaring up and the manufacturing costs rising sharply. Under this difficult situation, the legal representative of Gree Electric Appliances, Zhu Jianghong said with assertion that: "We should never do shoddy work and use inferior materials in order to reduce the production costs. We must ensure our users' interests. When there is a cost-quality conflict, the cost should be consistent with the quality." Thanks to Gree's unique management concepts, model and effective administration, the research & development in technology and supervision in product quality have been guaranteed. At the same time, Gree Electric Appliance also let the ideas about providing high quality products and services run deep in Gree's blood. Just because of the determinations that Gree made in ensuring the quality of its products, Gree continuously has been making new records in its performance indicators and has ranked No.1 for 12 consecutive years by virtue of its solid basis of technology, management and quality. This large-size air-conditioner maker has gradually become famous with its high reliability, low repair rate and has deeply engraved the idea of "Good air conditioner, Gree made" with quality products and services in the minds of consumers. It is the product quality that forged the popular brand of Gree air conditioner.

(2) The Best Service Is Providing Products Which Does Not Need After-Sale Services

The year 1996 saw a "service concept war" caused by the uneven product quality in air conditioners provided by domestic home appliances and the consumers' worry about the after sale services. Then the "service concept war" broke out in air conditioning industry, in which many enterprises started to hype their customer services that they were providing for the consumers, such as the star-class after sales services, and they were all beating the drum for their service concept around. Facing the "service concept war" breaking in fury, Dong Mingzhu went in the opposite direction by putting forward the concept that in air conditioner services: the most important are pre-sale and after-sale services, which was a whole new service concept at the time.

"The best service is providing the products which does not need after sale services." In the eyes of Dong Mingzhu, there are three aspects showing that the enterprise is responsible for its users, namely, pre-sale services, in-progress sale services and after-sale services. If you do a good job in product designing before sale and quality control the production, transportation in sale and installation quality well, the after sale services will be unnecessary. What is more, according to Dong Mingzhu, the maintenance and repair service is actually a trouble and disturbance to consumers.

Different from other enterprises, Gree has distinguished itself from other peers by giving priority to its before-sale services, i.e. strictly control and supervise the product quality. By doing this helps to reduce the pressure on the after-sale services and more importantly, saves consumers many troubles in repairing and fixing. Based on the previous concepts, since 2003, Gree has brought forward the following concepts of "the best service is providing the products which does not need after-sale services", "no customers' visit for repair in 8 years"; besides, it also took active measures in the important parts of manufacturing, like producing, manufacturing, logistics, selling and installation to achieve its goal. All the ideas and measures were pushing Gree to move toward its goal of providing the best service for the customers. From January, 2005, Gree found its way to proclaim the service guarantee of "6-year free warranty for a complete machine", meaning if a consumer buys a Gree air conditioner, during the first six years if any failure in the air conditioner happens, he/she will have the "6-year free warranty for a complete appliance". When the breaking news of "6-year free warranty" was made public, it immediately caused a public sensation in the home appliance industry home and abroad, for the service guarantee Gree made this time was far beyond the state standard and international standard, and it signified that Gree would take huge risks in carrying out the "6-year free warranty" policy.

But from Dong Mingzhu's point of view, "6-year free warranty for a complete appliance" is quite well-reasoned. Owing to the compete quality control system formed by Gree in so many years' practice, the quality of Gree air conditioners has already been up to the level that users can use them for six years without any maintenance and repair service. With this warranty policy, on the one hand, it is just because of the confidence in its product quality, Gree dared to make this promise to consumers. On the other hand, Gree's service warranty significantly raised the competitive threshold and promoted the reshuffling, healthy and orderly development of this industry.

As Gree made enormous efforts in product quality, innovation and service, it has stood out in the list of "Symbolized Brand in Chinese Industry" by China Branch Research Institute to become the leading enterprise indisputably from the three candidates of air conditioning brands. In the preliminary list of "China World Brands" issued by China Top Brand Strategy Promotion Committee, only four brands were nominated. At last, Gree was listed in the final list and become the only home appliance enterprise in the list. It is true, in recent years, Gree has made rapid strides in its development and its brand reputation has been gradually improved. As the forerunner in air conditioning industry, how did Gree Electric Appliances build its brand through services? Not long ago, the reporter from *China Business Times* interviewed Dong Mingzhu, the president of Gree Electric Appliances on the issue of Gree's customer services. The following is about the interview and Dong Mingzhu's comments on their customer services:

Reporter: How to interpret the phenomenon of those enterprises' beating the drum for their maintenance and repair service?

Dong Mingzhu: "Many brands claimed that they are providing 24-hour after-sale services for their customers. They will call their users and ask about the quality of the air conditioners through telephone follow-ups right after the installation of air conditioners. Then the next day, they will call the users again about the product quality. With respect to this practice, if you analyze it carefully with conventional thoughts, you will find something fishy here:

The first point is that apparently the enterprise has no confidence in its products. If they are quite confident of their product quality, there is no need for them to call the users again and again and ask about the quality of their products. It also needs money for making telephone follow-ups; it is never free of charge, but who is going to pay the bill for making phone calls? I believe the enterprise has no additional funding for it; the money for it has to be added into the costs of the products so the consumers have to pay for the costs, which is an irresponsible practice for the consumers. Secondly, consumers will probably think it is good that people from the manufacturer can fix their air conditioners. Actually, if there is a quality problem in their products, the manufacturer should undertake the responsibility to fix the quality problems. It is a must for the manufacturer to do so. The after-sale services can never be the attraction for consumers to buy a product. If a business is blindly engaged in the high-profile publicity of after-sale services, it will be proved to be lagging behind the time. When a customer buys an air conditioner, the most important work should be the installation of this air conditioner. Just providing maintenance and repair service is not enough. The job has been not finished yet when an air conditioner is just sold; what we need next is the installation service for the air conditioner. Regarding this aspect, Gree's task is to have a well-trained installation team to make sure that when the air conditioner is installed, it will be the best product which doesn't need maintenance and repair service."

Reporter: "Apparently, it is quite easy to know that you are very assured and confident of the quality of your products, but why Gree proclaimed that it would offer the service of '6-year free warranty for a complete appliance' from this year?"

Dong: "I do think it is an improvement for Gree's service. We sold more than 7 million air conditioners last year and I made a rough stab at working out the expenses, supposing 1% of the 7 million units have quality problems; that is, about 70,000 units need fixing, so there will be about RMB100—200 million to cover the expenses for repairing. Gree set the goal of "no need for maintenance and repair service for 8 years" the year before last. To reach the goal demands the workers' improving production skills and make the products free of maintenance and repair service for 8 years, which requires every one of us not to make any error in every link in the chain. After two years, we feel that our products are durable and will last for 6 years. Then we decided to provide 6-year free warranty, which is not just a slogan but a promise that we made to our users and we must fulfill it. If we cannot fulfill it, the consumers will be disappointed and they will never buy our products any more. If the product quality is bad, it needs lots of money for its maintenance and repair and we cannot afford the bill for the maintenance and repair service. Just because of our confidence in our products, Gree dares to put forward the slogan to prove that our product quality is quite high. To ourselves, we are also under the huge pressure to make our promise of the "six-year free warranty".

It is easy for us to see in Dong Mingzhu's interview from the reporter of *China Business Times* that to assure the product quality or to even reduce the after sale services into zero is the guarantee for the marketing plan of Gree Electric Appliances. As a matter of fact, when many air conditioner manufacturers were vying with each other for the market share with drumming for their wonderful "after sale services", Gree's customer service still was not put in the shade. The following points are the highlights of Gree's customer service:

(1)Universal Remote Control and Circuit Board

Most of remote controls and circuit broads in Gree products are universal. When the service personnel receive calls for repair from users, they can immediately arrive at the users' home and replace the failed components with the universal replacement parts. Those universal and changeable components show that Gree is trying all the means to make the consumers satisfied in a real sense. Contrarily, some companies like preaching their efforts that they made in their customer services but it turns out that there will be various types of circuit broads even in the air conditioners of the same types, not to say the air conditioners of different types. For those air conditioning enterprises of poor universality, it is without doubt that their after-sale services are unbearable and intolerable. Compared with some enterprises which only know hyping their customer service, Gree always tries to figure out what the consumers really need and tries its best to meet their needs, so it can win the consumers' hearts.

(2)Complete Accessories with Computer Coding Management System

The three major problems in the after sale services of air conditioners include: universality, the completeness of accessories and components for repair and maintenance service, and the quick settlement of maintenance charges. Gree's sales companies founded by Gree Electric Appliances and the local distributors have special warehouses and service stations for storing a large quantity of accessories, which laid a solid basis for Gree's after sale services. Moreover, Gree has encoded all the spare parts big or small and all the products and made sure that the codes in computer system match with every single component in the warehouses. For instance, if a compressor is needed for repairing the user's air conditioner, the service clerk just needs to know the code of the user's air conditioner compressor, then come back to give the code to the warehouse personnel. The warehouse personnel could quickly locate the accessory part in the warehouse according to the code, which greatly improves the work efficiency in Gree's after-sale services. In many provinces of China, there are still spare parts for the products made 5 or 9 years ago in Gree's special warehouses.

(3) The Quick Settlement of Installation and Maintenance Expenses

There is a saying about air conditioning products – for a normal use of an air conditioner unit, "the machine itself only accounts for 30% and the installation accounts for 70%", so Gree places great importance on the training and managing of after-sale service personnel, but more importantly for Gree is to bring more benefits to them. The cost of installation in Gree is the highest among its peers. At present, to install an air conditioner indoor unit needs about RMB 180 per unit (plus an air conditioner shelf), but for Haier which is famous for its customer service, its installation fee is RMB 130 per unit (plus an air conditioner shelf). Therefore, comparatively, the service staff members in Gree are more active in work than in other companies for the higher pay. Moreover, Gree always tries to timely pay the installation and maintenance fee to after service personnel and it seldom falls into arrears with those payments. Additionally, since Gree is very influential in its local partners; when Gree's users call for repair service of his or her air conditioner, all the local service staff can arrive at the user's home within 24 hours.

2. Set the Highest Global Service Standard

Air conditioners are usually known as the "semi-finished products", which needs installation and maintenance service far more than any other home appliances. In recent years, in order to attract public attention, many air conditioner brands began to hype the concepts of after-sale services, such as the concepts "8-year guaranty" "10-year guaranty" or even "15-year guaranty", which make consumers feel greatly confused and puzzled about it. The experts in this industry pointed out: as the level of consumption in China rose noticeably and the price of air conditioners was cut down under the new regulations two years ago, now price is not the last sharp weapon to capture the market share any longer. Supposing the life span of an air conditioner is 8 ~ 10 years, the after sale service standard of "6-year free warranty for a complete appliance" provided by Gree Electric Appliances actually means a lifelong free warranty.

1) The First One to Promise the "6-year Free Warranty for a Complete Appliance"

The service concept of "Customers' interests come first, Gree's profits come second" is the extension of Gree's concept of "service organization". Dong Mingzhu reiterated the point that, as long as the customers obtain the return from their investment in buying Gree's products, Gree can obtain its own profits. In this aspect, Gree has many valuable examples to illustrate the above point. For instance, Gree has a star-rating standard that Gree must bear the pressure at any time.

In the eyes of Gree, there are three steps for Gree to win profits: the first one is trying to discover the consumers' demand, the second one is to meet the consumers' demand, and the last one is for the enterprise to gain profits. The enterprise should consider everything from consumers' perspective, it should try to make high quality products, come up with sophisticated marketing and provide excellent customer services for its customers.

Gree began to publicly proclaim that, from January 1st, 2005, its warranty policy was officially changed into "6-year free warranty for a complete appliance", including all the functional parts, such as compressors, all the fan motors and control boards. According to the national mandatory standards, the warranty period of appliances purchased for home use purpose is "one year for the complete appliance and three years for the functional parts". Among all the air conditioner brands in China, the longest warranty for a complete machine is just 3 years, which means Gree's standard will exceed all the air conditioning brands' in

China. In this way, Gree will become the first air conditioning enterprise to provide the highest after-sale service standards in the whole world.

Air conditioners are usually known as "semi-finished products", which needs installation and maintenance service far more than any other home appliance. In recent years, many air conditioner brands began to speculate the concepts of after sale services, such as "8-year guaranty service" "10-year guaranty service" or even "15-year guaranty service", which make consumers feel greatly confused and puzzled. An authoritative experts in this industry explained, the guaranty service and "free guaranty" are two different legal concepts; the biggest difference is that "guaranty service" could be the paid guaranty service and the "free guaranty service" is totally free of charge.

Insiders in this industry pointed out: Supposing the life span of an air conditioner is $8 \sim 10$ years, the after sale service standard of "6-year free warranty for a complete appliance" provided by Gree actually means a lifelong free warranty.

It is said that Gree people have prepared for the after sale services of "6-year free warranty" for two years. They first started from implementing Six Sigma Management and recruiting related employees, then unveiled about 60 detailed rules and regulations concerning maintenance service and spare parts. Having done a drastic expansion and upgrade job in hardware and software in a full scale, with the large enterprise size and the competitive strength plus a long time preparation, Gree finally issued the surprising service policy of "6-year free warranty" on 1st January, 2005 with success. Since Gree is the pioneer in air conditioning industry, some air conditioning brands don't want to be lagged behind in market competition; so they also hastily followed suit. But "6-year free warranty" is more than a just empty promise or hanging the advisement banners, the construction of service network, adjustments in spare parts, recruiting and training employees, all the supporting work cannot be done in just few months. Apparently, Gree took an initiative completely in the adjustment of service policy, which fully demonstrates its leaders' foresight and sagacity.

The key point in providing good customer services is to put the service items into operations and the more difficult is to manage and supervise the whole process of the work. Sometimes, the customers may not be satisfied with the services, even though the spare parts and maintenance are well prepared. As the whole service process is servicing for the product, the service behaviors must be standardized and professionalized. With the purpose of providing good customer service, Gree timely controls and supervises the service effectiveness through every consumer's telephone survey.

2) Consumers' Interests Come First

In Gree's business concepts, compared with its after-sale services, the pre-sale services and in-progress sale services are far more important. "The quality product is the best service." In 2004, Gree launched a campaign of customer visit "caring about millions of users and concerned about the consumers' needs" as the theme on a global scale. It was the second massive campaign that Gree had launched since 1999.

The "massive campaign" once again demonstrated Gree's distinctive characteristics from others and offered a unique interpretation for its customer service. During this massive campaign, Gree provided free and standardized air conditioner maintenance service for 40 million old and new customers by introducing the general knowledge of using and maintaining air conditioners, handing out service supervision cards and collecting lots of helpful suggestions from the users. It is not hard to see that there was a world of difference between for the value brought to users in Gree's "massive campaign" and general after-sales services. Generally, the after sales service provided by many manufacturers is just for fixing the defects in the products, which does not bring any new value to users; contrarily, Gree's "massive campaign" is the sincere reward for all the users and it is fully illustrating the idea of "Organically combine the long term responsibility for consumers with the enterprise's long term goal," and bringing tremendous benefits to users.

Gree Electric Appliances always regards "Good air conditioner, Gree made" as its own duty and assiduously, whole-heartedly put all its energy in improving its product quality. For example, many air conditioning manufacturers use 0.75 mm thick of copper pipes in air conditioners for the purpose of lowering cost, in contrast, Gree only uses 1 mm thick of copper pipes in all the air conditioners, which effectively solved the problem of copper pipes leaking refrigerant. Knowing that outdoor units of air conditioners are easy to be rusty with cold-rolled steels, Gree is never hesitant to replace them with expensive galvanized steels because it won't get rusted easily even used in foggy seaside, though it will increase the manufacturing cost by tens of millions Yuan every year. Furthermore, in Gree's selecting factory, the task of 600 workers there is to check every component strictly; more than this, there are more than 400 quality control inspectors—the above two teams will be about 1000 people. The reason why Gree has so many people work together in the selecting factory is just for one goal: zero residual error in the products.

The vice chairman of Gree Electric Appliances, Dong Mingzhu pointed out that the consumers' interests should always be in the first place. In the "6-year free warranty" service declaration ceremony held in Gree's Chongqing branch company, Dong Mingzhu made a public disclosure about the reason for making this decision to the media and accepted interviews on the issues that consumers are concerned about at the mean time.

Reporter (R): Why did Gree make such a commitment of "6-year free warranty"? Is it just a speculation or hype?

Dong Mingzhu (D): Firstly I want to say that, every decision that Gree made so far is for the interests of consumers. Gree always gives the top priority to the consumers' interests. If we suppose the life span of an air conditioner is 8 ~ 10 years, Gree's after sale service standard of "6-year free warranty for a complete appliance" actually means a lifelong free warranty for all Gree air conditioners. In last year, Gree saw a substantial growth in its sales volume and it dared to make the promise of "6-year free warranty" service, which is not caused by a sudden impulse or for the purpose of hyping itself. This decision on one hand shows Gree's confidence in its products; on the other hand, this promise of "6-year free warranty" will be fulfilled with the guarantee of Gree's own corporate strength.

R: Gree once raised the goal of "no costumer visit for repair and maintenance in 8 years", and this time it proclaimed to provide the after-sale services of "6-year free warranty". Are the two contradictory to each other?

D: Actually, they are not contradictory to each other at all. "No costumer visit for repair and maintenance in 8 years" is our ultimate goal and the "6-year free warranty" is a guarantee provided by our after-sale services. Both of them are the manifestation of our full responsibility for our users.

R: Will the service of "6-year free warranty" provided by Gree lead to resentment of its peers? How will Gree do to deal with the inharmonious queries from the markets and outside world?

D: Gree always sticks to taking its own way of doing things. In the age of meager profit in air conditioning industry, the enterprises must be more standardized required by the markets. Many enterprises used to think they would be the winners if the products were sold out, but now we tend to believe the real winners are those enterprises who have won the recognition from our consumers. The air conditioning industry cannot win consumers simply with the "price war", not to say the speculation of "service concept". The most important decisive factor for air conditioning enterprises in market competition should be the product quality.

"Gree's standard, industry standard" has become a saying prevailing in China's home appliance industry. Being quite popular with consumers in the markets, Gree Electric Appliance became the first air conditioning enterprise whose sales revenues topped RMB 10 billion. In 2006, Gree still kept creating sales miracles in the fierce market competition by totaling RMB 23 billion to rank No.1 in the world. With all the efforts made, finally, Gree came to realize the dream of being the world champion with its steady growth in sales volume.

3. Beyond After-Sale Services

Usually there are three phases in the competitive strategy in a company: product competition—brand competition—service competition. As the science and technology are more and more advancing, the differences of similar products are becoming narrowing and product homogeneity is getting more and more serious. In today's world, it is hard to tell which the following ones like the product quality, price and branding of those companies is better. Therefore, the companies have to compete with their competitors with the customer service in the market competition. The service competition actually is "the higher level of production competition and brand competition" and it is based on the two competitions above. Today's consumers are not only satisfied with their material possessions; what they are pursuing is a higher level of satisfaction. They are eager to be regarded as the important ones and to be respected, praised and adored by other people, which is the central idea of the service economy era. In a word, our society has already entered the era of service economy, in which one of the basic characteristic is the service competition dominating the markets.

(1)The Campaign of Customer Visits

When recalling the campaign of Gree's customer visits, Dong Mingzhu said that: We visited 40 million customers with our concrete actions, which is different from the friendly service of after sale service. We made big investments in this campaign and it was really a worthwhile job. I did a rough calculation: if we had an advertising campaign, a half-page ad would cost thousands of Yuan; if we put this advertisement nationwide, it would cost tens of millions Yuan. Is it much better if we really invest the tens of millions Yuan in our users and make it change into the reward and our friendliness for our users?" In October, 1999, the first stop of Gree's "campaign of paying visits to 8 million users" is launched. Gree head office sent a maintenance team of hundreds of people to support the service stations and workers in Hunan to conduct these tour maintenance activities.

However, this campaign was an unexpected move to many people. When a Gree air conditioner user received the call for free maintenance service from Gree, she was quiet surprised and asked: "Is it really a free service? How can I never hear of it when I bought this air conditioner for so long a time; I didn't go to your service station for repair but you voluntarily come to my house for providing free maintenance service? " The real facts make consumers understand Gree's sincerity and consumer philosophy. Through this activity, she also got to know the importance of air conditioner maintenance. In this massive campaign of visiting customers, Gree not only provided free and standardized maintenance service for its regular millions of customers and offered the new users high quality follow-up service, but also introduced the general knowledge of how to use and maintain air conditioners correctly, distributed service supervision cards and collected lots of helpful suggestions from the users. In 2001, Gree Electric Appliances launched the "campaign of paying visits to 10 million users", and then in 2006, Gree's global users already reached 40 million.

Gree's large scale campaign is neither the kind of after-sale services just for fixing product quality problems nor the irresponsible product repair activity of "on-call service" or "24-hour service". Even though those services above mentioned are so called after-sale services provided by air conditioning enterprises, they are still quite different in essence from the value that Gree brought to their users during the process of its campaigns of "visiting customers". The common "after-sales services" is like to lock the stable door after the horse is stolen; it is nothing but a remedial action from manufacturers, which itself is an irresponsible attitude towards the users and won't create any new value for its customers. Whereas, Gree's big campaign has given a unique interpretation of its customer service from a whole new perspective. The value that it created is far beyond any ordinary after sales services. This value is, to combine the enterprise's long term goal with the enterprise's responsibility for its customers together organically; it is the actual interests, brought through a friendly way, to users, the enterprise itself and more users in the future. Those massive campaigns show Gree's distinctive characters in its own customer service from other air conditioning manufacturers'.

The chairman of Gree Electric Appliances, Zhu Jianghong explained, "Gree's concept was greeted with same responses from its consumers. It needs courage and vision for Gree to invest tens of millions Yuan to provide the sincere service this time. In China, Gree was the first one to start this campaign courageously with grand and spectacular scene and left a strong and deep impression on the public. This time, Gree's campaign introduced the consumers a new service model which is being improved and enahced by Gree day by day, in the same manner, this new service model opened up a new field which is beyond price war and the battlefield for being the first one to dominate the markets; that is a full competition in service. As there has been overall improvement in service concept, instead of those short-lived promotion activities appearing in the early stage of development in home appliance industry, what the consumers feel through this friendly and sincere campaign is certainly a sustained, long-term and in-depth service. Some people once asked me that since your Gree air conditioners are very good, why did we seldom hear you advertise that Gree's after sales services are good as well? I answered: If you are a consumer, are you happy to buy a product which does not need after sales services or a product which often needs after sales services? If the price of the former is RMB 500 higher the latter, you probably will buy a trouble-saving product. If the product is cheap in price but not trouble-saving in its quality, it must be the most ineffective consumption act. Therefore, our duty is to make our products to be the products which do not need after-sales services at all."

In the customer visits of the year 1999, workers in Gree Electric Appliances found there was an aging problem in Gree products. The problems appeared set up a higher demand for Gree: if the aging problem occurred in 5 years, can Gree make products which are durable for over 10 years and bring more tangible benefits to the consumers? The purpose of the down-to-earth advertisement is to let consumers understand the tangible benefits that the products bring, not a just simple product promotion.

In this customer visit activity, the biggest harvest for Gree was that many users felt confident in using Gree's products. Meanwhile, this result also posed a new problem for Gree: The target of after sales services is the users; while Gree has thousands of distributors in the whole country, it is rather hard for them to share the same awareness and idea when the distributors are providing service for Gree's users. Then, Gree made a timely summary on various feedback information collected from the users in the campaign and began to solve them one by one. In this process, leaders in Gree noticed some inappropriate practices in distributing products and some problems existed in Gree's home appliance service network; some of them were even about the product itself—the product problems. Fortunately, they have been all promptly notified through the users—"the sentry of quality" and thanks to the users, all the problems were immediately fixed.

On the necessity and the intrinsic force of Gree's "customer visits" campaign, the chairman of Gree, Zhu Jianghong has his own farsighted views on them. He summarized the background activities of this event into "five changes":

The first change is from passively providing services to actively providing services for Gree users. In the past, when there was a problem in the product, the consumers will visit the manufacturer for maintenance or repair service. Now, though there is no problem appearing right now, the manufacturer still actively visits the users. In the past, the manufacturer used to send people to handle the complaints from users. Now, there is no complaint but Gree comes knocking at the users' door to offer their services.

The second point is: the change from after-sales services to the all-in-one services of pre-sales, in-progress sales and after sales services. Gree was the first one to propose the ideas of pre-sales and in-progress sales services. Pre-sale service—should consider the design of the products, according to the four principles that Gree put forward for designing air conditioning products: the first is the product that the designer has designed should be suitable to the use of the consumers; then should be convenient for putting into a product, and there should not be any design problems in the process of production. The third is: when designing the product, the designer should take the servicemen's work into consideration, whether the design is easy for servicemen to install or to repair; and the last, but not the least principle is about considering the owner of the enterprise; designers' product design should yield profits and should not waste costs. If the pre-sales service is well prepared, the in-progress sale service is much easier and convenient both for the maintenance man and the user.

The third change is to impart the knowledge of how to properly use air conditioners to consumers and to let them support this campaign, i.e. the change from the company's own understanding on the campaign to the consumers' shared understanding.

The fourth one is the change from a corporate behavior to a social behavior. Making air conditioner products is not purely a corporate behavior any longer and a corporation cannot do all aspects of the service work very well, which needs every one's participation. Gree has deepened the integration with social forces, strengthen the maintenance and supervision 不 by letting the users be the supervisors for Gree's products and forcing Gree to do a best job in every step. In this way, Gree could win the consumers' recognition.

The fifth change is from paying lip services to providing down-to-earth services. It is useless for an enterprise to just pay lip service to their customers. What an enterprise should do is to provide the down-to-earth service by bringing tangible benefits to consumers, and let them feel satisfied and moved through the process of enjoying the service provided by companies.

Ai Feng, the director of China Quality Long March Organizing Committee and the famous economist, once talked about the customer service of Gree: Gree is an enterprise with its distinctive characteristics and a down-to-earth work style. It has expanded and deepened the service content by offering the after services of paying visits to tens of millions of consumers. Service is a very important factor in the market competition today. The importance of service lies in the point that the market is a battle field and the market competition is the battle for fighting for consumers; the core of the market competition is to seize the market shares. The enterprise which has the most consumers will be the winner of the markets. It is known that the product quality is the basic factor in the competition, but as the development in science and technology, usually there are no big differences in the product quality. Therefore, "customer service" becomes the decisive factor in fighting for consumers in the market competition. Customer service is the most important chip. Especially, after China's entry into WTO, perhaps the unique advantage for Chinese enterprises is the customer service. Service for enterprises is something which is the most direct, individual, culturally connotative and emotional contact with consumers. The success of the "customer visits" campaign firmly strengthens Gree's faith: price war or advertising competition is not a permanent solution for expanding the product market, only with high degree of quality and sincere services, can the users conceive customer loyalty towards the brand in a real sense. In a word, winning consumers' hearts is the key for the enterprises in China to play a leading role and to be in an invincible position in the market competition.

(2) Strengthening the Sense of Quality and Exceeding After Sales Services

In recent years, "the conceptual speculations of customer service" is nothing new to consumers. To sum it up, generally, there are three ways of speculations that often can be seen in the markets: One of them is the speculation about the promises made by manufacturers, such as "guarantee for replacement for X years", "lifelong maintenance" etc. The second one is about the speculation of "home maintenance services", e.g. "24-hour on-call service". The third one is that the service stations call the consumers day and night from time to time to ask about the use of air conditioners. Many consumers are becoming more and more tired of those commercial speculations. After all the consumers have had quite a few times' shopping experience, many of them began to realize: those easily made "promises" only bring the trouble back at home; repeatedly offering home maintenance service still cannot solve the problem and being enthusiastic towards comsumers means having other intentions; calling the consumers night and day and requiring about their air conditioning products clearly showed their lack of confidence in their products. They are just "making experiments on consumers". Here, we cannot help probing into the question: What kind of service are the consumers looking for exactly? On this question, Gree's answer is that the services that can bring consumers tangible benefits are the best service.

In essence, the consumers do not hope the manufacturers to provide after-sales services, because if the products that they provide are reliable in quality, consumers do not need after sales services and the home maintenance service is also unnecessary. Gree Electric Appliances advocates the idea that "When an air conditioner is sold, the users do not need any maintenance and repair service for 8 years". This Gree's unconventional idea, on the one hand, shows it is fully confident of its products; on the other hand it has raised a higher goal for itself – never rests on its laurels and keeps making the air conditioners which do not need maintenance and repair service. The "product" Gree refers to does not mean the products in the factory, for they are just semi-finished products. Those semi-finished air conditioners are only equipped with the professional in-progress sale design and installation can construct the complete air conditioning product concept.

The next story is about Gree's placing great importance on its after sales services while it is making products of good quality. Hebei Gree Electric Appliances has provided users free maintenance and repair service in off season for 8 consecutive years, in which Gree users can have an appointment by making a phone call or going directly to Gree store for an appointment of free service. The service includes: to check whether the air conditioner is proper functioning or not, whether the power system is safe or not and make sure the filter and the air conditioner indoor unit are thoroughly cleaned. People at Gree will bring the users the warmth like in the spring when in a cold winter. What they bring to consumers is zero trouble. Pleasantly, when the service workers come to consumers' house for home maintenance and repair service, the users even will get a small exquisite gift from them. Therefore, Gree has enjoyed a good reputation in the air conditioner market with the slogan of "Good air conditioners, Gree made". Just as one of its users once introduced about Gree's service, he said: "It was 11 o'clock at night and the air conditioner in my home was broken down. I immediately called their after-sale service department; soon after, they arrived at my house and fixed the air conditioner for me. At that moment, I really felt Gree's true honesty and sincerity. "

As to the complaints and feedbacks from the users, how does Gree handle them to assure the quality of its warranty work? Here, let's take a look at how Gree handled a real complaint case:

Name: Mr. Xiao

The content of the complaint:

After I had known about the "6-year free warranty" service policy provided by Gree Electric Appliances, Inc. of Zhuhai, Guangdong province, then I decided to buy a "split-type air conditioner KFR-32W/K" made by Gree Electric Appliances, Inc. of Zhuhai from Hengchang Computer Industrial Company in Cangxi County, Sichuan Province. But when I opened the box and began to install it, I found there was no manufactuer's warranty card and product qualification certificate. I asked the installers about it, they said they were just workers temporarily hired by Hengchang Company and they didn't know about the manufactuer's warranty card and product qualification certificate. Therefore, I called and asked Hengchang Company about it; then the people from the company promised me that they would send the manufactuer's warranty card and product qualification certificate the next day. But on the next day, I found there was no barcode on this air conditioner unit, and the serial numbers of its outdoor unit was erased on purpose. There were two obvious scratches on the indoor unit. The shells of outdoor units were mismatched with loosened screws and several blemishes on the heat sink, so I had to once again inquiry Hechang Company about those defects. They said those defects wouldn't affect the normal use of this air conditioner and they brought the blank manufactuer's warranty card and product qualification certificate. I found the machine number of the quality certificate was effaced, and then I wanted them to fill the warranty items on the manufactuer's warranty card, but I was told that they were unable to solve the problem because they were not the direct sale store of Gree Electric Appliances, Inc. of Zhuhai. Thereafter, I went to the company for solving the problems over and over again but the problem still remained unsolved. Then, I managed to find one of the local distributors of Gree Electric Appliances but they said that they couldn't give me a filled manufactuer's warranty card because there was no barcode and no factory number on my air conditioner and I should go to the company which sold this air conditioner to me to solve the problem. Now I don't know how to do to make this air conditioner with significant quality problems enjoy the "6-year free warranty" service policy and repair service from Gree Electric Appliances, Inc. of Zhuhai?

Complaint Handling Results:

Gree Electric Appliances, Inc. of Zhuhai, Guangdong province received the complaint on 18th, May. The following is about the handling of the complaint:

According the "three-guarantee policy" (guarantee of repair; replacement and refund of substandard products) of our company, we provide the user "6-year free warranty" after-sale services, and replace a new air conditioner immediately required by the user. We will strengthen the management of the distributing network of Gree air conditioning products. At present, the Sichuan Branch of Gree Electric Appliances, Inc. of Zhuhai has reached an agreement on the final solution with the user on this case. The user is very satisfied with the result.

From "Every little thing you are doing will be the big thing for Gree" to "never make experiments on consumers", form "Strengthening the sense of quality and exceeding after sales services" to "top class product + top class installation service = zero maintenance and repair"......Gree has made great efforts in selecting raw materials for its products, then provided perfect work in the all-in-one services of pre-sales, in-progress sales and after-sale services; the excellent work went through every step of production and marketing: design, trial-manufacturing, production and installation.

Now, Gree's campaign of "paying visits to customers" has become a distinctive feature of Gree Corporation, after it has been put into practice for so many years. The promise to the global 40 million users is not just a slogan, but the down-to-earth service made from 14-year hard work of absolute sincerity and professional control of quality and technology. We have every reason to believe that the "prevailing wind of Gree's work style of honesty and integrity" will grow stronger and stronger.

Review: Only Service Based On High Product Quality Can Really Win Customers

Speaking of customer service, there are two trends forming in our globe today: the first one is that providing service as a new industry and its proportion is getting bigger and bigger in the overall pattern of national economy; the second trend is the servicesation of manufacturing industry. The second trend is of strategic significance to the growth of manufacturing industry nowadays.

The so called manufacturing industry is that those enterprises which make and produce goods in quantities. There will be a multi-link process in which a product is produced by manufacturing enterprises then delivered to consumers. To know this process, there are at least three phases: 1. selling, to sell the products to consumers; 2. marketing, to make the products according to the demands of consumers; 3. service, to make consumers feel satisfied.

Gree is one of the few enterprises who realized the strategic significance of service. Its understandings of it can be summarized into the following points:

(1) Product quality is the foundation. If the product is of inferior quality, service is nothing but a means of marketing. As long as the product is of superior quality, the service of an enterprise can have its real significance.

(2) Service features the character of integrality. Service goes through every step of the process: the pre sales, in-progress sales and after sales service. It is not fragmented but it is a system of integrality.

(3) "Zero service" is the highest level in all the service forms. What the consumers need is the function of products and as long as the function can meet their demands, it is O.K. that they don't need any other services. This is the feature of the service of manufacturing industry, which is essentially different from the service industry.

(4) Providing service is an interactive process. Service is not one-way—the enterprise provides the services   and the consumers enjoy them; but two-way and interactive—the consumers also participate into the process of service. Once there is a saying: "Picky consumers are the treasure of an enterprise". In the early stage, consumers' participation in service is characterized by grumbles, complaints and fault-finding, but few companies really understand this idea "Picky consumers are the treasure of an enterprise". According to the result from an experiment carried out by researching fellows abroad: the picky consumers always remained the most loyal to an enterprise. The experiment result seems a little contradictory. In fact, it is not difficult to get a handle on the experiment result. Try to imagine, there are two guys who both are your customers. Customer A has the opinions and complaints about your product; if he never tells you about it, perhaps he will tell other customers about it. On the contrary, Customer B will tell you all his opinions and suggestions about your product, if you listen carefully, perhaps he will give you some helpful suggestions for enhancing your product. As time goes by, consumer B will become your loyal customer, and consumer A will probably become one of your competitor's customers.

Chapter 5: Overseas Market Expansion

1. Embarking on Globalization

On choosing the way of entering the global markets, Gree Electric Appliances is very "special" compared with other companies. When some enterprises try to increase their enterprise's global visibility or gain competitive advantages against multi-national corporations, Gree has formed its own idea: entering the global market does not simply mean the export of products or building a factory in another country. Going global should be the Chinese culture going global. At the meantime, there should be beneficial results when enterprises are making inroads into the international markets and the enterprises should not lose money by just doing loss leader business in the internation arena.

1) Going Global Resolutely

In the tide of economic globalization, it is hard for enterprises to find a harbor of refuge. If Chinese enterprises want to stay on solid footing in the stage of the future, they must be active and brave to enter the international market and join in the competition of the global markets. Only in this way, can we build our own global competitiveness and can the real world brands be made in China.

In the early 90's of the 20th century, Zhu Jianghong went to Europe for exploring and seeking market opportunities there. When he passed a security check in the Customs of Paris, France, at first, the Customs security officers were very polite and respectful towards Zhu Jianghong, for they thought that Zhu Jianghong was Japanese. But when they opened Zhu's passport and found that he was Chinese, the smile on their faces were diminishing, and they appeared to be deliberately unhelpful and obstructive towards Zhu Jianghong, the chairman of Gree Electric Appliances. It was this unusual experience that inspired Zhu Jianghong's courage and determination to put more efforts in the globalization of his enterprise and forge Gree into a world brand.

The possession of world brands has become the key index for measuring a nation's economic competitiveness in today's global competition. Whether a state or a nation can win respect from the international community or not largely depends on how many world famous brands this country has. Since World War II, Japan started its road of globalization with the well-known brands of Toyota and Sony; the enterprises of South Korea also had their early start of globalization with quite a few world-class brands, e.g. Samsung, Hyundai.

To Chinese enterprises, they should not only implement the "Red Ocean Strategy" in the domestic markets, but they should also carry out the "Blue Ocean Strategy" in the international markets. In the case of Gree Electric Appliances, it must find the new steady profit growth point in carrying out the "Blue Ocean Strategy". The industry experts pointed out that for the success of Gree's globalization, Gree must enter the global market and win the universal recognition and admiration from the consumers all over the world with the faith of "rely on the core technology, always be the pioneer in the industry" and the imposing manner of "promote China's national industry and create China's top brands". In 1998~2001, Gree Electric Appliances successively entered the shopping malls and supermarkets of Hong Kong, Philippine, Italy, Spain, Germany, USA and Brazil, as well as established a mature sales network in over 100 countries and regions around the world. With its graceful and elegant product image and reliable product quality, Gree finally won numerous admirers in the global markets. Here, let's review Gree's process of internationalization:

In March, 1993, Gree air conditioner made its inroads into Hong Kong markets and became "the only Chinese brand air conditioner entering into large Japanese shopping malls", which lifted the curtain on Gree's going global.

In 1994, Gree was certified by German GS, a well-known safety certification mark in Europe markets, especially, in Germany. Gree Electric Appliances was the first enterprise from Mainland China to hold "the pass for entering European home appliance markets", which ushered Gree into the European markets.

Still in 1994, Gree air conditioner was certified by Japanese JIS; another success entry into Japanese markets.

From 1995, the sales volume of Gree ranked No.1 in China for three consecutive years, meanwhile, its products were all over 100 countries and regions, also well received and praised in the markets of Western Europe, North America, South America and Southeast Asia.

On 28th December, 1995, as the first enterprise from mainland China, Gree honorably received the first CE Certification by European certification authority and had the legal basis to have access to selling products in 17 EU member states. Therefore, Gree finally catch the "Golden Key" to open the European markets.

In July, 1996, Gree passed the reexamination of ISO 9001, which marked Gree's holding of the "visa" to the international markets.

In November, 1996, Gree's supply of "cooling king" air conditioners fell short of demand in Western Europe, with the selling price equaling to the price of Japanese products. And this event totally changed the image of Chinese products which used to be sold only in street markets and won credits for China's national industry.

Still in 1996, Gree air conditioners were recognized as the "national recommended product" and the "Designated Air Conditioning Product for the Production Studio of Philippine National TV Station".

Since March, 1997, the sales volume of Gree air conditioners has been occupying the first place in air conditioner sales ranking.

On 30th June, 1997, Gree was awarded "The 22nd International Award for The Best Trade Name" by European Entrepreneurs' Association. It was the only grand award received by Chinese air conditioning industry from an international organizational authority in Europe.

In 1998, Gree air conditioner was certified by USA UL (Underwriter Laboratories Inc) then Gree made its inroads into US air conditioning market.

In January, 1998, Gree's passing EMC (Electro Magnetic Compatibility) certification exam marked that Gree air conditioners' anti-electromagnetic radiation and anti-electromagnetic interference reached the international level.

In 1999, topping the highest record in its history by 10% in sales volume and with its sales revenues amounting to a staggering $ 60 million, Gree exported 150,000 units of air conditioner to the international market and took a leading position in the handful air conditioning export enterprises.

In November, 1999, with the aim of localization of manufacturing and selling, Gree decided to invest $ 20 million in building a production base with the manufacturing output of 200,000 air conditioners in Brazil, which greatly increased its competitiveness in global markets.

On 27th June, 2000, the press conference on the establishment of Spanish Branch of Gree Electric Appliances & Gree's New Products Introduction and Promotion Conference were held in REYJUAN CARLOSI hotel of Barcelona, Spain. This big event helped Gree to enjoy a surge in its local sales in Spain in a very short time.

On 31st July, 2000, Gree and Trane Air Solutions—a subordinate company of American Standard Company signed an agreement on Gree's air conditioners exporting to American markets, which speeded up Gree's pace of its marketing development in the North American markets.

In December, 2000, Gree was certified by AS Security Authentication on electrical product and non-electrical product of Standard Association of Australia and in this way, Gree obtained the guarantee from the universal commonwealth business regulations for Gree air conditioners.

In May 2001, Gree was awarded the "Supreme Award Golden Prize of WQC International Star in Quality Field" from Business Initiative Directions (BID), which showed the great praise for the product quality of Gree air conditioners from the international markets.

In June 2001, Brazil Branch of Gree Electric Appliances, Inc. of Zhuhai had been officially completed and put into production. The state councilor of China, Ismail Amet, made a special trip to attend the ribbon-cutting ceremony and inaugurated this new branch company.

......

China cannot go global without world famous brands, which is not a dispute but a must for all the Chinese enterprises. Zhu Jianghong once said: "Chinese enterprises have the responsibility and obligation to enter the international markets and display our quality products and services to change the deep-rooted prejudices that people from other countries have towards China and Chinese people."

Therefore, people of Gree resolutely and determinedly took the road of globalization. In the list of "100 Most Valuable World Brands" issued by *American Business Week* in 2005, 58 of the "100 Most Valuable World Brands" were American brands, 9 Germany brands, 7 French brands, only 8 of the 58 brands from Asia with 6 Japanese brands and 2 South Korea brands. And it was great pity that there were no Chinese brands. In recent years, the GDP of China has ranked No. 6 in the world and the total trade volume of China ranked No. 3 in the world, but because there was no world class brand, the overall competitiveness of China in the evaluation of competitiveness indexes only ranked No. 49 in all the countries of the world. In the international commodity markets, the idea of "Made-in-China" meaning cheap, low quality products is still deep-rooted in people's mind. In European Union markets, some enterprises even labeled their products "Not-Made-in-China" to manifest the high quality of their products.

Fortunately, in the process of Chinese enterprises going globalization, people of Gree led by the chairman of Gree Electric Appliances, Zhu Jianghong and the president, Dong Mingzhu created the world's biggest miracle of selling 10 million residential air conditioners in 2005. Zhu Jianghong indicated that, China is the world largest air conditioner producer and exporter, as well as the biggest air conditioner consuming country. The top air conditioning enterprises and top air conditioner brands should grow in this beautiful land. "By the year 2009, the goal of Gree is to realize the 30% market share in the global home appliance markets. Our ultimate goal is to let all people from the world have faith in Gree products, just as they do in Mercedes-Benz and BMW. " Dong Mingzhu said. As a matter of fact, just as Dong Mingzhu said about the goal of Gree, the people of Gree are getting closer and closer towards their glory and dream with their steady strides and pragmatic work style.

2) Must Create Our Own Brands While Entering the Global Markets

Depending on the great achievements made in the international market competition,

Gree Electric Appliances has become an outstanding representative of "going global" in Guangdong province, a world class brand and a great winner in pursuing internationalization.

To the cool iron lady in Gree Electric Appliances, Dong Mingzhu, the globalization strategy of "must create our own brands while entering the global markets" is full of hardships and setbacks. It is not a simple and easy task as some people imagine it to be by thinking that the enterprises just need to cooperate with foreign companies; then the enterprise is "entering the international markets". To Gree, the idea of going global means building its own international brand. Few years earlier before the Brazil factory were put on production, the course of going global was very arduous and tough. The first two and three years to Gree the beginner in this arena is like the process of paying tuition and learning lessons in the international market, for it is not easy for Gree to adapt itself to the foreign environment because of those factors, such as foreign laws and regulations, policy and culture. In term of investment environment, Zhu Jianghong, the chairman of this state-owned listed company thinks that China has the best investment environment for many foreign companies, but things are different in forgein countries for there is no favorable policy and treatment and there even some irregularities which made Gree very hard to finish the work according to the schedule. But for the dream of building Chinese own brands, Gree finally got through those difficulties and stood put. When Gree knew that the Brazil branch realized the profits of RMB 25 million, at that time, it feel much relieved and the Brazil became a very solid step in the process of laying the foundation for Gree's future in the end.

Gree hopes to win the honor for Chinese people by creating world famous brands and making the electric appliances recognized by the whole world. To build self-owned brands in the process of going global is a very important factor in the success of Gree's internationalization.

In fact, the air conditioners manufactured by Chinese enterprises are being sold widely in USA and Europe and many of them are not under their own brands of those manufacturers but OEM products under a foreign brand. In the 90's of the 20th century, the international air conditioner market was the world of American and Japanese brands. As the late comer in this market, most of Chinese air conditioning enterprises are lacking of brand popularity. The OEM production is indeed a shortcut of going global for Chinese enterprises to make breakthroughs in a short time regarding the difficulties in brand development and the big cost input. At that time, Gree also made full use of the OEM advantages, i.e. low manufacturing costs and obtained many OEM orders from many multi-national corporations, such as Panasonic, Daikin, Whirlpool, Carrier, and Siemens, which facilitated the boost in Gree's exports and triumphantly achieving the great penetration in the international markets. In the process of OEM production, Gree effectively improved its own manufacturing technique and management ability and began to be gradually familiar with the "international rules of the game" as well.

When Gree was providing an OEM service for multi-national corporations, Zhu Jinghong already realized that although the OEM pattern was an inevitable choice in the growth phase of an enterprise, it should not be a good choice for actively meeting the challenges and for the new birth of an enterprise. If Chinese enterprises want to stand firm in the international market, they must rely on their own brands.

The self-owned brands are not just the signs of products, also the back-bone of a nation's national industry and the embodiment and carrier of a country's cultural heritage as well, just like those brands reflecting the cultural heritage of their birthplace: e.g. South Korea's Samsung, America's GE and Japan's Sony.

Mr. Zhu Jianghong pointed out: "China is a large home appliance manufacturing country, but not a powerful manufacturing country. Its weakness lies in its lack of self-owned brands, so it is very important to have proprietary brands in the process of entering the global markets." He explained, since the day Gree began to be engaged in OEM business, it had gradually promoted its own brands in exporting. Having gone through many hardships and struggles, the air conditioners of Gree brand finally could be exported to more than 60 countries and regions.

After Gree people made much efforts in Gree's brand building strategy, gradually, Gree's sales of own brand is getting bigger and bigger in the proportion of the sales volume of the global markets. What's more, Gree has also entered into the mainstream marketing channels and won the recognition of the consumers in the mainstream markets. For example, in Brazil, with the advantages of a great variety of products and excellent technology, Gree made a successful entry into major cities in Brazil, namely, Sao Paulo, Rio De Janeiro, Santos, Vitoria and set up concession counters in major supermarkets, which greatly promoted the image of Chinese home appliance top brands. Besides, Gree air conditioners often can be seen in the houses and villas of many Brazilian celebrities, such as movie and TV stars, football stars and government officials. For example, the famous Brazilian football star Ronaldo is also using Gree air conditioners in his home.

"Gree has grown from a small sapling into a towering tree, from an obscure small factory into a modern huge enterprise, from an OEM manufacturer into a Chinese top brand and a world famous brand. Now Gree has already been a big tree of 'flourish, sturdy and vigorous', but no matter how far-spreading her branches are, her root is always in Zhuhai." Said Zhu Jianghong.

2. Occupy the International Markets First, Build Factories Second

"First to occupy the markets then promote the brand, who said we cannot have them both?" In the end of 1999, four young people of Gree came all the way for the preparatory work of Gree's Brazilian production base from China to Manaus city situated at the hinterland of Rio Amazon in northern Brazil. On 11th June, 2001, the Brazilian production base officially was started to put into operations. In 2004, just over a short span of three years, the Brazilian production base ushered in its first harvest time with the profit of RMB 25 million, so it became the role model of "going global" among Chinese enterprises. With regard to this situation, Zhu Jianghong indicated that: "If Chinese enterprises want to gain a foothold in the stage of the future, they must be active and brave to enter the international market and join in the competition of the global markets. Only in this way, can we enhance our own global competitiveness and can the real world brands be made in China."

1) Market First, Factory Second

The insiders in this industry have various controversies over the pattern of enterprises' "going global" in Chinese companies. Every enterprise has its own plan about it. For example, Haier's strategy of "first difficult, then easy", TCL's strategy of "cross-border merger and acquisition" and Gree's adherence to its business idea of "market first, factory second".

Dong Mingzhu, one of China's leading business women, explained, the success of Chinese enterprises' "going global" depends on whether they can generate more profits for our country and they can continuously win the recognition of the consumers. Different enterprises, with different management concepts will lead to different results. Zhu Jianghong believed, for an enterprise's "entering the international markets", it must have the capability to cope with the risks. It is a steady and wise practice to invest and build a factory only there are market demands for the products.

Gree air conditioner entered the Brazilian market since 1998, with the advantages of excellent product quality and complete specifications, soon they had been well received in Brazilian consumers. Its sales revenues had been up to over $ 3 million in just half and two months. After three years of ardent and painstaking efforts for Gree's Brazilian production base, by the year 2000, the sales revenues of Gree air conditioners totaled $ 30 million, which catapulted Gree to be in the second place in the local market occupancy.

It was based on the market needs that Gree decided to invest and set up factories in Brazil. Then in 2001, the Brazilian production base was successfully put into operation. However, Gree's move this time has been proved to be a remarkable success. Currently, in Brazil, Gree's sales outlets have covered 24 states with more than 300 agents, 1000 retailers and 300 service stations and installation companies.

Facing the question of "why didn't Gree go to developed countries like USA or

European countries and set up factories there?" from the outside world, the spokesman of Gree explained: "Air conditioning industry is a labor-intensive industry; it only has the competitiveness and advantages to set up its production base in developing countries with comparatively lower salaries."

Seeing the emerging market, with its usual calmness, Gree chooses the soft and penetration strategies of "to navigate with a borrowed boat" and "to get eggs with a borrowed hen". In June, 2004, Gree signed an agreement with American Whirlpool on the export of air conditioners and 40,000 units of air conditioner would enter Indian markets, which is the biggest export order that Chinese air conditioning industry obtained from India so far.

With the purpose of boosting the pace of internationalization, Gree's production line in Pakistan was also officially brought into production. But different with the production base in Brazil, the Pakistan production line was invested by the local distributors and Gree was only responsible for providing the technical support and brand management. Zhu Jianghong indicated that, "When the Pakistan market becomes a success, we can gradually buy this production line back and make it the second overseas production base for Gree air conditioner. About the building of Gree's overseas factories, we firmly believe that instead of seeking quick results, we should work steadily and make solid progress."

Being in the competitive-oriented globally market, Gree people realized that they must forge Gree's own proprietary brand and build Gree's advantages in technology and management. Therefore, when Gree is going global, it won't have to take risks in investing much money in overseas projects, instead, it can cooperate with the local sponsors or manufacturers by the way of transferring technology and sharing its managerial experience with them. Gree does not wish to pay too much "tuition" in expanding the overseas markets and to Gree, it will be a steady way for it to find about the market needs first and then to consider setting up its factories next.

When many Chinese enterprises are making overseas investments, they are mostly out of their strategic plans. That is, they are pinning all their hopes on setting up factories or mergers and acquisitions in developed countries or regions to build its brand image of internationalization, subsequently to realize their bigger expansions and profits in domestic markets and the market of developing countries. However, to Gree Electric Appliances, the one who is always remaining stable and steady style in expanding overseas market has a different attitude towards this approach mentioned above:

"We don't play speculations in the every step we made, e.g. many countries, such as, India, Turkey all wanted us to build our factories there, and they even had ready-made factory buildings for us, but we didn't go instead of doing that , we chose to tell them it was risky to do so. Some of the risks were beyond our control. Thus, we would rather choose to make air conditioners in Zhuhai and then sell them to India. We won't easily set up the factories until we find it is very necessary to do so. The precondition for us to set up our factories in forgein countries is to make sure there are market demands for our products and we can obtain our own niche market by establishing our factories there, only when the market share reaches a certain level and we have the economic strength accordingly, can we consider setting up our factories there."

2) Going Global With The Brand

When will Chinese enterprises truly become internationalized? In the context of today's economic globalization, if Chinese economy wants to keep its prosperity, Chinese enterprises must involve themselves in the process of internationalization and globalization. For those enterprises that are successful in going global will become the most successful enterprises in China. From TCL to Haier, many of Chinese businesses are engaged in cross-border mergers & acquisitions and overseas investment, nevertheless, according to some experts, the biggest obstacle for China right now is the difference between its enterprises and foreign enterprises in the management mode and culture. At present, Gree has formed its characteristics in its technology and management; in the mean time, it also attaches great importance to the exploiting the overseas market.

The accomplishment of the global distribution does not necessarily mean that Gree can become the world first-class multinational corporation. To build the first rate international competitiveness, Gree needs keeping constantly optimizing and improving its management and business operations at all levels so as to forge a global brand. However, the task cannot be completed in a very short time.

The industry experts suggest that after Gree finished its international distribution, actually, its global branding was like an arrow on the bowstring—there was no turning back.

About how to build a global brand, what the executive leaders in Gree Electric Appliances should consider is that firstly, to establish a business management system corresponding to the process of internationalization. Gree needs to optimize its management process and management institution in order to complete its management system and to build the managerial capacity for group internationalization management strategy. In accordance with the requirement of internationalization, Gree needs to enhance the enterprise's internal organizational system and management system and to proceed with the global enterprise resource planning, so as to improve its global managerial capacity. Meanwhile, the globalization of an enterprise needs international talents as the foundation, so Gree should build a team adaptable to the international management and business operation through internal training employees and the talent introduction from the markets as well as try to learn, innovate, understand and master the rules of international operations in the changing global market and accumulate the international business experience, thus to adjust the enterprise itself to the requirement of the enterprises' globalization.

The second step for Gree Electric Appliances is to integrate and construct a globalization research and development system. Through the integration and mergers& acquisitions, research & development, design center and Gree's original R&D center, the synergy effects of global research and development could be produced inside Gree and the company could realize the global R&D resource sharing, thereby to improve the enterprise's R&D and innovative capability in the core technology.

Moreover, Gree needs to build a competitive global supply chain system. Making a full use of Gree's advantages in speed, efficiency and cost control, raising the efficiency of every stage in work as well as strictly controlling and optimizing the operational costs of every regional market, Gree could bring its competitive advantages from domestic markets to the whole global markets and build the supply chain system of global integration through the integration of purchase, manufacturing and logistics. Currently, in the fully competitive markets, Gree can keep its leading position in cost control and shape its competitive power by relying on its excellent supply chain management.

Lastly, Gree should make high-end brand products to increase the product value and brand value. Talking about the high-end brand products, Gree should improve its brand image by the promotion in the product design and core technology as well as the development and sales of high-end products and diversified products. And Gree shall take this opportunity to promote its value-creating capability and increase the added value of products.

To most Chinese enterprises, globalization is just a starting point. How to create and keep the long-term competitive strength, make world top class products and build first class brands will be a more arduous course. In the course of globalization, Chinese enterprises' setting up factories in foreign countries is a process of spreading their management culture. They could bring Chinese outstanding culture into other countries and try their efforts to make others accept Chinese culture through the process of building factories and communicating with the local people.

Gree once encountered some labor problems when building the production base in Brazil. In China, in the 8-hour working time, if a worker doesn't do the work that he is supposed to do according to the labor contract, he should do other task that his superior asks him to do as long as the assigned task is in his working time. But this is not allowed in Brazil, if today the work that he is supposed to do according to the labor contract has to come to a stop for the reason that there are some problems in the raw materials needed in the production line, the workers of this production line can have a rest according to the local law, but if you ask them to do other work, like doing cleaning or sweeping the floor, it will be a violation of their rights and they will report the enterprise to the local labor union. As a result, the company will be fined by the local labor union for it. However, while abiding by the local law, after communicating, sharing with each other and setting examples, Gree finally made the Brazilian workers feel and understand the devotion and dedication spirit which is always advocated by Gree Electric Appliances. Gradually over a long period of time, the Brazilian employees began to accept Gree's way of management. Certainly, different countries have different corporate culture. It is hard to tell which one is superior to the others or not. We should also learn from the advanced foreign corporate culture, but the most advanced corporate culture is the one which is most suitable for the enterprise itself.

The past several years witnessed Gree's success management in its Brailian production base, but Gree's success in Brazil does not mean it can copy its Brazil management model in other countries. Instead of building factories in India and Russia, Gree is just selling air conditioners in the two countries by cooperating with the local distributors, for the local market demand and environment are not really suitable for Gree to make direct investments.

Gree now is devoting itself fully to manufacturing. If Gree wants to go global, besides establishing its own market channels, the more important for Gree is to build its own production base. In line with the strategy of "market first, factory second", early in 1999, Gree worked hard to exploit the overseas markets. It not only introduced its direct sales stores into the overseas markets, but also made direct investment in building production base in Brazil, South America. By the year 2004, the production base in Brazil realized the annual output of 300,000 units with total profits of RMB 25 million.

One of the strong points in the Brazil model is that the products are easily to be trusted and well-received by the local consumers. With this business model, Gree's market occupancy has been increased quickly, its brand reputation has been tremendously enhanced and the image of Chinese products has been totally changed.

On the issue of Gree's going global and building factories in foreign countries, many experts think that the first important thing is to find out the local market needs. If Gree wants to lower the risks and costs in entering the international markets, it firstly must rely on the existed market to survive and win the recognition of the brand Gree from the local people. For instance, Gree now is doing a wonderful job in India. It is not only directly exporting its products through middlemen, but also it is cooperating with the local dealers to sell its own products by opening Gree's direct sale stores.

To avoid a lost battle in overseas market investments, Chinese home appliance enterprises must have a thorough understanding of the local consumer culture and then customize themselves to the local market. One of the approaches to have the penetrating understanding of the local consumer culture is to navigate with a borrowed boat—to use external support to develop the company itself and then to make every endeavor to realize the customization of the products through "local design, local production and local sales".

Just to take a close look at the whole situation of the international markets, it is easy for us to find that the anti-dumping is the trick that foreign rivals often employed to counterattack and frustrate their competitors. The next stage for Gree to consider is to overcome various obstacles and barriers, such as EU Directive on the protection of the environment, recycling fee for used household appliances, special safeguard measures and Social Accountability 800. In the long run, an air conditioning manufacturer cannot have a long-term development without the profit-making prospects. For Chinese air conditioning enterprises, it is advisable for them to devote more time and energy to improve product quality, technique, stability and functionality as well as to construct their regulatory corporate governance structure and raise the awareness of information disclosure with the attitude of sticking to high quality and high standard; to handle matters in strict accordance with the local market rules as well. On this point, the most crucial factor is that the enterprise's management team should build a complete series of system, including the supervisory control of the management team itself.

With the aim of changing foreign people's view about Chinese enterprises and Chinese products, Gree tries to show people of this idea via its excellent product that different enterprises have different products, thus, the quality of the products is different too. The goal for Gree's resolutely going global is to change the world's opinions about Chinese products.

3. The Localization Strategy of Globalization

To Chinese enterprises which are entering or ready to enter the international markets, the most basic thing for them to do is to acquire the success in the markets outside of China. But to Gree, the task is even more specific, that is to pursue the transaction model in the overseas markets. None the less, it is a hard and difficult task. Along with the development of global economic integration going deep and international competition getting fiercer and fiercer after China's entry into WTO, Chinese industrialists have to face many thorny problems and challenges one after another.

1) Showing Potential in Pakistan

In 2005, while many Chinese enterprises were still "cautious" about the overseas expansion, Gree eventually had a new move in its overseas expansion. In March 2006, Gree announced that its production base in Pakistan was put into operation and began to turn out air conditioners on a large scale. It is the second production base that Gree has established in the overseas markets after the production base in Brazil.

Different with the production base in Brazil, the one in Pakistan is a cooperation project between Gree Electric Appliances and the largest professional air conditioner dealer in Pakistan—Digital World Pakistan (PVT) Ltd.(DWP). In this project, Gree provided this production base its full technical support. This production base is located at Lahore, the capital city of Punjab province, a site of strategic importance in Pakistani air conditioner markets. The base is exclusively engaged in the production of Gree brand air conditioners with the annual output of 100,000 units and it has enjoyed the largest production capacity in Pakistan ever. This project is totally invested by DWP and the rights and interests also belong to DWP. Gree Electric Appliances is only responsible for exporting air conditioner production line, equipment, air conditioner spare parts and providing the technical guidance. Plus, Gree also fully supports the manufacturing of Gree brand air conditioners by the way of assembly processing and the selling of the products in Pakistan. By the time the operation of this project reaches its designed capacity, the volume of air conditioner spare parts that Gree is exporting to Pakistan could increase to $ 20 million every year. At the same time, the brand of "Gree" will have the market share of 15% in Pakistani markets. Additionally, the production base in Pakistan is able to effectively radiate and cover neighboring countries and regions like India, etc.

Mr. Fan Luke, the CEO of DWP once commented on this production base: "It was very lucky for DWP to cooperate with China's No.1 air conditioner brand also the leading brand in global air conditioning industry, we will strive for the goal of promoting the brand of "Gree" a household name in Pakistan in two or three years. And to let Gree become the top brand in the local air conditioner market and make it a success in Pakistan as much as it is in China.

In the meanwhile, the conference of 2006 Gree air conditioner --Pakistani new product launch was held grandly in Lahore city. At the conference, the latest product series of residential air conditioner and commercial air conditioner were displayed through the forms of the model air conditioner units, real units and picture demonstrations, which greatly met the requirements of Pakistani distributors for Gree air conditioners and received high praise and warmly welcome from more than 300 Pakistani distributors present.

The settlement of Gree's air conditioner production base in Pakistan will be better meet the local distributors and consumers' needs and will certainly have the great impact on its local market occupancy. In 2006, the market capacity of Pakistani market was 600,000 units including their own brands and OEM products. So far, Gree has received a large number of orders and can hopefully become the Chinese air conditioner brand which will win the most market share in Pakistan.

Compared with some Chinese enterprises which are keen on promoting their products with "lower price and better sales" strategy, Gree has always been carrying out the development strategy of "playing for safety" and high-end product positioning with the dynamic integration of own brand products and OEM products to develop the market. By means of excellent product quality as well as the delicate and various styles of Gree air conditioner, Gree Electric Appliances quickly established its good reputation in local dealers and consumers. With a soaring sales volume, Gree air conditioner soon became the best seller in Chinese high-end air conditioner brands. By the end of 2005, a team formed about 40 Pakistani distributors paid a special trip to visit Gree Electric Appliances Inc of Zhuhai. In Zhuhai, the 40 Pakistani distributors were deeply impressed and encouraged by Gree's No.1 production scale in the whole globe and its world first-class professional air conditioner R&D center, the strict quality control system as well as its scientific and standardized modern management. And after their inspection tour in Gree Electric Appliances in Zhuhai, all of them signed the order agreement for the next whole year with Gree one after another.

2) The Unmatched One in Brazil

On June 6th, 2001, Gree Electric Appliance (Brail) was officially put into operation. A blue and white huge factory building stands in the Manaus free trade zone in the north of Brazil, on which the English characters "Gree" are very eye-catching. In the wake of the first Gree air conditioner born in the land of Brail, the history that Brazil was not capable to produce split type air conditioners came to an end. The first Gree air conditioner made in Brazil was also a milestone indicating Gree's important step forward in its globalization progress. Brazil is a country with vast territory, large population and strong buying power. the popularizing rate of home appliances, like TV set, refrigerator, radio, etc has reached 80%, but the ownership rate of air conditioner is only $5\% \sim 6\%$ with unitary variety and slightly higher price. As early as in 1998, Gree had already begun to export air conditioner units to Brazil and established a perfect sales network in Brazilian markets. Therefore, as far as Gree's globalization strategy is concerned, to build factories in the sales market is a way to lower customs import duty and production costs, also favorable to provide after-sales services. In the mean while, the Manaus free trade zone where Gree's Brazil factory is in is close to other countries in South America, which helps Gree to cover the whole South American markets.

At present, Gree brand has ranked No. 2 in more than 10 air conditioner brands in Brazil. Many of socialites, celebrities and big shots in Brazil all prefer to use Gree air conditioners. In Brazilian markets, Gree air conditioner has two strong points: 1. Advantages of product categories. Gree air conditioner enjoys a full range of specifications, from window unit to split type unit, portable air conditioner, floor standing air conditioner and ceiling mounted air conditioner. The product sizes and specifications of Gree cover every product category that any air conditioning manufacturer is selling in Brazil. 2. Quality superiority. In terms of the product quality and exterior design, Gree air conditioner has already won wide recognition after so many years' market tests.

When Gree's Brazil branch was put into operation, at that time the winter was approaching Brazil, even though, the sales revenues of Gree air conditioner in 2002 still reached RMB 7 million with over 20% of the market occupancy. According to the plan made by Gree Electric Appliances, the production of Gree air conditioners in Brazil is targeted for 100,000 units in 2007 and in 2008 the production capacity is expected to be 200,000 units. Meanwhile, the prospects of Gree products in South American countries, such as Brazil, are growing promising day by day. The brand of Gree is gradually becoming the dominant air conditioning brand in the areas of South America.

From the purely exporting products in the past to today's transnational investment, Gree Electric Appliance is speeding up its international market expanding. Since Gree entered Brazilian markets in 1998, up to now, the distribution outlets of Gree have had covered 24 states with more than 300 agents, over 1000 retailers and more than 300 service stations and installation companies. Now Gree has made a successful entry into the key cities in Brazil, namely, Sao Paulo, Rio De Janeiro, Santos, Vitoria and set up concession counters in major supermarkets and shopping malls, which is greatly helpful to promote the image of Chinese home appliance top brands.

3) Marching Into Tunisia

Enjoying the reputation of the largest air conditioning enterprise in China, for so many years, Gree has been committed itself to developing the overseas markets with relying on its superior product quality and delicate designs to completely change the foreign consumers' prejudice against Chinese products. And Gree also has broken the monopoly of American and Japanese air conditioning enterprises in core technology for many times, which greatly boosted the morale of Chinese enterprises and encouraged all the Chinese people around the world. In May 2006, Gree had another piece of good news in its international market development: on 22nd May, 2006, after one year's meticulous preparatory work, in Jiuzhou Harbor of Zhuhai city, five big containers of Gree large central air conditioners were hoisted abroad on an ocean-going freighter from Italy and they would be transported to Tunisia.

This export of Gree's central air conditioners to Tunisia included: two air-cooled screw chillers, 24 water-cooled household air conditioners, 12 packaged air conditioners and 130 air conditioner terminal equipments. It was the first time for Gree to export large central air conditioning units with its own brand name, which was a landmark in Gree's history of exporting large central air conditioners and facilitated Gree's building its benchmark image in the overseas markets. This batch of air conditioner units would be delivered to a large hotel subordinated to TANIT Group in Tunisia. In Tunisia, TANIT Group enjoys high popularity and its business scope includes: property management, real estate, electric appliances and elevators, etc and 20 subordinate branch companies. This group was constructing a large and luxury hotel and this hotel was near completion. As the hotel needed an air conditioning system, in order to purchase the air conditioning system to meet the demands of the hotel, the general manager of TANIT Group, Mr. Sami went to China for several times to make on-the-spot investigations into those famous air conditioning enterprises including Gree Electric Appliances. During Mr. Sami's investigations in China, he was greatly impressed by Gree's international leading research and development level, strict quality control system and products of complete categories. After repeated comparisons and investigations, TANIT Group finally chose Gree's central air conditioner system for their luxury hotel. Meanwhile, TANIT Group decided to join in Gree's oversea distribution team and sell Gree air conditioners in Tunisia. During this investigation tour, TANIT Group also placed an order of 1000 Gree residential air conditioners right way; consequently, it became Gree's first distributor in Tunisia. Before Gree's cooperation with TANIT group, the distribution pattern of Gree's residential air conditioning products had been sold through OEM partnership in Tunisia.

As Gree's key economic growth engine, Gree central air conditioners have been well-received by the consumers of the international markets, and continuously harvested big overseas orders for Gree.

Besides the Tunisia export project, currently, there are several large overseas projects of Gree central air conditioners, such as, the screw machine project with Vietnam and India, the centrifuge project with India and Caribbean Area etc. Along with the international market development, the export of Gree central air conditioner is gathering its development momentum and it is expected to compete against those air-con giants in central air conditioning markets, such as, USA and Japan to fight for bigger market share in the global central air conditioning markets.

Review: Stability and Steadiness is the Seed of Success for Globalization

We have already read more and more stories about Chinese enterprises' "going global". Especially their globalization process with the way of cross-border merger and acquisition is always the hot topic and the frontpage news that the finance media are rushing to report. For example, Lenovo's buying of IBM's PC business and TCL's purchase of Thomson's television and DVD player operations once were the front-page stories attracting people's attention. However, they are just the "tip of the iceberg" in Chinese enterprises' "going global" strategy. There are still many Chinese enterprises which are taking its internationalization road with a quite steady and down-to-earth manner and they tend to keep everyting a low profile and do not want to be the focus of the media and the public.

Behind the two phenomena are two types of different internationalization/multinational ideas: the former ones think that the chance of cross-border merger and acquisition is a once-in-a-blue-moon opportunity. Once they succeed in doing it, the enterprise will become a famous multi-national corporation "overnight"; the latter ones think that internationalization/multinational operation is a long process and they need to advance steadily step by step in order to win the final victory.

With the down-to-earth manner and attitude in the intnernationalization business operations, obviously, Gree belongs to the second type. The characteristics of Gree's manner and attitude are reflected in the following points:

1. The choice of the target market. Gree started the implementation of its globalization strategy first in the developing countries; then gradually penetrated into the markets of developed countries;

2. The export of products. Gree started its globalization from OEM products, then began to promote its own brand;

3. The way of internationalization. Gree firstly exported its products to other countries, when the production and selling were up to a large-scale or gained a big market share in the target market, then it began to consider building its factories in the local markets;

4. The way of investing and setting up Gree's own factories. Gree adopted the both ways of autonomous investment and technological cooperation. One thing to be worthy of mentioning is that Gree firstly made autonomous investment in Brazil, then cooperated with its Pakistani partner in building the production base. It can be seen that the decision-makers in Gree must have learnt from the failure that the loss occurred in the investment in Brazilian project in the first three years. Therefore, in Pakistani project, Gree made a "half step" back and proceeded with the project with a steadier and more stable manner.

Alough it seems that the merger and acquisition strategy is a very quick way and short cut for Chinese enterprises to going global, the writer is still in favor of steady and progressive internationalization strategy. Considering Chinese enterprises without any practical experience in globalization or under the circumstance that they have not drawn any lessons from the forerunners' mistakes yet, the success of large scale mergers and acquisitions can only can be "accidental", or even "miraculous". The miracles do happen sometimes but the chance is slim. Even there are miracles, they only take place in a very few enterprises. To most of Chinese enterprises, a steady and progressive internationalization strategy should be the perfect choice. In this respect, Gree has set another good example for all Chinese enterprises.

Chapter 6: Confronting Channel Intermediaries

1. Breaking with GOME and Fight for the Final Say

Regarding the event of Gree's breakup with GOME, in the case of Gree Electric Appliances, it is really like grasping the shadow and letting go the substance to give up cooperation with Gome, the golden channel, and to build its own sales networks, strengthen the channel penetration and nurture the second and third-tier channel intermediaries to replace Gome, one of the largest privately-owned electrical appliance retailers in Mainland China and Hong Kong. However, for GOME Electrical Appliances Holding Limited, it must have the feeling of unsupported or isolated to let go Gree, a well-established brand in China, and to drive the growth of the business with the second and third-tier air conditioning brands. Nevertheless, the higher level leaders in both sides all have a determined attitude towards it; and "would rather give up" becomes the shared comment for both sides. How to interpret this situation? It is better to make the comment that the two sides are stacking against each other with "future" as the bargaining chip in this unrestrained gamble rather than the two are engaged in "two-horse race--loss at both sides".

1) The Truth of The Break-up Between the Two Powerful Companies

Is the warfare between Gree and GOME on "business models" or "old and new concepts"? Here, let's replay the whole process of the event over again: dispute--upgrade--breakup--self-improvement--continuation.

(1)   Dispute. On 17th February, 2004, Chengdu GOME held a conference in which local air conditioner distributors were informed that that GOME would start "a price war of air conditioners" and made it clear that GOME would put in RMB 2 million for this campaign. Subsequently, on 24th February, 2004, Chengdu GOME started the large scale promotion campaign, with the price of one of Gree air conditioners down by 40%, ranking No.1 in all the bargains. So Gree Electric Appliances officially informed Chengdu GOME and required "immediately to terminate the low-price sales practice", but Chengdu GOME insisted that it was a normal promotion activity of the GOME store and they still went on with the price reduction of Gree air conditioners. Since there was no   mutually satisfactory negotiation result, Gree decided formally to cease to supply air conditioning products to GOME anymore.

(2)   Upgrade. On 9th March, 2004, GOME sent an emergency notice of "selling all of the remaining stock of Gree air conditioners" to all its branch companies, requiring that all the branches should clear up the stock and terminate business deals with Gree. Then Gree head office began its counterattack against GOME by announcing that if GOME did not honor the rules of Gree Electric Appliances, GOME would be removed from Gree's sales system. As a result, the struggle between the two giants was escalating.

(3)   Breakup. On 11th March, 2004, all of GOME stores in the whole country were clearing up Gree air conditioners and Gree's comment on it was to stop cooperating with GOME. The two sides finally broke up. In the middle of March, 2004, Gree announced that it would join in selling 70,000～80,000 units of Gree air conditioners with Dazhong electronics(another popular store to buy electric appliances in China) and realized its sales revenues of RMB 180 million. Meanwhile Gree would reinforce the cooperation with those large home appliance retailers in China, such as, Sunning etc. Obviously, the conflict between GOME and Gree was becoming white-hot.

(4) Self-improvement. At this point, Gree started to make enormous efforts in building its own marketing channels with the "joint-stock regional sales companies". Firstly, it strengthened the control of all the branch companies by means of increasing the investment and buying stakes then enhanced the control of direct-sales stores through branch companies; the core part in the marketing policy was the interlink strategy. At the same time, in order to provide better services for its distributors, including: shop design, shop assistant training, service training, Gree Electric Appliances has set up many direct sales stores nationwide with a elegant and neat, unified shop design, standardized service specifications and personalized services, which are all for Gree's competing against the crazy expansion of home appliance chain stores in China. This time, Gree was trying to improve itself in an all-round way. On 24th February, 2005, Gree released its annual report of 2004. According to the report, in 2004, Gree's sales revenues totaled RMB 13.832 billion, up 37.74% over the previous year; achieved a net profit of RMB 420 million, up 22.74% over the previous year. The year 2005 got off to a flying start with the Return on Equity in last year up to 17.24 %.

In the whole process of from the cooperation between Gree and GOME to the rupture in their partnership, the media reports were split up in two groups: one group thinks there were defects in Gree regional marketing channels; the other group believes that GOME's chain channels are too powerful and overbearing. In fact, the two views are leading to various misunderstandings:

Misunderstanding No1: Mistakenly overestimated that the home appliance chain channel is the only development direction and future trend for home appliance distribution and GOME model has the overwhelming advantages compared with Gree, which made

GOME a big overlord in the distribution channel and underestimated the brand power of manufacturing products in the air conditioning field.

Misunderstanding No.2: Mistakenly overestimated the advantages of GOME in the first tier city markets, and underestimated the channel advantages of leading brands, e.g. Gree in regional markets, especially, in the marketing channels of second and third tier cities.

Misunderstanding No.3: Misunderstood the concepts on channels by thinking that the distribution channel of home appliances was equaled to air conditioner distribution channel, which caused the confrontation between GOME and Gree.

As a matter of fact, under the trend of home appliance industry integration, the conflicts can be often seen between manufacturers and distributors and it also happened in the transition process of American retail industry before. Some experts commented that, currently, China's home appliance industry is in the transition period; when the power of the manufacturers matches the distributors', the conflicts between the two sides usually will break out. However, both sides want to change their current sales pattern and neither of them wants to be manipulated or dominated by each other. Nevertheless, the smell of gunpowder in the conflict between Gree and GOME is not as strong as it is described by the media that: How domineering GOME was and how arrogant Gree was. It is just a conflict between two different distribution patterns and it is by no means a conflict between the two enterprises. The problem appeared will be eventually solved under the market rules.

GOME so far is the largest home appliance retailer in China. Everywhere it goes will always arouse a high tide of low-price promotion campaigns. So many small and medium sized retailers and department stores are washed away by GOME. Thus, GOME's powerful sales force and generosity in placing big orders always make itself enjoy VIP treatment from many home appliance manufacturers and many manufacturers always try every effort to cultivate their friendship and partnership with GOME by offering GOME the best supply conditions. Even those big brand air conditioner names, such as, Haier, Midea, AUX all regard cooperating with GOME as the first important matter in their marketing and they even set up the Key Account Department to deal with the business relationship with GOME. In order to compete for the order of 100,000 air conditioner units from Gree, for the second-tier brands, like the Hualing air conditioner, its senior executives all turned out in full strength for obtaining orders from GOME.

Despite the facts that many air-con makers are competing for GOME's big orders, Gree is still a latecomer to GOME. It did not build relationship with GOME until 2001 and its business partnership with GOME was only confined to 5 sales companies on a provincial level, those areas like Hubei etc. But Gree Electric Appliances, Inc. of Zhuhai never becomes the direct supplier for local GOME stores. Till March, 2004, when the conflict between Gree and GOME broke out, GOME's order only accounted for 3% of Gree's whole sales volume, in Beijing area just up to 5% in its whole sales volume and with a slightly bigger figurer in Chengdu up to 8%. Some people think that, the March of 2004 is the time for the jumpstart of the selling air conditioners for all the air-con makers. At this critical time, Gree should keep pace with its peers, namely Haier and Midea to intensify the cooperation with GOME and to boost its air conditioner sales in GOME stores so it can set a new and higher record in its sales volumes in the year 2004. But on the contrary, Gree chose to break up with GOME. Therefore, many industry insiders and home appliance industry experts all expressed that their worry that Gree's losing GOME, this golden channel, would make itself lose its market share and its leading position in the industry. When there was a rupture in the relationship between Gree and GOME, Gree's view was that GOME would not obey Gree's channel marketing policy, but GOME's comment was that Gree was not willing to take the business model of "manufacturers supplying directly", as it did with Haier and Midea. But, behind the complete break between Gree and GOME, there are some deep-seated reasons for their breakup:

(1) Gree's marketing channel chain is relatively stable with its flexible market operations, so it will not be subjected to distributors' dominance. If Gree surrendered itself to GOME this time and abandoned its present marketing system, perhaps Gree would lose even much more market share because Gree's pyramid distributing system has been put into practice for a very long time and it has been already deep-rooted in Gree's sales system. At the end of 1997, Gree Electric Appliance first established the Hubei sales company with Gree Electric Appliances and major distributors in Hubei as the main shareholders of the sales company, from that moment, the sales company played a dual role as the general agent and the local market governing body for Gree Electric Appliances. After that, Gree continually promoted this model of regional sales company to the nationwide market. At present, Gree has dozens of this type of regional sales company over the whole country. In this manner, Gree Electric Appliances and its distributors are interdependent and become a community of interests; they are trying to make concerted efforts to enlarge the market share and win satisfactory returns. With this system to supervise and manage the marketing channels, Gree could maintain and enhance its brand power and gain a wholehearted support in capital fund and market promotion from the local distributors. All the support that Gree has all contributed to Gree's leading position in market share in this industry. Even in recent years, although the air conditioner brands, namely AUX and Chigo caused some unrest situations in the markets, Gree still could keep its brand image of high quality and high price as well as its first place in the market occupancy, in which the significant role of sales companies could not be ignored. The year 2003 saw that 90% of Gree's sales volume came from its direct-sales stores and end-user retailers' contribution under the model of sales

company.

(2) Gree regards the price war as the important means in today's market competition. It requires itself to have the absolute control of price-setting and price regulation; only in this way can Gree take the initiative to wage the price war and make a quick counterattack against its competitors' price sudden attack with an easy manner.

Since the latter half year of 2003, the price of the core raw materials for air conditioners, such as steels and compressors had skyrocketed and Chinese government also had lowered the export tax rebate rate by 4%. In the meantime, as the energy efficiency rating system for air conditioning products was issued by Chinese government, all the factors aroused the "visibly" increase of production costs in making air conditioners. Because of the SARS outbreak in 2003, all the air conditioner manufacturers had no choice but to accumulate a huge stock. According to the incomplete statistics, about 10 million units of air conditioners were still in the warehouses. As the new refrigeration year began (From September 2004 to July 2005, during which is called the refrigeration year of 2005), the major air-con makers in China, namely, AUX, Midea, Gree, heavily invested in their business expansion in succession. Galanz Enterprise Group Co. of Guangdong (the largest producer of microwave ovens in the world) even claimed to build the biggest air conditioner production base with RMB 2 billion investment. Some inferior or discredited air conditioner brands dared not to continue their business because of the rise in the raw materials for making air conditioners, costs of export sales and state industry standard. So the market space was left when they exited from the markets and the left market space would be the target that all the big brands are struggling for. On the one hand, the continued expansion of big brands could offset the increase in the raw materials and costs of export sales through the scale effect, so as to curb the increase in the price of products; on the other hand, the expansion of all the manufacturers and the huge stock must bring the pressure in the selling of those products. So under the condition of serious product homogeneity, the best way to increase sales turnover is still the price war.

Thus, the product price reduction was the main theme of the year 2004. As early as in February 2004, Haier air conditioner also decided to wage a price war and divorce from its former tradition of only participating in the value wars. Then it joined hands with Suning, one of the large Electrical Appliances retailers in China to launch a vigorous and grand price war in the air conditioning market. However, Gree had already put aside its pride in 2004 and began to participate in it and even initiated a price war itself. Since Gree has taken the price war as the important tool in the market competition, it must make sure that itself has the absolute control in price-setting and price regulation. Only in this way can Gree wage the price war and make a quick counterattack against its competitors' price sudden attack with an easy manner. For this reason, in the final say in controlling the product price, Gree definitely does not allow GOME to challenge its authority in price-setting.

(3) Gree is the leading enterprise in the air conditioning industry and its unyielding attitude towards the retail giant is trying to tell all the enterprises in the industry that as the manufacturers, they should have the final say in price-setting issues as much as the retailers have.

As a matter of fact, in recent years, as Gree's peers came to be the direct suppliers for GOME one after another in a rush, Gree also has been rethinking its marketing channel pattern. Just as many experts said, since the air conditioning industry is turning from the times of extravagant profits to low profits, it is not advisable for the manufacturers to have a long distribution channels, which would make the price of the products higher for the end users after the products go through layers of commissions and the long marketing channel will lead the producers to lose the market share in the repeated occurrence of price wars. Here, let's have a close look at Gree's marketing channel   is: Gree   Electric   Appliances—regional   sales company—agent—retailer—consumer. Compared with the product price of Haier, and Midea which are directly selling to GOME, Gree's product price is obviously much higher after going through its long distribution channels, but it has to be higher than others otherwise it could not meet the interests and demands of all layers. Having seen the risks in the long distribution channels, Gree Electric Appliances has started to adjust its marketing policy. In August, 2003, Gree increased its holdings of the shares of the regional sales companies in Guangzhou and Shenzhen and made the two companies completely under its control.

Before this move in the regional sales compies in Guangzhou and Shenzhen, Gree had bought more stakes in the regional sales companies in Anhui, Hubei and Guangxi with the excuses of their poor performance in sales and coping with the market competition. The final goal for this reform is to change the regional sales companies into management and service organizations which are only responsible for logistics, brand maintenance and providing service. After the reform, the regional sales companies become the management organization and do not withhold any profits from the sales revenues, so they can have direct contact with the second level and third level distributors. In this way, the channels could gradually become flattening. However, Gree's reform did cause a big stir inside its marketing channels. In order to prevent the big stir from affecting the air conditioner sales volume in 2004, Gree suspended its reform in a wider range. At this crucial point, GOME made requests of direct selling products to Gree, which were apparently against Gree's principle of slowing everything down in its adjustment in the marketing channel policy. Certainly, the truth for Gree's magnanimous attitude is also for comforting those big distributors who always remain loyal to Gree Electric Appliances.

(4) It was at the crucial time that the distributors at all levels decided whether they would pay the producers or not. As early as in November 2003, Gree changed its old image of never involving in a price war, and started to launch price wars. In Guangdong province, Gree cut the price of 1 horse power air conditioner to RMB 1099 per set. Meanwhile, in Beijing, Gree also cut the prices of 6 types of air conditioners by 50% of its original price. Gree's launch of this price war made other air conditioner brands, such as, Midea, Kelon, AUX follow up one after another. And the purpose for Gree's starting the price war is to attract the attention and tempt the distributors to pay for the products. Therefore, Gree certainly would not let GOME ruin its well-designed plan to let the distributors pay for the products as the time when the problems were about to be settled was arriving. Turning down the requirement of being the direct supplier for GOME and resolutely settled the problem of GOME's unauthorized price reduction of Gree air conditioning products all showed Gree's ability to control its own market channels and to protect the interests of its distributors at all levels, which could make its distributors continue to remain their loyalty to Gree. When Gree got the payment of the goods, it could make its production according to the demand in the markets, so Gree could ease its financial pressure and feel more confident in dealing with the fierce market competition in air conditioning industry.

(5) Usually, there is only a precedent of a manufacturer's full development promoting the development of a large group of retailers, but there is no fact showing that a retailer's abandonment of selling a certain brand products restrained the development of a manufacturer. Gree's product distributions in the first tier city markets, besides depending on its own marketing channels, are mostly depending on the regional cooperation with large home appliance chain stores, for instance, Gree has signed a cooperation contract with Sundan in Guangdong, with MKD in Shenzhen, with Tongcheng Market in Changsha, with Yongle in Shanghai, with Sanlian in Fujian and with Dazhong in Beijing. As GOME has so many manufacturers coming to its door and wanting to be its suppliers, it naturally would not attach great importance to Gree which did not want to be its direct supplier; not even to say, it would take Gree's products as the featured products in GOME stores. What's more, GOME does not accept Gree's term of payment in advance. But contrary to GOME, Tongcheng Market paid Gree in cash in advance; Dazhong also accepted Gree's supply model of non-direct supply and payment in advance and claimed that it would improve Gree's ranking in sales volume of top 20 in its stores before to be top 3 by increasing Gree's sales volume.

These regional big home appliance chain stores are the No.1 in the local area and they are all strong enough to compete against GOME, one of the largest electrical appliance retailers in China. Cooperating with these partners who are willing to play the game by Gree's rules, Gree eventually gained its final say in the market channels. Therefore, it is natural for Gree to have the confidence in its cooperation with those retailers in the markets of first tier cities. Just for this reason, Gree had so strong reactions to GOME's action of "lowering prices without permission and disturbing Gree's price system" and immediately severed its relationship with GOME at all cost. In fact, even though Gree overlooked GOME's price cutting activities and gave GOME the green light on it, other big home appliance retailers, such as, Suning and Dazhong, etc, would force Gree to stop GOME's unauthorized price reduction. Otherwise, Suning and Dazhong would be bound to follow suit after GOME's pratice; as a result, the price system of Gree was doomed to fail and collapse in the end.

In 2004, the focus of Gree's business plan for this year was central air conditioners (especially, commercial air conditioners). The design and installation of central air conditioning systems requires very professional skills that GOME was incapable of completing the installation job. The sales of Gree's central air conditioning products mostly rely on Gree's direct-sales store. The changes in the main business of direct sales stores from residential air conditioners to commercial central air conditioners paved the way for Gree's next important task of shifting focus from its selling of ordinary air conditioners in its dierect sales stores to cooperating with large home appliance chain stores. Evidently, it was the very first move for Gree to carry out its reform in the marketing channel policy.

Additionally, in 2004, Gree Electric Appliances laid a special emphasis on the sales areas of the markets in second and third-tier cities, in which Gree did a really wonderful job. But for GOME, it still needed a few more days to finish the allocation of the sales network and to dominate in the markets of the second-tier cities, like Zhongshan, Dongguan, Foshan and Wuxi. And the expansion of third tier cities had not been on GOME's agenda yet. Since GOME's sales network played a very insignificant role in Gree's business achievement and its regional distributions in 2004, Gree did not have to show the white feather to GOME, which was the deep-rooted reason for the breakup of Gree and GOME.

2) Right Decision to Stop Supplying GOME

As the industry experts commented, Gree's giving up GOME, the increasingly powerful big marketplace for electric home appliances would lead to Gree's losing the market share. Contrarily, if Gree surrendered itself to GOME at this point and gave up its current marketing system, probably it would lose more market share. The pyramid distribution system of Gree has gone through for many years; the difference between Gree and second tier brands, like Hualing, TCL lies in their lack of the high efficient nationwide distribution networks or complete sales networks.

Take Hualing as an example, Hualing air conditioner is quite famous in Guangzhou, but people outside Guangdong province don't know about this brand much. For many years, there is not any improvement in constructing its sales network in the northern market of China. With the help of GOME-- one of the largest home appliance chain stores in China, Hualing finally could enter all the markets all over the country to expand its brand influence and find opportunities for itself to build its own sales network. Although GOME tried to undersell Hualing aircondtioners for many times with very low prices (certainly GOME would not suffer losses in price reduction), the influence of Hualing brand on the sales network of Northern China still has been insignificant. And the Hualing's price behind GOME's underselling is that Hualing was forced to provide even more favorable conditions for GOME, as long as the products could be sold in quantity in GOME stores and Hualing would not grudge the meager profits (in January 2004, Hualing signed a 100,000 units of big order with GOME) .

But in the contest with GOME, Gree won't allow that GOME cut the product price of Gree air conditioner at will, or its sales all over the country would be affected. So some industry experts think that Gree's giving up cooperating with GOME is not seeking its own destruction but a wise move. The following are the reasons for supporting the view above:

Reason No.1: The manufacturer would defend and strengthen its position in the commercial circulation and it would by no means willingly give up its dominant position and the right to control the situation when dealing with distributors.

For example, in the dispute of Chunlan air conditioner, also a large air-con maker in China and Carrefour, one of the largest international hypermarket chain stores in the world, Chunlan showed a strong objection towards Carrefour for its sudden advertisement of big promotion, in which the price of 1.5 horse power Chunlan air conditioner was priced as RMB1799 lower than the price of RMB 199 that Chunlan Group had for this type of air conditioner countrywide and the price provided by the Carrefour store was even lower than the original wholesale price about RMB101 . The purpose of Carrefour's cutting the price was for the promoting the whole products in the supermarket and attracting customers' attention by lowering the price of home appliances. Thus, Carrefour would not care about the sales volumes of Chunlan air conditioners. Carrefour's disturbing activity seriously damaged the price system of Chunlan air conditioner in Nanjing market at that time, which also affected the interests of other distributors to a certain extent. While Chuanlan Group was making its resistance to Carrefour, it also even began to consider investigating Carrefour's legal liabilities in "low price dumping beyond agreed areas".

Both the dispute between Gree and GOME and the battle between Chunlan and

Carrefour were all caused by the retailers cutting the product price greatly without the permission from the manufacturers. Coincidently, the two retailers all encountered the manufacturers' resistance and the results of the two events were also similar: Carrefour reverted the original price of the Chuanlan air conditioner in Nanjing area and Chunlan Group would not pursue the investigation into Carrefour's legal liabilities in "low price dumping beyond agreed areas"; GOME took the excuse that the ultra low-price air conditioners had been sold out and it would fully reverted back the original price of Gree air conditioners in all the stores of GOME. The manufacturers' toughness and channel intermediaries' compromise reflected the actual strength of the manufacturers.

Reason No.2: the subtle changes between producers and intermediaries show that the interests become the bond between the two sides, which means that the game playing between intermediaries and manufacturers has entered into a brand new stage.

The present producer-retailer relationship is neither the relationship that is dominated by the producers or the two sides were competing with each other in the past, nor the relationship of separation of the industrial enterprises and commercial enterprises as some people predicted or mutual cooperation, but the relationship is more characterized by the relationship of coopetition(a combination of cooperation and competition) or their mutual exploitation and mutual dependence, with the interests as the bond and with the goal of seeking the "win-win situation".

Reason No. 3: The marketing hype is more and more employed in the market competition. Both the manufacturers and retailers all want to enhance their reputation by means of the media hype. As the competition is heating up, in order to win the market share and obtain the opportunity to survive and develop themselves, the manufacturers and retailers will inevitably exploit all the resources to be engaged in commercial hype and make the event that they are involving in sensationalized to attract the public attention so that they can acquire the preemptive market opportunity and occupy the markets. Just take the event of "Gree refusing to supply GOME" as an example; GOME became the media circus through the hyped issue of fighting with Gree. During this event of Gree's confronting GOME, GOME obtained the following benefits: attracting the public attention, improving its commercial brand image, expanding its market influence, boosting the sales volume of its products as well as sharpening its competitive edge.

To Gree, this much hyped issue might affect its brand image and caused some chaos in its market price order, but as the issue was not a fundamental threat to Gree. Actually, this kind of event could serve as the "free" advertisement for Gree's products-- half a loaf is better than no bread. What's more, it was a free one. Therefore, once such events are happening, the manufacturer tends to take advantage of this situation and make the full use of this opportunity to express that they will investigate this matter and consider punishing the retailer severely; or issue official letters on this event and stop supplying goods to the retailer as a protest. After measuring swords with each other, the brand image for both the manufacturer and the retailer will be imperceptibly enhanced.

Reason No. 4: The event of "Gree's refusing to supply GOME" is a very effective "event-based marketing", in which the dominant brand always could seize the preemptive opportunity.

Along with the consumer concept becoming rationalizing day by day, the Chinese marketing is quickening its pace to enter the "era of brand consumption". In the "era of brand consumption", the consumers not only wish to buy the products of "excellent quality and reasonable price", but also they expect the product of high brand reputation. However, the popularity and reputation of small and medium-sized product brands are not wide and high enough; their power of influence and appeal are much to be desired and the channel intermediaries could not achieve greater market influence and better actual results by cooking up the hype of the small and medium-sized product brands. If the channel intermediaries want to enhance their image and make a promotion of their products via "event-based marketing", they must find some big brand names, even the products of the leading enterprises in the industry to cook up the hype, which can cause a sensation and arouse huge social echoes. In fact, both the Carrefour event in Nanjing or GOME and Gree event, the leading roles of the hyped issues are the well-known brand names in the air conditioning industry: Chuanlan air conditioner once ranked No.1 in the sales volume of Chinese air conditioner for many years; Gree is the new champion in air conditioner sales volume in recent years. The two brand names have great influence in the markets. Once the channel intermediaries are involved with them in an event, it is very easy to catch the public's and the media's attention. Sometimes the event even causes a big earthquake in the whole industry and the dominant brands can be quicker to size the preemptive opportunity in the market than those small and medium-sized product brands.

The events similar to "Gree's refusing to supply GOME" not only just happened in the home appliance industry, but also in other fields, they are not uncommon. Through summarizing the past experience and lessons in those events, the manufacturers could be enlightened and inspired by them, and then they can put what they have learnt in to practice, which is the best way for the local manufacturers to survive and to form a sustainable development.

2. No Regrets in Breaking With GOME

In April, 2004, as the first electrical appliance enterprise which dared to challenge the powerful and dominant channel intermediary, under the leadership of the iron lady, Dong Mingzhu, Gree Electric Appliances decided to withdraw all of their products from GOME. Subsequently, Gree's marketing pattern, including the vice-chairman Dong Mingzhu herself was facing a new round of challenges: whether Gree could go on as Dong Mingzhu said "check around the world is not to rule the world, but to fight side by side with every one." It is still doubtful that whether Dong Mingzhu could make Gree tide over and survive with the marketing model of "commission agent system" which was already abandoned by many electrical appliances enterprises long time ago. In electrical appliances industry, as the only company which "stepped forward" to confronted the overbearing and powerful enterprise in circulation field, Gree's courage compelled the universal admiration from numerous home appliances enterprises in China.

1) "We Are Not Afraid of GOME Entering into the Markets of Zhuhai"

"In the case of GOME's entering into the Zhuhai market, we are not afraid of it at all. There is only one GOME store in Zhuhai, even if they have dozens of stores in Shenzhen or hundreds of stores in other places, we are still doing what we should be doing and our sales volume still will be the No.1 in many places for many years. What differences will one GOME store make? " Zhu Jianghong claimed with a firm attitude.

"At present, although we are still keeping building our own marketing channels, some people commented that the cost for us to build our own marketing channel is too high but in fact we did not spend any money building our channels. It is our distributors who opened their own purse to run the Gree direct-sales stores. Can we take control of them without investing our money? I believe we still can make it."

Zhu Jianghong said, Gree's special stores and direct-sales stores are all very loyal. Currently, the sales of Gree stores accounts for 70%~80% in Gree's overall sales volume and the percentage of the sales in big malls is very low. "Up to now, the percentage of the sales in GOME and Suning is less than 3% in Gree's total sales."

After the clean break with GOME, Gree's choice in business model of building its own marketing channels with direct sales stores cannot be simply considered as returning to the "traditional" marketing channels.

Firstly, the current trend of marketing channel development is going towards the direction of polarization—large and comprehensive, small but specializing. The trend of marketing channel development cannot be just large and comprehensive. In the change of the trend of market channels, the traditional home appliances market is shrinking, not the brand stores. The cases of many industries could provide us the evidence to prove it. Seeing that the cheese of the old marketing channel is going stale, Gree does not want to surrender and give in but bravely and firmly chooses the strategic direction of building its own direct-sales stores and precisely grasps the trend in the development and evolution of the marketing channel in the future.

Secondly, from the macro environment for the choice in marketing channel strategy, considering the status quo and environment of the present China's markets, there should not be just one marketing model dominating the whole markets in China and the current situation of Chinese markets has determined that there could be a overlapping of direct sales and distribution model when enterprises are dealing with retailers in choosing marketing model. It is quite wrong to over emphasize the importance of certain end user stores. As for Gree stores, the network of those stores is controllable, which is its competitive advantages; needless to say there are so many reliable and loyal distributors all over the country, with whom Gree could cooperate with to build their own direct-sales store channels.

Thirdly, from the perspective of displaying the brand image in the end user stores, although the size of direct sales stores is comparatively small, they are still superior to GOME stores. For example, which brand could have the chance to open a brand store inside a GOME store? Even if it is allowed to do so, the cost of opening a brand store will be rather high compared with the practice of it setting up its own brand store next to GOME. An expert once gave a very proper comment about Gree's stores that Gree's direct sales stores have a resemblance to GOME's chain stores. Supposed if someday Gree puts the word "chain" before its stores, are the two very similar? The differences between the stores of Gree and GOME are just the product variety and the size of the stores.

The industry analysts believe that, there is no such marketing channel model as strong as the iron, but only the market strategies of flexibility and adaptability. If the producers don't seek competitive advantages in the following aspects of consumers' needs, product quality and brand appeal, but entrust the above key factors and their own life to something insignificant rather than the product and brand, it is bound to have the result just like the ending of the story in our primary school textbook that a man cut a mark on the side of his boat to indicate the place where his sword has dropped into the river (means that one takes measures without regard to changes in circumstances or to be stubbornly unimaginative).

Since Gree has already chosen the business model of building its own direct sales store channel, to the questions from some experts concerning about the use of regurgitation feeding of terminal information and the brand image all can be answered. On the one hand, there are many ways to solve the problems, e.g. to collect more information about the end user markets, competitors and consumers; on the other hand, without the advantages of GOME's channel, to those customers who are uncertain or not loyal to a certain brand, Gree Electric Appliances could put more money and efforts to do some ad campaigns and brand promotion activities, which will be greatly helpful to build Gree's self-sustaining marketing channels. It is high time that Gree should work hard to build its brand loyalty and brand association as well as cultivate consumers' preference and trial rate by means of emotional marketing and event marketing.

As the development of the world economic integration, the markets and the competitive environment are changing every day. The competitors and consumers are also changing and everything is changing every day. Facing the future, the "gomers" should think more about that the design of their marketing strategy should be based on the value chain and give a comprehensive consideration to the interests of suppliers, themselves, consumers and society etc. The competition in future is not only the competition of a single enterprise, but the competition model based on the every link of the value chain. Only in this way, will the life of Chinese enterprises be longer and sustainable, and gradually they form their competitive strength and core capability to compete with those international retailer giants. The vice-chairwoman of Gree Electric Appliances, Dong Mingzhu indicated that, Gree's industrial spirit should be the internal spiritual quality and soul to support Gree brand to become a world class brand. Furthermore, the more important spirit is the rare and commendable spirit of "feeling proud even in defeat" in Gree and Dong Mingzhu—which is the spirit that the industrialists of our national industry don't have in current China.

2) Advanced or Backward

When talking about Gree's business model, Zhu Jianghong shared his view with us, "We are always sticking to Gree model; that is the combination of sales companies and Gree direct sales stores, which has increased Gree's sales volume by a wide margin every year. Some enterprises depend on GOME to sell their products, if this marketing channel is good, the sales volume of those enterprises should grow much faster and greater than Gree, but why the result is still not satisfactory? Although we don't depend on GOME and Suning for selling our products greatly, our sales revenues don't drop a little bit. On the contrary, there has been a growth of 30% every year in our sales revenues. Doesn't the growth rate explain everything and make the problem clear? Some people said, that Gree doesn't enter Suning, GOME means that Gree would encounter the big slide in its sales achievement and it will not be one of the mainstream brands anymore or it will no longer in the top 3 in home appliance industry. These views are all ridiculous. Our sales growth is not made up or stolen or robbed from others, but evidently from the efforts of our direct sales stores. And we are not only the No.1 in the whole nation; we are also the No.1 in the whole world. The fact has already shown that our sales model and direct-sales pattern are all very good and quite suitable to the market conditions in current China. We had no regrets in breaking with GOME in the past also have no regrets at all for now. Quite the other way, we believe if we had withdrawn our products from GOME earlier, we could have taken more initiatives."

For a single enterprise or a circulation field, if it cannot be flexible to change itself according the changes of the markets, it only can be regarded as a traditional and backward one. As long as it could adjust itself to the changes of the markets, it can be considered an advanced one. To a manufacturer, the cooperation with distributors is a traditional model, but the cooperation with those outlets or supermarkets is an advanced model; this classification is not quite correct and scientific. Dong Mingzhu believes that to judge a marketing model is advanced or not mostly depends on what the consumers need. With Gree's advantages in its product quality, if Gree cooperates with large home appliance stores in an overall way, the short term interests and profits will be considerable beyond all doubt, but what Gree truly wants is a sustainable and long term development, not just the short term interests.

Therefore, Gree chooses to build its own self-sustaining marketing channel. It not only to build the channels, but also to manage the channels via its own efforts and to change the management philosophy of the retailers so as to make them realize that to provide services for the consumers is the most important. With the idea of providing services for consumers as the focus, despite the big marketplaces or small marketplaces, they all will be the winner at last. The marketing model is not the crucial factor in determining the winner in a very short time and the decisive factor for an enterprise's sustainable development should be the right business philosophy.

The "Gree model" is not a traditional model, but the outside world keep regarding Gree's sales model as a traditional sales model, thinking that it is a backward one and the burgeoning big home appliances chain store is an advanced model. Dong Mingzhu does not deny the fact that the home appliances chain store will be the trend in the future, but according to her, across the world, all the high-grade products have their own exclusive shops. What Gree is selling is the products of elegant taste and high quality. If Gree determines to forge the world class brand and make products of superior quality, it must choose a way suitable for its own development. Thus, the sales model of Gree Electric Appliances is an advanced model which could be adaptable to the market needs and changes as well as continuously enhancing and improving itself in the dynamic markets.

3. There is No Eternal Enemy In Business World

It has been three years since Gree Electric Appliances, Inc. of Zhuhai broke up with GOME Electrical Appliances Holding Limited. After three years' cold car, Gree and GOME finally chose to mend their relation first from the regional cooperation. But as more than 90% of Gree's products are being sold in its own self-sustaining channels, it is quite impossible for Gree to go into an all-around partnership with any retailers of home appliances chain stores. At present, the large-scale procurement between Gree and GOME is still restricted to Guangzhou area. In the areas of Shanghai, Beijing, Gree still adopts the model of cooperating with its distributors as usual. The industry experts said, this time that Gree products reentering into GOME stores does not mean the two sides make peace with each other; after all the channel intermediaries are still considering making profits as their final goal. Hence, the partnership between the two sides is just for the shared goal of seeking win-win situation and common interests.

(1) He Who Laughs Last Laughs Best

After two year's break-up of Gree and GOME, the year 2006 witnessed their new round of cooperation. When the press was having an interview with GOME store in Guangzhou, they all found that Gree air conditioner had already been sold in GOME stores. According to informed sources, "The cooperation between Gree and GOME in Guangzhou is just the pilot program. If this one goes smoothly, this cooperation model will be promoted in the rest of China." Besides Guangzhou, the GOME stores in Henan, Fujian all confirmed the news that the press got from Gree Electric Appliances.

It is reported that from November 2005, Gree air conditioner made its entry into the GOME stores in Guangzhou. The two parties were Guangzhou GOME Electrical Appliance Holdings Limited and Guangzhou Gree air conditioner sales Co. ltd. In terms of the cooperation model, Gree still directly supplied GOME and Gree's sales agents with a uniform price; then in the end of the year, according to the sales volume, Gree would offer GOME stores and its agents the rebates. The cooperation model is quite different from Gree's cooperation with others and GOME's current sales model with other partners before. The industry analysts suggest that this cooperation between Gree and GOME is not comprehensive cooperation, but it is the curtain raiser for the two giants' brand new partnership. In that case, will Gree make friends with GOME again?

Regarding this question from the outside world, Gree Vice-chairwoman, Dong Mingzhu emphasized: "He who laughs last laughs best." After losing GOME, under her leadership, the "professional distributor and direct sales stores model" has proved to be fruitful. More than 600 professional distributors rapidly helped Gree air conditioner to improve its market occupancy and the constant technology innovation made Gree's competitive advantages prominent in the specialized industrial clusters. After Gree being the first enterprise in Chinese air conditioning industry with sales volume exceeding RMB 10 billion, in 2004, Gree air conditioner realized its sales revenues of RMB13. 832 billion, up by 37.74% over the previous year with the net profit of   RMB 420 million, jumping 22.74 % over the previous year, which was unmatched and unequaled for those manufacturers who only have relied on the modern chain store marketing model. The unique pattern of regional sales company created by Dong Mingzhu is praised as "the brand new revolution in the 21st

economic domain" by the economic circle and the theory circle.

However, as the two giants in its own industry, the cooperation between the two is inevitable. About the partnership between Gree and GOME, when interviewed by *China Business News*, the deputy general manager of GOME operation center, Mr. He Yangqing denied the statement of the cooperation between GOME head office and Gree head office, but he admitted that there were many GOME branch companies cooperating with Gree branch companies. "There are no big conflicts between the two sides, if there are common interests for both the two sides, it is better for the two companies to work things out based on the mutual interests." He Yangqing said.

As to whether Gree would cooperate with GOME or not, the spokesman of Gree Mr. Huang Fanghua also expressed the similar views: "As long as GOME plays the game by our rules, the cooperation between the two sides is possible. But so far there is no plan about the comprehensive cooperation between Gree head office and GOME head office yet."

The analysts inside the industry also pointed out, on the foundation of the current cooperation model, GOME serves as one of Gree's distributors in Gree's distribution channel so that Gree can greatly reinforce its control in the end price. At the same time, GOME deals with Gree's regional sales companies, compared with dealing with Gree's sales agents; the price is more flexible to GOME.

The facts showed us there is neither eternal friend nor eternal enemy in the marketplace but only the eternal interests and profits. Some experts indicated that the markets in second and third tier cities are the common interests of Gree and GOME. For GOME, after finishing the market layout in the markets of top tier cities, the markets of the second and third tier cities become its development priorities at the present stage, and Gree has powerful brand influence in the markets of the second and third tier cities. According to the informed sources, on the very day when Gree's financial statement analysis was released, Gree held a conference about the issue of the nation-wide direct sales stores. At the meeting, Gree further confirmed that its market expansion strategy in the markets of second and third tier cities. From this aspect, "GOME's dependence on Gree in entering the second and third tier city markets is continually growing".

In the meanwhile, after the reshuffling of the air conditioning market in 2005, about 20 air conditioner brands were phased out through this reshuffling. The air conditioner brands which have the strength and capability to enter the home appliance stores and supermarkets are becoming fewer and fewer. Considering the aspects of brand, sales volume, GOME does need Gree in its stores. The principal consultant, Mr. Pang Yahui from Shanghai Zhuoyue Marketing Consulting Company believed: "to GOME and Gree, they two are the leading enterprises in their own industry. It is impossible for the two giants not to be partners and their cooperation depends on the results of the game playing between the two." He continued to point out that the advantages of "Gree's model" lie in the second and third tier city markets, but the market share of chain stores is expanding day by day, which is a trend that Gree cannot ignore. When those chain stores like GOME fight with Gree and make the market share of Gree regional sales company drop and decline in the second and third tier city markets, it will be too late for Gree to adjust its distribution channels at that time. Therefore, the cooperation between Gree and GOME is also in accordance with the interests of Gree. Moreover, following Gree's example, Midea air conditioner also has set up some sales companies in some cities of some provinces and TCL launched the Happy Tree (Xing Fu Shu) electric appliance chain stores, too. Mr. Pang Yahui thinks, as the benchmark in this industry, if Gree is cooperating with GOME, their cooperation certainly will have impact on the above-mentioned enterprises which are trying to build their own self-sustaining marketing channels. Thus, the cooperation will bring Gree handsome profits. Judging from the present situation, building the partnership between the two giants is not so urgent, but from the long term strategic perspective, their partnership will be a mutual interest.

Sun Weimin, the President of Nanjing Suning Electrical Appliance Chain Group Co., Ltd, said: "There is no eternal cooperation or non-cooperation between the manufacturers and retailers. If the two sides can work things out and reach an agreement, they will cooperate with each other. If they cannot reach the agreement between the two sides, they will not be the partners. The key point is whether there are mutual interests between them or not."

(2) It Is More Than A Contest on Game Rules

Huang Guangyu, the founder of GOME Electrical Appliances Holding Limited, is generally known for his taciturnity and cold-bloodedness. But when the name of Dong Mingzhu is mentioned in the conversation, his eyes betray him and show affirmation and admiration towards this stubborn woman. When a tough man meets an even tougher woman, it seems that the tricks of the trade usually used between men do not work anymore. This is also the same for Huang Guangyu who has experienced numerous trials and hardships in the business world for many years. When Huang Guangyu meets Dong Mingzhu for the second time, the game between the two enterprises begin to have some new rules, but this time, the rule maker is Gree's cool iron lady, Dong Mingzhu.

Under the current trend of the strong becoming more powerful and the weak becoming even weaker in the production and sales of air conditioning industry, Gree and GOME, the two leading enterprises in its industry, once the two sides put each other in their blacklist without any hesitation and at last broke their relationship openly. Finally, in the morning of 14th March, 2007, the two giants came to shake hands and make it up. The general manager of Guangzhou GOME, Gao Jiqun and his counterpart of Guangzhou Gree,

Wang Weiquan signed the joint agreement of "The Strategic Escalation of GOME and Gree" and announced from that day, the Gree air conditioning products would appear in all the 33 GOME stores in Guangzhou. And GOME also placed a RMB 200 million purchase order of Gree air conditioners for the first time. "Business is business; the most important thing is profit." Gao Jiqun the general manager of Guangzhou GOME expressed his views to the press. "Although GOME is holding the lion's share of 30% in the south air conditioner markets of China, if there is no air conditioner of Gree, the air conditioning industry leader, "it will be a great pity for both parties and the consumers".

Actually, from November 2005, some of Guangzhou GOME stores already began to directly sell Gree products. In 2006, the sales volume of Gree air conditioners in GOME stores even reached the highest level ever compared with the sales before the two's breakup in 2003. The two parties chose to have strategic upgrading cooperation at this very moment; obviously, their cooperation was mostly driven by the market competition and business profits.

Did the all-around partnership this time between GOME and Gree mean that the two would be "from hostility to friendship" and cooperate with each other in a nationwide level? Gao Jiqun said to the media, he did hope the cooperation would be in a nationwide level, but the cooperation for this time was just regional. And Wang Weiquan, the general manager of Gree, said, about Gree's entry into GOME stores, on the hand it was because of GOME' huge sales force in air conditioning products, on the other hand it was because that Guangzhou GOME respects and identifies with Gree's market rules. "I can be very sure that the prices are all the same in any distribution channel in Guangzhou, including GOME or its chain stores."

The industry experts analyzed the prerequisite for the cooperation between Gree and GOME is just out of the business profits. Because GOME cannot do its business without Gree, if there is no Gree product in GOME stores, a considerable amount of cash flow will be cut. Gao Jiqun said the sales revenues of air conditioning products accounts for 20% in GOME's annual sales revenues. He referred the ice-breaking move in the two's relation as "it will be GOME's pity, if there are no Gree products in GOME stores", which shows his great sincerity in this cooperation. Wang Weiquan also expressed a similar view: if the sales achievement of Guangzhou GOME is excellent, he "is willing to be the regular customer of Mr. Gao."

When talking about the most sensitive price issue between the two sides, Gao Jiqun made it very clear that, GOME respects Gree's market rules. He claimed that, as GOME has already been the No.1 in the whole country, it is not necessary for GOME to wage any price war. When asked about "whether it means even if GOME cuts the price for promotion like before, it will not cut the product price of Gree air conditioners any more", Gao Jiqun and

Wang Weiquan are all smiling and shaking their heads in a tacit agreement.

According to the experts, for the second time that Gree is cooperating with GOME, Gree will face a hard choice. It is understood that, at present 90% of Gree air conditioners are sold via its direct-sales stores and retail outlets. However, since 2000, the large home appliances chain stores had begun to capture the market share in many big and medium-sized cities all over the country. The statistics indicate, home appliance chain stores like GOME, Suning, they have at least monopolized the 50 % market share in the home appliance markets of many cities with a high retail concentration degree, like Beijing, Shanghai and Guangzhou. Under this circumstance, Gree is facing a very hard choice.

Some analysts believe, as the power of distribution businesses is growthing stronger and stronger, there will be subtle changes between the manufacturers and the intermediaries: the two sides will be more dependent on each other with the "interests" as the bond and the two sides will seek for a "win-win situation" together. Does it mean that GOME and Gree will completely resume their business relationship as before after the ice breaker case in Guangzhou? Both Gao Jiqun and Wang Weiquan did not give us the answer, but from the point that the producers and intermediaries are from the open strife and veiled struggle to trying to mend the relationship between each other, it indicates that the business relationship of the producers and intermediaries is going through a new round negation of the negation in their game playing.

Review: The Interest of Customers is Paramount.

As the Prefect of the Grand Scribes of the Han Dynasty and the father of Chinese historiography, Sima Qian wrote in his great book *"Shi Ji/ Records of the Grand Historian"*: "Jostling and joyous, the whole world comes after profit. Racing and rioting, after profit the whole world goes!" (translated by Burton Watson) The famous quotation tells us that the eternal theme of the business world for every person and every company is only for the purpose of pursuing profits.

In today's market economy, the conflict between companies is for nothing but profits.

The PK between Gree and GOME is also for their own profits and interests. But the two dared to challenge each other openly, for both of them are the leaders in their trade backed by their tremendous strength. The so called fighting for the final say in the value chain actually means the fight for profits. As the two sides become friends again, what they did and what they fought for are still driven by the commercial profits.

But where does the profit go to? We have seen that when Gree "broke up with" GOME, the two parties were only considering their own interests: Gree wanted to control its own price system and couldn't put up with GOME's cutting the price of Gree products without its permission. GOME wanted to implement its promotion strategy and did not allow Gree "to keep itself clean and not to be involved" in GOME's promotion activities. We still have seen that, when Gree and GOME had their cooperation for the second time, it showed that when the emotional feelings of "overbearing" and "arrogant" dispersed and disappeared, the two parties started to regard the interests of the consumers as their main consideration. GOME as the largest home appliances retailer in China, if there is no Gree product, the No.1 top air conditioner brand in China, on its shelves, apparently it cannot bring the benefits for consumers; despite that Gree has its own distribution channel, if it does not enter GOME stores, it is also can not do a very good job in serving the consumers.

The struggle between Gree and GOME is just the "brief interlude" in their cooperation and it will never be "the central theme". To producers or to retailers, there is only one central theme-- to bring the most interests for the consumers as much as they can, which should be the fundamental element for the sustainable development of enterprises.

Among Chinese enterprises, the excellent enterprises which really care about the interests of the consumers are not many. In recent months, the hyped issue of the fight between Danone(Groupe Danone, a French food-products multinational corporation) and Wahaha(Hangzhou Wahaha Group: a private group of companies, and the largest beverage producer in China), the core of their dispute is still about their own interests. During their fight and dispute, which side really cares about the interests of the consumers?

Many westerner enterprisese tend to believe that: "The customer is God." All the activities of enterprises should be customer-oriented and serve the customers. The history of Chinese enterprises is not long but there were once many market opportunities in the transformation of Chinese economy. Although quite a few enterprises had not had this idea of taking the interests of consumers as the first priority, they still made much money with the market opportunities. This kind of situation only happened 20 years ago for at that time Chinese enterprises and markets were not mature. But in the future, this kind of situation will not exist any longer. Only those enterprises which truly regard the interests of the consumers as the top priority, can they gain a foothold in the global markets in the environment with increasingly fierce market competition and increasingly rational consumers.

We hope that both product manufacturers and retailers in the circulation field, when they are thinking about the cooperation strategy with their partners, or when there is conflict in their cooperation, could take the interests of consumers as their first priority, especially, the long-term and long-lasting interests of consumers. Thereby, the word "champion" can have a new extended meaning: the champion enterprise is the one which could put the interests of consumers in the first place in its marketing strategy. So we can say that he who can consumers the most satisfaction will be the real winner in the end.

Chapter 7: Facing Three Major Difficulties

1. Breaking through the Markets of First Tier Cities

The industry experts believe that Gree's direct sales stores are completely in a weaker bargaining position when cooperating with Gree Electric Appliances, the big company, which is a typical model of "the big manufacturer bulling the small stores", but this model conforms to Gree's control strategy of its marketing channels. Under the context of the fierce market competition, Gree must do something to make up for the weak position of Gree direct sales stores; otherwise, this model will lose the foundation of its existence. Currently, the market size of Chinese home appliance market reaches RMB 500 billion. In Chinese home appliance market, the markets of first and second tier cities make up 53%; the markets of third and fourth tier cities account for 47%; that is about the market capacity of RMB 235 billion. So far, the home appliances chain enterprises, like GOME, Suning, haven't developed their business in the third and fourth tier cities. But Gree's present achievement exactly has benefited from the markets in those areas. However, along with that the market layout of home appliances chain enterprises has been completed, once the keen competition is created between Gree and GOME in the markets of third and fourth tier cities, the channel risk of Gree's marketing channels could cause the risk of affecting the whole business operations in Gree Electric Appliances. As a result, Gree itself will under the huge pressure brought about by the risk: the great impact on Gree' sales achievement, the less and less huge sum of advance money and the deteriorating cash flow.

1) Gree's Regional Agent System Finds Hard To Be Adaptable to the Future

When Haier, with the largest market share in white goods, and Midea, the sizeable conglomerate specializing in the manufacturing of household appliances develop a comprehensive and deep-rooted partnership with new chain channels, Gree is particularly noteworthy for its own marketing channel strategy. Under the situation that the great changes are happening in the channel pattern and the market space will be occupied with a large margin, it will be very unfavorable to Gree indeed. If Gree still sticks to its regional agent system, it will inevitably meet big challenges brought by its own marketing system. The analysts in this industry indicate that China's all appliances retail enterprises will eventually make the whole markets for home appliances into the chain store operations and any markets cannot skip this process. At present, the chain operation of Chinese home appliance retail industry is expanding from cities to rural areas. The chain network in the cities at provincial level has already taken shape. To Gree, it is workable to maintain the present agent system, but, it must cooperate with GOME, those chain store retailers. If it still forces itself to maintain its present regional agent system, Gree will definitely bring at least 5 great damages to itself:

First, the fatal injury brought to the Gree brand. If Gree does not develop its partnership with those chain store retailers, such as GOME, it will totally lose its brand image and parts of market share in the markets of first tier cities. If the situation is going on and on, it will continue pose serious damages to the brand of Gree; for GOME, those chain store enterprises have already become the runway for powerful brands. If Gree does not make its appearance in the new channels, the markets will be left a mistaken impression that the brand is fading and consumers also will have the impression that Gree is disappearing from the frontline of the markets in the first tier cities, which not only affects Gree's sales in first-tier city markets, but also bring negative influence to the second and third-tier city markets. Consequently, Gree probably will be more and more like a rural brand of first and second-tier markets, which will become an adverse factor for its business expansion. Hence, in the changes of the market channels in the top tier cities, how to avoid the earthquake in its branding is not the problem only concerning sales volume but the problem that Gree should treat carefully.

Second, Gree's regional sales volume will be affected. The chain channel is leaving the impression of a "price basin" to the markets, which is a direction for consumption in the first tier city markets. If Gree is not in this channel but in other channels, even its price is much lower than those in the "price basin", it will be very hard for consumers to find out. In this way, Gree's sales volume will be affected by its own marketing model hugely.

Thirdly, there is no price advantage in Gree's own regional sales system. Compared with the selling price of the brands, namely, Haier and Midea, etc, which are directly supplying GOME, Gree has not any price advantage as Gree's distributors are cooperating with GOME, for the price advantages have been eaten up by the regional agents. As a result, the price momentum is not strong enough to capture the market increment.

Fourthly, sluggishness in Gree's marketing system. Cooperating with chain store enterprises, the manufacturers will get optimized in the process of from gaining information from consumers to the product manufacturing. The current state of Gree's marketing channels objectively creates the inaccurate grasp of the actual consumption, but Haier pays more attention to the market demand information via the cooperation with GOME. Although the cooperation is challenging, it is still worthwhile for the home appliance manufacturers to do so. While the rivals are trying to optimize their process of production,

Gree's current marketing channels limit itself from going in for innovations; compared with other brands, Gree is obviously lagging behind in this aspect.

Fifth, it is difficult for Gree to lower the cost and make a full use of its scale merits. The present state of Gree's marketing channels causes the operation cost very high, e.g. the logistical cost. Presently, Haier, a multinational consumer electronic and home appliances company, has already begun to send its products directly from its production line to GOME's distribution center. There are no warehouses of regional companies in Haier, but on the contrary, the number of Haier's warehouses is declining. However in Gree model, the product flow pattern is that the products firstly arrive in the warehouses of the manufacturer then go to the warehouses of regional sales companies and lastly to the distribution center of GOME, which means that Gree has already been defeated in the logistics chain. The vacant market place left by the small and medium-sized air conditioner brands does not necessarily mean there will be a natural increase in the market share of big air conditioner brands. The price adjustment of Haier air conditioner has once been regarded as the helpless choice after it encountered the disturbance of low price air conditioners. Actually this opinion has been proved to be rather superficial. Behind the price adjustment of Haier is the significant reduction in its multiple costs. The profits of the price cutting activities come from the cost reduction; contrarily, many enterprisers cannot low the cost when they are doing price adjustment, so they have to cut their profits to lower the product price. But Haier's practice in fact is redefining the law of competition in the era of competition among the big air conditioner brands. And now Haier is doing an adequate preparation for its marketing expansion in its price, marketing channel, brand and manufacturing. With this view, the situation in front of Gree is not optimistic. So in order to enhance the competitive strength, Gree must improve and upgrade its own market channel system.

Just as an old saying goes: "there is no flawless thing in the world", so is Gree's business model. The industry analysts indicate that there are some defects in Gree's model in terms of in theory or in practice.

Firstly, theoretically, the old grudges left by the previous fights for the market share between Gree's large distributors plus the unequal regional sales company shares held by the share holders—the perfect shell of regional sales companies cannot conceal the conflicts between those share holders inside, which sets the scene for the sharp contradictions in regional areas.

Secondly, the undue dependence on the large distributors has led Gree to overlook the construction of its sales terminal and Gree's strict channel control makes the number of products very limited in sales terminal. Thereby, the gap and distance between consumers and Gree products are gradually becoming widening, which is particularly obvious in the three major cities: Shanghai, Beijing and Guangzhou. For example, in Guangzhou, the local manufacturer Hualing Group occupies 50% of the market share in Guangzhou air conditioning market, and the global giants, Panasonic which is entrenched in Guangzhou markets deeply and Mitsubishi Heavy Industries which is located in Jiangmen both have a large group of followers who are very loyal to Japanese products; the giant Midea from the neighborly city Shunde considers Guangzhou as the door of its home and even the business of Haier from the north of China also begins to take shape in Guangzhou. There, the marketing channels of all the manufacturers are everywhere. By contrast, Gree's distribution outlets are much rarer compared with its competitors. And the problems are widely prevailing in the markets of those key cities, namely, Chongqing, Wuhan, Shenzhen, Zhengzhou and Shenyang etc, where Gree has relatively done its business quite well before.

Thirdly, in the practical operations, because of the difficulties in supervising, the distributors who took part in the setting up of the regional sales company are succumb to violating the regulations and abusing power for their personal gains, which certainly has damaged the interests of the joint venture companies and Gree's share holders. At the same time, due to the restrain in the local market competition, Gree's distributors have showed inertia in the less fierce market competition, and have no effective work in developing the terminal channel. Most of them have the attitude of over optimistic towards the market expectation of the products and they are appearing to be insensitive and sluggish towards the competition and the market changes.

Fourthly, the non-standard paperless operation in Gree has aroused considerable controversies. It cannot be denied that Gree Chairman Zhu Jianghong is always persistent in practicing the principles of honesty trade and good faith that he always advocates, which indeed has been integrated into Gree's corporate culture. But China's current credit standing does not allow unilateral credibility in the business transactions, for when one's own economic interests are involved, especially under the circumstance that there are no written contracts, many problems and disputes unavoidably become complicated and complex.

Surely, almost all the domestic air conditioning enterprises in China are engaging in "paperless operations", because of the cut-throat competition in air conditioning industry. As those business spies and commercial rumors are everywhere and pervasive, the pricing policy and rebate policy of every air conditioning enterprise are considered as "the nuclear button". If those terms written in paper are revealed and exploited by those competitors, the marketing channel will be collapsed and the pricing policy will be broken down and the enterprise which unfortunately encounters all the bad situations will be very vulnerable to be attacked. Therefore, in order to prevent the trade secrets from disclosing, Gree has to adopt some stringent precautionary measures with Chinese characteristics. But, Gree should never take it as an excuse for its paperless operations, which is against its corporate image of being a large enterprise in the industry.

2) The Management of the Direct Sales Stores Needs Standardized Administration Urgently

After Gree and GOME the two giants had become hostile to each other, Zhu Jianghong said: "Gree never feels regret in withdrawing our products from GOME. Although, at the beginning, quite a few people worry about us thinking that what we are doing is just like cutting our own throat. But it turns out that, in the third quarter of 2004, Gree's sales revenues totaled RMB 12.9 billion, which almost is the whole sales revenues of 2003. To a large extent, the success is accredited to the thousands of Gree's franchise stores and special stores all over China." It seems that, despite the odds, those franchise stores and special stores have become Gree' arsenals for fighting against GOME and Suning and winning the victory in the tough competition. Although Gree won the championship in its field, Gree Electric Appliances still appears to be lacking of in-depth planning and analysis on its direct sales stores and it does not pay enough attention to promoting those non-store aspects. Among the defects in Gree's model, the management of those direct sales stores espeically needs reinforcing urgently. The followings are the reasons why the management of those direct sales stores needs reinforcing urgently:

Firstly, the standard of services is quite different in the 2500 Gree stores nationwide. Although the storefronts and store designs are unified, the service level is unevenly mixed with some good ones and some bad ones. According to Huang Fanghua, the spokesman of Gree Electric Appliances, the main sales task of Gree has always been accomplished by the 2500 direct sales stores: the direct sales stores are dealing with the regional sales companies and the regional sales companies are responsible for Gree head office. The regional sales companies of Gree serve as the subsidiary management organizations and the direct stores in those areas usually call the regional sales companies as the Gree office of those areas.

The Secretary of Board of directors and the spokesman of Gree Electric Appliances, Huang Fanghua pointed out, "The price and all the marketing channel policy are strictly controlled and formulated by Gree head office. All the activities against Gree's regulations, such selling products beyond the agreed areas and reducing the price without permission are forbidden and Gree head office has the absolute right to control all those activities." On the surface, Gree Electrical Appliance head office is protecting the rights and interests of its direct sales stores and trying to construct a fair competition environment, but it is not always the case. According to an anonymous source from Gree's Beijing direct sales stores, although Gree head office refuses to cooperate with GOME, its regional sales companies are still keeping their partnership with the local stores of GOME and other home appliances chain stores, such as, Yule, Dazhong and Five-star Appliance.

The head of Beijing direct sales stores said, those big appliances chain stores, e.g.

Beijing Dazhong take delivery of goods directly from Gree regional sales companies, and they enjoy same delivery price and marketing policy with Gree's direct sales stores. Compared with Gree's direct sales stores, the large appliance stores have the advantages of store size, marketing and price. After made the comparison, the consumers tend to choose the large appliances stores instead of Gree's direct sales stores. He alleged, now he has the overstock worth of more than RMB 3 million in the warehouse.

After Bestbuy, an American specialty retailer of consumer electronics bought up Five-star Appliances then many foreign appliances enterprises began to find their way into Chinese home appliance industry. It seems that appliance chain industry has become the inevitable trend for the future distribution channel of home electrical appliances. Therefore, Gree's direct sales stores will be under bigger and bigger pressure when facing the aggression of the big appliance chain stores and Gree Electric Appliances' attitude towards home appliance chain stores will be more ambiguous.

Second, Gree Electric Appliances itself is constantly exerting pressure on direct sales stores. It is said that the rebate promises that Gree has made are all realized only by restock product quantity. If the products are sold well in this store this year, at end of this year, the owner of the store will be given high product quotas for restock just like this back and forth. But the more serious is that Gree's head office is getting harsher and harsher when it is making the policy of direct sales stores. As is understood by the writer, Gree head office used to offer 4 percentage rebate points in 2003, but now, the rebate points have been lowered to $1\sim2$ percentage. The category of restock products for the rebate points can be selected by the owner of the stores freely before and now the products for the rebated points are specified by Gree, which means the stores have no right in choosing the products for their restock. At the same time, the direct sales stores must paid the double money to purchase the products for the rebate points, for example, if the store has the rebate points worthy of RMB100, 000, the sales store must pay RMB 200,000 to buy the products; that is to say the store pays RMB 200,000 for the products worth of RMB 300,000.

Third, the cost of direct sales stores cannot be amortized. At present, in Gree direct sales stores, except the exhibition stands are arranged by Gree, the owners of the stores have to bear all the related costs, such as the rent for the house of the store, inventory costs and office supplies. One thing makes all the owners of the direct stores feel hard to accept is that when Gree was doing the cost accounting for the rebate points at the end of the year, the above costs would not be counted into the costs of the direct stores. With regards to this problem, about 100 Gree's direct sales store owners from Beijing have sent their representatives to negotiate with Gree head office in Zhuhai at the end of last year, but the problems still remain unsettled.

The industry experts said that Gree must strengthen the management of direct sales stores, so it can open a new prospect for the direct sales stores. The specific measures are including:

First, in order to build a positive image of the direct sales stores in consumers, improve their credibility and enhance their competitiveness, the direct sales stores should intensify the construction of "three points": emphasizing the chain store features, unified management and relevance construction.

The Second point is to build excellent direct sales store culture of Gree and to promote the development of the direct sales stores under the guidance of the culture. Gree should establish a set of complete and effective rules and regulations to make the stores meet the market demands and be self-assured, self-enhanced and self-disciplinary. At the same time, the stores should serve as a role model in the following aspects: firstly, to be the role model of stabilizing price; secondly, to be the role model of after sales service; thirdly, to be the role model of observing the rules and regulations formulated by the sales companies; fourthly, to be the role model of persisting in honest management; fifthly, to be the role model of Gree brand promotion.

Thirdly, the Gree direct sales stores should work as the bridge and bond that closely connect Gree brand with the consumers: care for the interest of the consumers, address the consumers' concerns and try to build a close contact and close relation between Gree and consumers.

"It seems that Gree Electric Appliances now is a very big and strong manufacturer, who begins to bully its small direct sales stores." Quite a few owners of Gree direct sales stores complained, "Recently, Gree has added some harsh terms in the sales of Gree air conditioners and requested that directs sales stores should sell other small household electrical appliances. The channel policies are similar to air conditioner products; just the model machines of those small household appliances have to be purchased from Gree at the discount of 20% of its original price." Gree direct sales stores are going into a vicious circle, many owners of Gree direct sales stores in Beijing all express the same opinion that they will not follow Gree's channel policy any longer and when the stock products are all sold and they are going to gradually terminate the cooperation with Gree Electric Appliances. However, it should be pointed out: the direct sales store is the most important factor that Gree can live by and always is proud of.   If there are problems appearing in Gree's direct sales stores, the marketing channel model that Gree firmly advocates will be like the castle in the air and it will be no more than a fantasy.

2. Cutting the Big Distributors and Forging the Terminal Brand

Once fighting side by side with Gree to capture the market share, now, some of the distributors are going to be cut from Gree's marketing channel, which is a cruel fact to those distributors who are not well-prepared for it, but this is the laws of the markets. Luo Qingqi, the Senior Director of Pal Consulting, who always pays close attention to the marketing trends in home appliance industry, said the factor in deciding the channel model is the profits of products not the market size. If the present profits cannot support so many distribution channels, it is an irresistible trend for the manufacturer to remove them.

1) Channel Flattening or Channel Revolution

In 2005, Gree Electric Appliances quietly conducted a significant reform of marketing model—adjusting Gree headquarters' proportion of shares in Guangdong and Shenzhen sales company. It is understood that this has been the first large-scale reform in the sales model since 1997 when Gree created the sales model of joint-stock regional sales company.

According to the analysts in this industry, Gree is planning to make a large-scale adjustment in its sales model (the two sales companies in Guangzhou and Shenzhen): on one hand, to make investment in the two branch companies so as to realize the Gree headquarters' controlling the shares of the company; on the other hand, to reorganization of the dispersed regional sales companies: Let Conghua, Panyu, Huadu and Qingyuan branches be under the leadership of Guangzhou sales company; let Huizhou and Dongguan,etc under the leadership of Shenzhen sales company. Gree headquarters will appoint the new board chairmen and sales directors to the two companies and one of the shareholders from distributors will assume the position of the General Manager.

According to the industry experts, Gree Electric Appliances now is conducting a marketing channel reform, which is seemingly calm on the surface of it. The reform is to cut the claws of those big distributors in key provinces and directly have deeper cooperation with sub-dealers. Since Gree has implemented the "joint-stock regional sales company mode" for many years, this reform inside Gree might be easy for many other electrical appliance manufacturers, but to Gree, which keeps "insisting on having its own way", it means a difficult transition.

The analysts pointed out that to Gree's original provincial first level distributors, it probably means that they will be turned into a mere figurehead in Gree's marketing channel and their business must be transformed. If a product has enough profits, we will find the number of levels in the marketing channel will be bigger and bigger; on the contrary, if the profit of a marketing channel becomes less and less, the enterprise will find it very hard to support such complicated marketing channels. Under the circumstance of todays' market condition, the marketing competition is just like a razor shaving the profits off layer by layer, and the marketing channel is like the layers of clothing to be stripped off layer by layer by the stiff market competition. The razor-thin profits in air conditioning industry do not allow air conditioning manufacturers to have extra money to support the long channel system of many levels.

Since Gree's regional sales company is different from other appliance manufacturers, it is a joint-venture formed by Gree head office and several big distributors in the key provinces. Therefore, Gree has given much thought to increasing the shares in the sales company, which is a reform that Gree made to be adaptable to the market competition.

Although Dong Mingzhu once said, the purpose of Gree's increasing shares in the sales company is not for profits but for providing better services for consumers, this move can still be regarded as Gree headquarters' strengthening its control in the sales companies. The experts in the industry all believe that as the profits of air conditioners have been continually shrinking, the producers must cut down on circulation intermediates to obtain enough profits. In this sense, this move of Gree reflects its wish to skip the first-level distributors at the provincial level and to have a direct contact with distributors at a district and county level. As Dong Mingzhu remarks, under the precondition of making profits, this reform probably will not be independent of people's will. Though she said that so far Gree has not had any plan to make reforms in other areas yet, it seems that the reform in Gree's sales company model will come sooner or later.

In China's air conditioning industry, Gree's case is not unique, but there are quite a few similar cases. It is reported that AUX air conditioner recently also has cut down on its general agents at the provincial level, and has direct marketing channels in the second and third tier city markets. According to a manager from the marketing department in an air conditioning enterprise, two years ago, about 200 general agents at the provincial level of major air conditioning enterprises have been losing their former status of "provincial agents" and gradually becoming the district-level agents.

Whoever is the real retail end of the business, the manufacturers should deal with him. Haier and Midea both have done it long before; in this regard, Gree is apparently a late starter.

Now, the air conditioning industry is no longer in the era of profiteering. Instead, it is stepping in the era of marginal profits. At the present stage, various air conditioner brands are continuously emerging and the market share is becoming dispersing. In the meanwhile, the channel pattern is undergoing huge changes and the nationwide home appliances chain stores have already formed scale advantages. The growing commercial capitals are more and more eager to have a direct contact with producers and have a direct supply of products to reduce the cost through the cutting of intermediate links.

As a matter of fact, the rapid development of these household appliance retail ends, like, GOME, Suning, is the process of replacing the manufacturers dominating the retail price. Certainly, this replacement is to help the price to be lower not the other way round. The Senior Director of Pal Consulting, Luo Qingqi believes that under this background, it is meaningless for the regional sales companies of Gree to do the wholesale business in its own area. If these branch companies are insisting on gaining profits from it, the retailers that they are facing only have to commit suicide. Thus in the new market situation, there are only two development directions for Gree's marketing channel: one is to expand the scale of the cooperation with GOME stores; the other is to have a direct cooperation with retailers. As to those first level distributors at the provincial level who have already lost or are going to lose the support from the manufacturers, Luo Qingqi suggests, they had better withdraw from the marketing channel as soon as possible and then they can either be the distributors of other brands or give the logistics support to their current brands.

For the past few years, Gree has been consistently carrying out its own business model of unique joint-system regional sales company and relying on the powerful branding and channel advantages of the major shareholders in each sales company to maintain its market share and position in top brands. But now the development trend in the air conditioning markets forces Gree to make a series of adjustments and reforms in its own marketing pattern. Judging from this trend, the experts in the industry commented, "The Gree marketing model is coming to an end." "To Gree Electric Appliances, the current adjustment in its marketing channels is by no means merely an operational improvement but a revolution in its marketing channel."

2) Facing The Future with A Long-term Perspective

Many people inside the industry think that Gree's marketing model of Joint-stock regional sales company has been out of date. The reforms in Gree's Huishen sales company actually is the beginning of Gree's campaign in cutting its first level distributors on a large scale. Here, the word "cut" means that Gree will have some adjustments and reforms in the stock holding of Huishen sales company and other sales companies, not simply "to deprive of the shareholder distributors' right to have a say for themselves". The industry analysts indicated, for the longer term interests, Gree must "cut" some of its distributors. The following three points illustrating the reason why Gree must cut some of its distributors:

Firstly, the layers of commodity circulation are too many, so Gree must cut some of them off.

In the case of Gree's adjusting the proportion of shares in Huishen Sale Company, the vice president of Guangdong Kelon Electrical Holdings Company Limited, Yan Yousong said: "As the profits of air conditioning industry are shrinking, the air conditioning enterprises have to keep cutting the layers in the commodity circulation to earn profits. Therefore, Gree's move this time can be interpreted as Gree's determination to cooperate with the second and third-level distributors directly. That is to say, Gree wants to gradually skip the first-level distributors at a provincial level and have a direct contact with the dealers at a district and county-level."Both the directors of Kelon and Midea think, Gree's reform in its regional sales companies this time is an intensive and meticulous adjustment in its marketing channel.

As the market competition is getting tougher and tougher, the profits of air conditioning industry are also getting thinner and thinner and for other air conditioner brands, there are only two layers in their marketing channel and only Gree has three layers—the sales company as a stakeholder which eats a large share of profits. Therefore, it is the time for Gree Electric Appliances to take back this share of profits. The person, who is in charge of Guangdong Kelon Electrical Holdings Company Limited said that, to cut off the big distributors step by step, focus on the cooperation with the second and third tier distributors and have a direct contact with the second and third tier distributors are the inevitable trend in today's market competition. Making the channel flattening is the big trend in the air conditioning industry. "As early as last year, Kelon has already begun to be engaged in the reform in our channel. After all, it is also a wise move for Gree Electric Appliances to do the same."

Gree's vice-chairwoman Dong Mingzhu said, they will strengthen the supervision of these sales companies (Dong thinks it will be more accurate to position them as a governing body) and urge them to improve their service. She believed that, if the old sales company is just an organization for making profits, now the new sales company with Gree having bigger shares is not just simply for profits, but for providing services. Thus the sales company will not withhold any profits; what it gets is the reasonable service fee and the value brought by the enhancement of Gree brand. In light of the market needs, the shareholders are requested to closely integrate with factories at a higher level.

Secondly, the channel strategy is lagging behind the market trend, so Gree Electric Appliances must explore a new pattern.

Because of restricting the competition in the regional markets, Gree's distributors are becoming inertia in the loose and comfortable market competition. As a result, they are showing sluggishness in developing its terminal markets. Plus the difficulties in supervising the practical operation of Gree direct sales stores, the distributors tend do have some non-standard practices to damage the interests of the joint-venture company and Gree Electric Appliances as well as to corrupt the solidarity and fighting capacity of the whole company. Additionally, though Gree is working together with the big distributors in each area and has formed the regional sales company, instead of coordinating with each other, the shareholders still have conflicts among them.

In contrast, the burgeoning home appliances chain enterprises with GOME, Suning as the representatives are very eye catching. At present, GOME has covered about 25 cities in the whole country with 125 chain stores, among them 91 are directly operated stores， 34 are franchisees and GOME is also planning to open more stores in Hong Kong. Suning has also covered about the capital cites of 15 provinces with more than 100 retail outlets in the markets at a district level in Jiangsu province. While consolidating its Sunan base, Jiangsu Five-star appliance is expanding its business in Subei, Anhui province. Zhongyong Tongtai is expanding rapidly and absorbing new members; Yongle successively has become the shareholder of Dazhong, Tongli and Dongze and controlled its members by holding the stake in those members. These professional home appliance chain enterprises have brought about huge pressure to the local manufacturers. It is known that, just in the same year after GOME and Suning had entered in Guangzhou and Shenzhen, about 300 small and medium-sized household appliance stores went bankrupt and the profits of home appliance sector of huge department stores are also quickly being peeled off. In Chongqing, GOME and Suning have already divided the whole markets with Chongqing Department Store and Chongqing General Trading Group equally. Those situations to the big distributors of each sales company of Gree are no doubt the real crisis, which make Gree have to face a tough choice in its existing marketing channel.

Whether to cooperate with GOME and Suning or not in the future, according to the game rules of the commercial circulation—the stronger one will be the leader, Gree must keep adjusting its strategy and exploring a new model to make itself grow up and be strong as soon as possible; then it could have the hope to continue its success in the future.

Thirdly, being over independent on big distributors in the past, Gree must intensify the construction of its retail outlets.

As all the air conditioning manufacturers are attaching great importance to the second and third tier city markets, they are also making its increasing investment in the markets. However, the markets of top tier cities stil remains the core area that all the air conditioning enterprises are competing for, especially to those top and second-tier brands, like Gree. The significance of the efforts in first tier city markets are: 1. the concentration of consumption in the first tier city markets is the profit growth point for every manufacturer and the proportion of market share is large. 2. Either in a busy season or a low season, the sales volume is always large. So the manufacturers' market-building activities can be continued, not like in second and third tier city markets; they only can conduct market-building activities in the busy season. 3. The first tier city markets always receive most attention so it can influence other markets in the country, and its driving effects are remarkable. But Gree's model of regional sales company makes it to be far away from the first tier city markets. Because Gree's over independence on the big distributors, it has overlooked the construction of the sale terminals plus the strict control in marketing channel, which causes the limited number of products in sale terminals and the huge gap as well as the distance between Gree products and consumers. The gap and distance are especially notable in those major cities, like Beijing, Shanghai and Guangzhou.

Chang Cheng, the Deputy General Manager of Guangdong GOME, gave his honest opinion about Gree's reform: "Gree's adjustment in the company's share of Huishen sales company this time is Gree's reform to adapt itself to the market competition and let the intermediate agents perish of themselves. Otherwise, the big distributor's snatching profits will elbow Gree off the first tier city markets; to Gree, what it loses will be the main battlefield." What Mr. Chang said does make sense.

Perhaps, through the reform at this level, Gree will reposition its regional sales company, realize its value, reduce the links in the circulation field and lower its marketing costs so as to seize the preemptive opportunities in the "reshuffling" of air conditioning industry.

3. Facing the Internal Control Dilemma

There was a time when Gree Electric Appliance was famous for its outstanding product quality in air conditioning industry and in consumers' mind as well. Gree also enjoys the reputation of "Good air conditioner, Gree made" in the world. However, the year of 2003 seems "an eventful and trouble year" to Gree with its scandals frequently breaking out and too many disputes making Gree too busy to attend to all of them. That year, Gree dazzled people with too many events. But the first event to raise people's attention was the corruption scandals of its senior executives, which touched off a public uproar and casted the doubt about whether its enterprise management system and internal control were strict and standardized. After that, the uncertainty in the use of trademark right caused the internal strife between Gree Electric Appliances and its little brother, Gree Household Electric Appliances, which all belong to Gree Group. Through seeing these events, we can get to know the chaos in Gree's internal management is rather noticeable.

1) The Lack of Supervision Encouraging the Corruption of Senior Exclusives

Many Chinese enterprises are sharing one characteristic: laying great stress on marketing, but pay little attention to the internal management and control of the enterprises. Therefore, an enterprise usually appears to be very successful in its marketing, but its internal management and control is in a great mess. Compared with some multi-national corporations, Chinese enterprises generally bow to no one in marketing, but in terms of internal management, Chinese enterprises are lagging behind a lot of multi-national corporations for years, which is a very obvious defect in Chinese enterprises. It is the same with Gree Electric Appliances, its internal management poses an obstacle standing in the way of Gree's further development; especially the exposure of the corruption event turned all Gree's pleasant impressions into ashes in an overnight. In the morning of 23rd May, 2003, Yuan Guangli, the former deputy director of the research institute of Gree Electric Appliance Co. Ltd of Zhuhai, was on trial for corruption charge. The local procuratorial organ announced in the indictment: During Yuan Guangli's tenure in Gree Electric Appliance Co. Ltd of Zhuhai, through using fake brand-names and jacking up the product prices in collusion with his relatives, he embezzled and defrauded the company of state property totaling RMB 4.619 million as well as accepting a bribe of HK$19,800.

The event should be traced back to the year 1996. Yuan Guangli began to assume the post of the deputy director of the controller affiliated factory in Gree Electric Appliances from 29th March, 1996. On 2nd November, 1998, he took up the post of the deputy director of Gree's research institute, responsible for and in charge of the development, verification and confirmation of controllers and electronic components for Gree Electric Appliances. Taking the advantage of his post and in collusion with his relatives, Yuan Guangli purchased those electronic components under fake import brands at a high price in order to realize his purpose of recklessly embezzling and defrauding the company of huge state property with his relatives. During the process of purchasing, Yuan Guangli only confirmed the materials supplied by his relatives' company and kept the competitors out; he even directly appointed "his own company" as the supplier without informing and discussing with Gree's supply department. But at that time Gree had already stipulated the rule that the relatives of the middle-level cadres shall not do business with Gree. Yuan Guangli clearly violated the relevant rules and regulations of Gree. During Yuan's vilation and defrauding, in order to avoid suspicions, his relatives signed the contract with Gree Electric Appliances under a pseudonym. Thus, the monopoly of material supply was formed, which allowed the company of Yuan Guangli's relatives to supply raw materials to Gree at an abnormally high price and caused the huge economic losses of RMB 46.19 million to Gree. According to the agreement between Yuan Guangli and his relatives, his commission will be 10% of the profits that their company earned, i.e. RMB 4.619 million.

The procuratorate thought that, as one of the staff members in a state-owned company, in order to pursuit his personal gains, Yuan Guangli took advantages of his position in the company and colluded with his relatives, under the cloak of trading, to defraud the company of huge state property. He should be prosecuted for his corruption crime according to the law. Moreover, in collusion with his relatives, taking advantages of his position and power in confirming and vivificating in raw materials, Yuan Guangli sold the electronic components of fake import brands to Gree in large quantity at a price far exceeding the market price, which was a purely defrauding.

Ironically, three days later after the former deputy director of Gree Electric Appliances had been charged of corruption by the law court, a very influential media company in Guangdong area published its interview of Gree's general manager. The writer of this article introduced "three trumps to help Gree to win in the market competition" in detail and "the first trump is its strict control in cost". In this artile, Zhu Jianghong introduced Gree's strict control policy in his interview: from October 2002 to April 2003, the price of raw materials kept rising, but Gree didn't shift the increase in the costs onto the consumers. Instead, Gree adopted a more strict control in cost and carefully controlled the purchase cost. To make a Gree air conditioner needs to purchase about 1500 components from hundreds of suppliers home and abroad and the most reliable approach was to "sieve" every component one by one. Zhu Jianghong even said, there was a difference from those home appliance enterprises in Pearl River Delta which just let their relatives undertake the purchase of the raw materials, but Gree's purchase of raw materials were very transparent. In this way, the procurement costs were much lower than other home appliance enterprises naturally.

On the one side is Yuan Guangli's charge of having business deal with his relatives, on the other side is that the chairman of the company claimed they are "very careful in controlling the procurement costs". As a state-owned listed company, which side of story should the investors trust? And it is pity that it took Gree seven years to find about the huge corruption. The public cannot help but doubt deeply about Gree's enterprise management system.

According to the analysts in the industry, in the business expansion of high-speed growth, Gree must have a stringent internal supervisory system to guarantee its normal operation. If there is no strict supervisory and control system, the smallest negligence will lead the large ship to sinking.

2) Internal Strife in Using the Brand, Mess in the Strategy

According to China's "Company Law", the management of a listed company must have an independent legal representative management structure and management system. But, since there is no complete legal representative management structure, Gree has the same team in the management of Gree Group and the listed company, which causes the confusion in the role of management. "The internal strife in Gree" is the focus of the conflict that broke out between Gree Group and the listed company.

Having experienced the disgrace of the senior executive's corruption case, after the big storm, Gree finally could be in peace with itself for a short period of time. But its good times did not last long, since November 2003, Gree which always tended to keep everything a low profile had once again become the focus of the media's attention. It was due to the statement that Gree Electric Appliances made in the press. From 4th to 5th November, 2003 Gree issued a "solemn statement" in the front page of authoritative medias in Guangzhou, Zhejiang and Hubei, etc; in this "solemn statement", Gree Electric Appliances announced that Gree was only making air conditioning products and it was not producing any small household electric appliances, which attracted many people's attention.

The "statement" tried to deny that the truth of some stories about "Gree's entering the kitchenware market" and "Gree has built three small household appliance production bases" reported in some presses. According the "statement", tn these articles, the stories about "Gree Electric Appliances entering the small household appliance market and kitchenware market" were nothing but a sheer fabrication, which was seriously misleading the numerous investors and consumers. Gree Electric Appliances proclaimed in the "statement"that at present, they were only producing air conditioning products and they were not making any small household electric appliances.

As a matter of fact, Gree Electric Appliances and Gree Household Electric Appliances are both the subsidiary companies controlled by Gree Group. The brand "Gree" was created by Gree Electric Appliances but the brand belongs to Gree Group. Gree Household Electric Appliances is the "child" "adopted" by Gree Group, with its production base located in Zhongshan city. The statement issued by Gree Electric Appliances made the public have doubts about the legality of Gree Household Electric Appliance (Zhongshan) Co., Ltd. and posed a negative impact on the sales of Gree Household Electric Appliances (Zhongshan) Co., Ltd.

When the "solemn statement" made by Gree Electric Appliances had been published in the newspaper, Gree Household Electric Appliances received numerous inquires about "the legality of Gree Household Electric Appliances" from its distributors of the whole country. Facing the doubts and inquires, Gree Household Electric Appliances immediately started to seek the emergency help from Gree Group. Later, Gree Household Electric Appliances (Zhongshan) Co., Ltd also submitted "the instruction for using the trademark licensing of 'Gree' "to some presses with the signature of the major shareholder of Gree Electric Appliances—Zhuhai Gree Group. Gree Household Electric Appliances (Zhuhai) sent the statement to the distributors all over the country and some presses at the first place in order to quell the crisis. On 11th November, 2003, Gree Electric Appliances of Zhuhai published a full page of an article on "an Endeavor Enterprise—Zhuhai Gree Electric Appliance". In some parts of the article, Gree Electric Appliance made a public "clarifying" and responses to the doubts from this newspaper and the markets. And it admitted that Gree Group authorized Gree Household Electric Appliances (Zhuhai) the right to use of the trademark licensing of "Gree", which denied the content of its previous "solemn statement".

Along with the successive appearance of Gree's statements, "Gree event" caused a great disturbance and sensation in home appliance industry and the news media. The series of problems inside Gree Electric Appliances also were unveiled and uncovered. Why did Gree Electric Appliances issue the statement with such vehemence? What is the problem with Gree Household Electric Appliances? What on earth are the secrets hiding behind the brand management of Gree Group? It is easy to see that Gree Electric Appliances and Gree Household Electric Appliances (Zhongshan), the subsidiary companies of Gree Group are having "an internal strife". On the one side, it is the fact that the Gree Household Electric Appliances (Zhongshan) is trying very hard to lean on Gree Electric Appliances, this "money bag" in its advertisement, on the other side, we can see that Gree Electric Appliances spared no efforts in clarifying that it has no relationship with Gree Household Electric Appliances (Zhongshan). Then Gree Group quickly and eagerly gave the evidence to prove that the two are from "the same root". The mixture of feints and ambushes makes people feel difficult to distinguish the true from the false. At one time, inside Gree, the war of words, confusions and chaos were prevailing and out of control.

The experts in the industry gave their own opinion about this issue: the fight in the using of the brand between the two subsidiary companies not only reflects the conflict between the future development of Gree Electric Appliances and its holding (parent) company, but also mirrors the widespread phenomenon of the indifferent attitude towards state-controlled property and the internal control tendency in the state-owned listed companies. The problems highlighted in front of people are multiple and profound, which can be concluded in the next four aspects:

Problem No.1: The use of the trademark and resource sharing. This "Gree event" on the use of the trademark, on the surface, is the internal strife between Gree Household Electric Appliances (Zhongshan) and Gree Electric Appliance. In essence, it is the discrepancy between Gree Group and its subsidiary companies in resources integration and development strategy. A trademark is the embodiment of credit and prestige and the beacon light for the marketing strategy. A famous brand has enormous promoting effect for its product selling. Therefore, how to make a good and full use of a trademark to promote the production and sales is the important issue for the business operators. Gree Group as the owner of the trademark "Gree" endeavors to make the good and full use of the trademark "Gree" which has been established in the markets for a long time and tries to develop its own diversity product management, which is a wise and reasonable move from the future perspective of Gree Group. At the same time, the reputation that Gree Electric Appliance has established is just for air conditioning products in Gree Group's product category. When consumers are choosing products labeled with "Gree" brand, they still will draw a distinction between Gree air conditioning products and other products. Hence, perhaps it is an overstatement of the fact that Gree Group's road of diversity management will hurt the brand "Gree" that Gree Electric Appliance has established with years of concentrated efforts. Furthermore, the decision is made by Gree Group purely out of the reason for expanding the business scope. Gree Electric Appliance as a subsidiary company of Gree Group has no right to interfere the decision made by the parent company for it is not the owner of the trademark. Surely, since the two companies all belong to the same "family", in order to avoid the over use of the trademark and bringing harm to the good reputation of products (air conditioner) which has already been established, it is very necessary for the products of other categories to constantly improve their quality.

Problem No.2: the property control and management constraints. Gree Electric Appliance as the subsidiary company, dared to challenge its parent company, which is unimaginable in a mature property right market. Due to historical reasons, Gree Group and Gree Electric Appliance have cultivated the relationship of a "weak central Group" and a "powerful principality". This situation between the two is very unfavorable for Gree Group's optimization and integration of the resources as well as for the long-term development of Gree Group. It is reasonable to say that, Gree Group as the absolute controlling party and the major investor of Gree Electric Appliance has the powerful property binding force to Gree Electric Appliance and also has the absolute right to decide the appointment and removal of chief responsible persons in its subordinate company as well as its enterprise strategic decision making according to the law. Under the normal circumstances, the internal strife of the using trademark shall never appear between the parent company and its subordinate company, for the subordinate does not have the capital to be evenly matched with its controlling company. Who invests the money, he will have the right to make the decision, which is perfectly justified. Even though at the very beginning Gree Group only invested RMB 1 million and today the capital assets of Gree Electric Appliance is up to RMB 10 billion, Gree Electric Appliance still only subjects to Gree Group. This is the power of property right and capital and also it is the inevitable ecology in a mature market.

Problem No.3: standardized administration and lawful business operations. Gree Electric Appliance as a state owned listed company has set up illegal and concealed accounts for a long time. Historically, it has its objective reasons for it. But in any case, the behavior of Gree Electric Appliance's setting up illegal accounts and destroying its concealed accounts, to Gree Group, is the reflection of the non standardized administration, but from the angle of law, it is a serious violation of law.

The problem in Gree Electric Appliance is a universal phenomenon in the state-owned enterprises in China. For a long time, in order to evade the heavy tax and to obtain the necessary "public relations fund" for the development of the enterprises, most of state-owned companies have to set up an "illegal account" for the convenience of their flexible and for avoiding the investigation of the audit department. Just because of this reason, it opens the door for the corruptionists and bribers, so the enterprises also have formed many bad habits. Therefore, it can be said that, the non-standardized administration is one of the sources for those illegal business operations.

Problem No.4: diversification strategy and professional spirit. Behind the internal strife in Gree is the struggle for power and strategy. From the contribution rate in profits, Gree Electric Appliance's contribution to Gree Group is up to over 90%. The number tells us Gree Electric Appliance's contribution to Gree Group is huge and amazing. Gree Group has three industrial pillars in its business operations: electric appliances, real estate and petroleum trade. Among them, Gree Electric Appliance is the flag enterprise as well as the most powerful supporter for the brand of "Gree". After Gree Group suffered the chaos and internal strife in its internal control, finally there came some adjustments in management level. According to Gree Group's announcement, Zhu Jianghong, the board chairman of Gree Electric Appliance will hold the following concurrent posts: the board chairman, legal representative, president and the Party Committee Secretary of the major shareholder Gree Group. Since then, the "internal strife between the father and the son"—Gree Group and Gree Electric Appliance had come to a complete end. And the former president of Gree Group, Chen Yuanhe will be transferred to Zhuhai State Asset Regulatory Commission to be the vice president. Even so, does it mean that Gree Group has to conform to Gree Electric Appliance or its development strategy and take the corporate culture of Gree Electric Appliance as the guide? Obviously, no matter how big contribution Gree Electric Appliance made to Gree Group, its status of being the subordinate company to Gree Group does not change. Before Gree Group gives up or loses its controlling status, the status of Gree Electric Appliance cannot possibly change. Therefore, under the circumstance of Gree Group making the overall deployment, even if Gree Electric Appliance has different opinions, it must take the interests of the whole group as the top priority and it should respect and accept Gree Group's arrangement.

The core culture and development strategy of an enterprise are all made by the decision-makers of the enterprise. As for Gree Group, its corporate strategy and culture are made by the board of directors in Gree Group. To Gree Electric Appliance, as a subsidiary company of Gree Group, it should inevitably be influenced and constrained by the corporate strategy and culture. In fact, it is not contradictory between the "diversification strategy" made by Gree Group and the "professional spirit" advocated by Gree Electric Appliance. The former is the development strategy and the latter is the work attitude. The two principles should not be contradictory to each other; instead, they should be combined into one. Gree Group wants to forge the brand "Gree" into a world famous brand. It is unimaginable without professional spirit, for professionalization and specialization has already become the winning weapon for an enterprise in the fierce home appliance market. But if Gree Electric

Appliance wants to take "professionalization and specialization" as the excuse to make a last-ditch defense in the battlefield of air conditioner making in the context of the profits declining every years, it will be harmful to the overall development of Gree Group.

There is no doubt that this "statement scandal" will inevitably create confusions in the market and the distributors' mind, also make the investors have questions about "is there any problem in Gree's brand management" and then they will doubt the managerial quality of the whole company. All of these situations will have a direct impact on the evaluation of Gree's whole brand image. What's more, Gree's adopting the measures of openly handling the conflicts inside the Gree big family will give opportunities to its rivals and bring harm to the interests of the whole Group. In the wake of those events, consequently, the falling of Gree stock price and the serious damage will be resulted in the brand image of Gree Group and Gree Electric Appliance. At present, the contest between Gree Group and Gree Electric Appliance has come to an end, but the conflict reflected between the Group Company and the listed company has got people to think deeply. On the surface of the "internal strife" event, it is just a dispute between the Group Company and the joint-stock company on the issue of using the trademark; more profoundly, it has reflected the problem in the management and internal control of Gree Electric Appliance. When the "war of words" between the Group company, Gree Household Electric Appliances and Gree Electric Appliance was becoming increasingly fiercer, the crisis management system in Gree should be established, but from the situation that when Gree's "internal strife" event had been in the vortex of the medias and on the horns of its internal control dilemma, it is easy to know what Gree lacks is the explicit brand management system and the effective communication mechanism.

Review: Great Efforts Should Be Made by Gree

This chapter demonstrates three major problems existing in Gree Electric Appliances: the first one is that how its current sales system faces the future trend of home appliance chain stores; the second is that how Gree should make efforts to improve its internal management and control; the third problem is that how Gree Electric Appliance and Gree Group work together to forge the "Gree" brand. The three problem are also the general problems that today's Chinese enterprises need to solve when facing the future.

About the applicability of Gree's model in the future, according to Gree Electric Appliance, the regional sales company and direct-sales stores as the main body in Gree sales pattern is the key factor to helping Gree grow from a weak latecomer to the champion enterprise in China and the whole world. In the future development, this model will continue to play its important role in Gree's marketing. About the first point, we agree with Gree. As for the second point, that is, the applicability of Gree model in the future development, it remains to be seen. The continual success of Gree model depends on the following factors: first, the simplification or diversification of the home appliance circulation, if just like what people said, the big home appliance stores will be the only model of the future home appliance distribution, Gree model will be facing serious challenges. Secondly, speaking of Gree's capability of "keeping abreast of the times", any sales model will constantly adjust itself in light with the changes in the demands of market environment and consumers. Gree model is no exception. If Gree is able to regard the consumers' interests as the top priority and increasingly improves its sales model, in that case, Gree model will be an innovative business model to continually exist in Chinese home appliance industry.

About the issue of improving the managerial capacity, in recent 30 years, the growth of Chinese enterprises is mostly market-driven. There are many market opportunities emerging each day and the opportunities have been seized by those entrepreneurs with courage and insight, then through introducing equipment technology and learning-by-doing marketing management, in this way, they bring their new products to the markets and consumers. As a result, their enterprises get the chance to grow up and become mature, which is totally different with American enterprises' growing up based on their own capacity after World War II. Growing under the special circumstance, Chinese enterprises have to face the consequence of generally lacking a solid foundation in their managerial capacity. Frankly, there are not many excellent enterprises possessing strong organizational capacity in China. Facing the future, Chinese enterprises must make up the missed lesson of "basic management". Just as Wu Xiaobo, the noted financial writer in China, talks about in his article "How Many Management Lessons That Chinese Enterprises Should Make Up": "Today, although China becomes the real 'world factory', we did not have any significant breakthroughs in our management and even 'the update' in management is also rare. Mostly, we are just zealously following others… In the past, we are proud that we only use less than 10 years' time to experience the 100-year development history of the enterprises in western developed countries, but we do not know, perhaps just in the less than 10 years' development, we have overlooked the initial management origins supporting the modern industrial system of the western countries. Behind the high speed growth, the hiding destructive breakdown may come suddenly someday and this is the last thing we want to see undoubtedly."

As for the brand-sharing between Gree Group and its subsidiary company, it is also a universal problem existing in Chinese enterprises. Once a certain brand started its reputation in the markets, we immediately put the label of the brand on other products without hesitation, which is called brand extension strategy in the brand theory. China is the "quick worker" in the brand extension strategy but not a "master hand" in it. China is the manager of a single brand but it is in short of managerial capacity in multi-branding strategy. The brand "Gree" is facing the same challenges as well. Logically speaking, it is not a bad idea for Gree Electric Appliances which has grown and thrived from making air conditioning products to extend its brand into making small household appliances, but the problem is that Gree Group lacks the managerial capacity in the single brand. So it is quite normal for Gree Group to find difficult in sloving and handling the situation, when the multi-product problem plus the one that Gree Electric Appliances was trying to defend its pureness of the "Gree" brand appeared at the same time. Therefore, the contradictory and conflict were shown in Gree Group's internal management control. Appointing Zhu Jianghong the chairman of the board for Gree Group is just the expedient plan for solving the problems. According to the writer, the fundamental solution should be the construction of Gree Group's brand management system and the enhancement in its managerial capacity.

Chapter 8: Future of Gree

1. Gree's Sprinting for World Number One

According to the statistics released by the authoritative journal of global air conditioning industry *JARN* and Japanese well-known investigative agency Fuji Economy, in 2005, the sales volume and revenues of Gree's residential air conditioning products have already become the No.1 in the world. So far, Gree Electric Appliances has successfully realized its goal of "to be the champion in 2005". In 2005, facing the extremely severe competitive situation in China, Gree still saw its success in winning the championship for the tenth time straight and kept its leading position in the air conditioning industry: the sales revenues of Gree were higher than that of the second place air conditioner brand by roughly RMB 3 billion globally; domestically its sales revenues were twice as many as the second place air conditioner brand's.

1) To Speed Technological Innovation and Forge Competitive Strength

In 2006, Gree realized sales revenues of RMB 23 billion just with its air conditioning products and kept its leading position in the air conditioning industry. In order to better consolidate its leadership in the market, Gree daringly entered the High-tech Zone of Chongqing municipality; then, Gree successfully completed its strategic layout of the four production bases in Zhuhai, Chongqing, Danyang of Jiangsu and Brazil. With the annual total capacity of hitting 15 million units, Gree Electric Appliances has become the professional air conditioner manufacturer of the largest size in the world.

The president of Gree Electric Appliances, Dong Mingzhu pointed out: "the fruitful results were achieved through speeding up technological innovation, forging competitive strength and concentrating on all our capacities and materials in this field." Since 1991, Gree has grown from a small company with less than annual capacity of 20,000 window-type air conditioners to a large national listed company with the total capacity of 15 million units. And it was the No. 1 home appliance enterprise with sales revenues topping RMB 23 billion, which helps Gree to maintain its leading position in the air conditioning industry. In the list "Top 100 Tax Payers in Listed Companies" issued by the State Administration of Taxation, in this list, Gree Electric Appliances has topped all the tax-payers in the Chinese air conditioning industry. In 2003, Gree was put on the list "Top 12 Listed Companies with Greatest Investment Value" issued by the famous global investment bank---Credit Suisse First Boston; for three consecutive years, Gree had been named in "China 100 Top Listed Companies" by *Fortune China*; in 2006, Gree was included in the "Red List of Import and

Export Enterprises" of 70 enterprises by the General Administration of Customs…

The analysts in the industry indicated that, the reason why Gree could retain the title of championship for twelve consecutive years lies in its persistence in winning the markets with superior quality products and in order to realize the enhancement in brand core technology, Gree has been keeping inputting human resources, materials and funds in the introduction of production equipment and the innovation of air conditioning technologies. When the president, Zhu Jianghong was interviewed by *Business China*, he emphasized that only by strengthening technological innovation can Gree stay in the leading place and become the winner in this industry. In accordance with this idea, Gree spares no money in science and research in the past years. They keep increasing investment in the research department and introducing professional staff in air conditioning research field, in order to build the world first-class laboratory with about tens of millions yuan spent in research and development annually.

As the fourth-stage project of Zhuhai production base was completed, so far, Gree has finished building the largest air conditioner R&D center which has more than 170 laboratories. The professional research center makes the conditions of research and development greatly improved. At present, Gree has the possession of 357 patents; among them, 25 patents were obtained internationally, e.g. the remote control technology and the air leveling technology, etc.

In developing the overseas markets and building Chinese national brands, Gree Electric Appliances has made its cautious and resolute steps in entering foreign soils. A few years ago, the decision-makers in Gree already targeted on the international markets and were ready to enter the overseas markets to build Chinese brand at an international level. In order to achieve the goal of "to be the world champion in 2005", Gree increasingly intensified its efforts to export the products under its own brand and successfully put Gree air conditioners on the market places of about 40 countries and areas, such as, UK, France, Brazil and Russian etc. Among them the products under its own brand accounted for one third of the total commodity export of Gree. Now, the products that Gree are exporting to Brazil, Russia and Australia, etc, all have been under the "Gree" brand. From now on, Gree will take measures to expand its export of self-owned brand products and change the markets which were initially gained with OEM products into the markets for Gree's self-owned brand products.

With the goal of entering the American markets, Gree laid great emphasis on American outdoor air conditioners and split air conditioning units, which were well received by American distributors there. Moreover, Gree also signed a contract with Whirlpool Inc. that Gree would specially develop and produce 200,000 air conditioners for the American markets, which is another business opportunity for Gree to gain a foothold in the markets of

Europe and South America. In the markets of Europe, South America and North America, Gree Electric Appliance is forging a real Chinese brand now.

2) Strengthening the Dominant Position and Occupying the High-End Air Conditioner Market

In recent years, the competition of home appliance industry has been becoming tougher and tougher. Especially, after the "reshuffling" of the air conditioning industry in 2005, quite a few small disadvantaged businesses exited the markets, which made the vitality of strong and powerful enterprises be more vigorous and energetic. Although the price war is becoming increasingly intense, Gree Electric Appliances still reaches a new level in its achievement year after year to outshine all other air conditioning enterprises, with its sales revenues from RMB 7 billion few years ago to RMB100 billion in 2003, then RMB 13.8 billion in 2004, lastly RMB 2.3 billion in 2006. Regarding to the whole situation in the air conditioning market of 2006, one of the stakeholders in Gree said, since the top ten air conditioner brands leading by Gree in domestic air conditioner market have occupied about 70.5% market share, and the rest of 71 air conditioner brands which are not in the top 25 can only fight with each other for the market share of less than 3%.

The goal of Gree is to pursuit No.1 in the world, just considering the figures in Gree's production and sales: its sales revenues and profits in 2005 maintained the growth rate of over 30% and completed the goal of 10 million units in production and sales. With no doubt, Gree successfully won the world championship in the production and sales of air conditioning products. In July 2005, the latest issue of American *Fortune* magazine (Chinese version), released "Top 100 Chinese listed companies of 2005", Gree ranked No. 56 on the list with its brilliant achievements: the sales revenues reaching RMB 13.832 billion, the net profits hitting RMB420,000 billion, the market value topping RMB 12.76 billion with the total assets up to RMB 5.347 billion. It was the fifth consecutive year that Gree had been included in the list.

If Gree wants to have got the upper hand in the high end air conditioner markets, it must set a premium on its technical innovation. In July, 2005, the non-drip water and controllable humidity technology firstly invented by Gree, which means the research in the technical problems of dripping water and over dried air in the use of air conditioners that had long troubled the common people's daily life had made a significant breakthrough.

On 24th August, 2005, the first large central air conditioner—water-cooled centrifugal chiller with own intellectual property rights in Chinese home appliance industry left the production line of Gree Electric Appliances. It was sent to the five-star hotel—China Huizhou Hotel of Huangshan, Anhui province and would be installed and tested there. The water-cooled centrifugal chiller so far has the highest energy efficiency ratio in the world.

Currently, only few American enterprises have mastered its core technology and production method. Thereby, Gree broke American central air conditioning enterprises' technological monopoly in the field of making the large central air conditioners and filled up the gap for Chinese home appliance enterprises in the large central air conditioning research field.

The beginning of 2006 witnessed that Gree's sales momentum was even stronger compared with last year. At the same time, the market share of air conditioner is becoming more and more concentrated for the top brands in China with Gree as the leader in the markets. In this process, the market share of top air conditioner brands was raised by a large margin. Meanwhile, because the implementation of the global brand construction strategy led by Dong Mingzhu effectively improved Gree's market occupancy in the overseas markets; additionally, the export of Gree also experienced a rapid growth.

In the eyes of Dong Mingzhu, the enhancement of market concentration to Gree is not merely a challenge but more an opportunity, because Gree is not only leading in the scale and sales and its advantages in technology and brand are also beyond compare to many enterprises plus its market occupancy rate in the high-end air conditioner markets, which naturally allowed Gree to share more the positive results from the reshuffling of air conditioning industry. It is not so hard to see that Gree Electric Appliance, the largest professional air conditioning enterprise in the world, apparently has been taking the development road of competing with its rivals in the innovation field.

3) Facing Up To The Huge Changes in The Industrial Pattern

According to the data released by the Development Research Center of The State Council, in 2000 there were once about 400 air conditioner brands, but in the year 2004 there were only about 50 brands survived in the competition of the air conditioning industry. Among the survived brands, the first tier bands of Gree, Kelon, Midea and Haier are holding a lion's share about more than 60% of the markets. The marketing competition will be entering the new phrase of the competition with the "brand + technology" as the main theme. The development trend of the air conditioning industry demonstrates that the three consecutive years' "reshuffling" in Chinese air conditioning industry has produced some huge changes in the industrial pattern.

In accordance with the research reports on the demand condition for air conditioners of Chinese urban consumers released by the authority organizations, namely, Development Research Center of The State Council, etc, the "three powers in Guangdong Province" continued to be the "top 3" for the second consecutive year, but in 2004, the ranking was slightly changed. The "top 3" were Gree, Kelon and Midea (before 2004, the ranking was Gree as the No.1, then followed Midea and Kelon) with their market occupancy rate respectively 12.1%, 11.0%, 10.9% and Haier ranking No.4 in the list.

The analysts in the industry pointed out, since 2002, Gree had relied on distribution channels, Media had relied on marketing and Kelon had relied on its technology innovation, so the three controlled the places of top 3 in the air conditioning industry, but Haier entered the first camp of air conditioning industry through the process of building its brand with its refrigerator products. According to the analysis, the air conditioner market suffered the rare the outbreak of "SARS" in 2003, which made Midea and Haier's healthy air conditioners become greatly popular with consumers. The typical characteristic "the electricity shortage" in 2004 created a great opportunity for Kelon's energy saving air conditioners and brought huge sales volume to Kelon air conditioners.

According to the industry insiders, the sharp price increases of the raw materials for making air conditioners and the great price reduction of top brand air conditioning products kicked some brands of small and medium-sized enterprises out of the markets. Additionally, the compressors are becoming a scare resource, which compressed the living space of the brands of small enterprises. The experts argued that after decades' growth of domestic air conditioner markets, rural and urban consumers are having higher and higher level of brand awareness and the continuous power shortage forced the consumers to pay high attention to the energy saving of air conditioners. It can asserted that after the price war and vying with each other in controlling the raw materials from the upstream end market, what the air conditioning giants are competing for next will be their brand and core technology.

Zhu Jianghong says, as the only enterprise which always specializes in making air conditioners in the numerous home appliance listed companies, Gree Electric Appliances is persistently concentrating its major resources on the advancement in the research and development of new products and the product quality. As to this point, we believe that this advantage will help Gree Electric Appliances calmly to face the huge changes in the industrial pattern, because as the consumers' trust in the brand of "Gree" is growing with each passing day, the sales and profits of Gree certainly will continue to be the No.1 in this industry.

2. Forging the Number-one National Industry Brand

Being the person in charge of Gree's industrial sector, Zhu Jianghong said to a reporter in an interview: "Since the industrial sector led by Gree Electric Appliance has taken shape, there will be broad space for the further development both to the Gree Electric Appliance and Gree Group. Therefore, we are confident that 'Gree' is not merely the proud of Zhuhai, but also the proud of China. It will become the real No. 1 national industry brand.

1) Exploring Overseas Markets, Building Chinese Brand

In Gree's assembly workshop, people can see the floor as clear as mirror glass, and the workers are assembling the components in an orderly way at their own posts. According to the president of Gree Electric Appliances, Dong Mingzhu: "Gree's production workshop in Brazil is just as standardized and clean as this one."

The Brazilian production base of Gree Electric Appliances has already become the second largest air conditioner brand in Brazil with the annual output of 800,000 units. The next step for Gree is that the production base will continually increase its productivity and strive for expanding the market of Gree air conditioning products to whole North America. It is the Gree air conditioning products that changed Brazilians' traditional idea that Chinese products are inferior goods, which is another successful move for Gree's entering into the international markets.

Gree Electric Appliances is going global with cautious and steady strides.

As early as a few years ago, while quite a few air conditioning enterprises were fighting for the market share of the domestic markets, the decision makers of Gree had already aimed at expanding the overseas markets, going global and forging the Chinese brand at an international level.

Everything is difficult in the beginning. At the beginning of Gree making its expedition in the international markets, especially in the European markets, it also tried the method of making OEM products under foreign brand names like many enterprises usually do for the purpse of increasing their export volume. Labeling Gree's products with foreign brands made everyone in Gree felt painful at that time, but in the meanwhile, they also felt encouraged when they knew that the air conditioners made by Gree were well received in European markets with the excellent product quality and graceful exterior design. People in Gree finally came to realize that: to enter into the international markets should not only rely on the export volume, but also should rely on the brand of "Gree" itself.

Now, all the products that Gree is exporting to those areas, such as Brazil, Russia and Australia, etc have been all under the "Gree" brand. From now on, Gree will make more efforts in exporting of self-owned brand products by turning the market share initially for the OEM products that Gree once earned for other brands into the markets of its own brands. Finally, Gree hopes it can realize the dream that one day other air conditioner manufacturers are producing OEM products under the brand name of "Gree" for itself.

In order to enter American markets, Gree Electric Appliances also signed a contract with Whirlpool .Inc—the largest home appliance manufacturer in the world. In accordance with the terms stipulated by the contract, Gree would specially design and produce 200,000 air conditioner units for American markets, which is another business opportunity for Gree to gain a foothold in the overseas markets after entering in the markets of Europe and South America.

People often describe the business world by quoting the saying that "Business is war without bullets". No doubt, in that very year when Gree Electric Appliances made the decision to explore the overseas markets, at that time, this decision has already helped Gree gain the preemptive opportunity for those decisive battles.

To Gree Electric Appliances, the overseas marketing expedition is just a beginning for its long term development. When talking about the highest goal of Gree Electric Appliances, the chairwoman Dong Mingzhu said without hesitation: "To establish the Chinese brand and build a century-old enterprise."

With the brand "Gree" as the core cohesion, Gree's industrial sector led by Gree Electric Appliances will definitely have a greater development.

Zhu Jianghong said if Gree wants to become the real No.1 national industry brand, it still needs a very long time to perfect and temper itself. Being the leading group enterprise and facing the new development opportunities, Gree Electric Appliances will take "to make the national industry brands greater and stronger" as its own responsibility and continue to strive for its goal with steady and careful strides.

2) Expanding Business Only in the Air conditioner-related Area

The chairman of Gree Electric Appliances, Zhu Jianghong once gave his opinion that the growth of an enterprise should follow the economic laws. It cannot neither reach the goal in just one step nor try all the means to seek the quick success and instant benefits. If so, it will bring about a fatal blow to the enterprise itself. At the initial stage of Gree's development, fortunately, it did not blindly pursue the exceedingly fast growth rate, but steadily laid the ground work for its development – by constructing an unobstructed market network for its products, mastering the core manufacturing technology and building a scientific management system; then launch attacks on its rivals in the market competition with strong force. Although Gree once also encountered the difficulties in funds and markets, it's faith of "making good air conditioners" with its down- to-earth attitude has never been shaken, that is, to win the market trust with reliable product quality.

Thereupon, just as what people know about the home appliance industry that Chinese home appliance industry has the most brutal competition. Despite of the brual competition and various difficulties, Gree Electric Appliances has explored a clear development road for itself with its steady and stable strides in its work style. With its development path, Gree not only created the unique Gree business model, but also won the reputation of "individual champion" in the air conditioning market.

For the goal of carrying out Gree's specialization strategy, Gree purchased the four business segments' stakes of Gree Group's four subsidiary Companies, namely, Landa's compressor, Greewire's enamel-insulated wire and Xinyuan Electronics' coating capacitance and Zhuhai Landa Compressor. On Gree's new purchase of four companies, the experts in this industry began to have the question: Does Gree's new move go against Gree's principle of sticking to its specialization strategy and does it mean that Gree gives up its own original development objectives and take the road of diversification business operations? As the core of the industrial sector of Gree Group, how will Gree Electric Appliances balance the relation between the acquired business and the major business of manufacturing air conditioners? What is the development strategy that Gree Electric Appliances will make for the acquired four business segments? Can Gree Electric Appliances turn the operating loss of the four businesses into the profitable ones?

About these questions and queries, Zhu Jianghong sonorously and forcefully answered. "Gree Electric Appliances never fights a war that it is not confident of. If we want to take part in a war, we will win a brilliant victory. " Then what makes Zhu Jianghong so confident in the future development of his business? He explained, this purchase of four subsidiary companies of Gree Group is not a simple takeover in a general sense, or the related party transaction of the controlling shareholder's "dumping the burden" in some habitual thoughts, but the implementation of Gree's important development strategy after Gree Electric Appliances has become the most powerful air conditioning enterprise through its specialization development. Both to Gree Group and Gree Electric Appliances, this takeover is a wise move to achieve the win-win situation.

Zhu Jianghong believes that specialization is the only path in the corporate development, but when the development of an enterprise reaches at a certain stage with some capacities such as, mature technology, talents as well as tremendous strength, the diversification strategy, the extension of the industrial chain will further broaden the development of this enterprise. To Gree Electric Appliances, making air conditioning products will be remained as its main business consistently, but the new purchased businesses will help to enrich Gree's industrial chains and its market space. In view of this point, even if Gree is taking the road of diversification operation, it still regards the "strive for the goal with steady strides and a down-to-earth attitude" as the guiding policy for its development.

In the acquisition of the four companies, Landa's compressor, Greewire's enamel-insulated wire and Xinyuan Electronics' coating capacitance all can be directly used as the accessory products in the industrial chains of Gree air conditioning enterprise. Far from causing the market risks, this acquisition has enhanced Gree's industrial chains and its self-supporting capacity and realized the sharing of the following aspects, such as, capital, technology, market share and talents. As a result, it has achieved the goal of further saving the production cost and improving the operational efficiency.

The chairman, Zhu Jianghong gave an example to illustrate his points, if Gree builds a large compressor company, the investment in factory buildings, equipment and personnel training will be tens of millions of Yuan. However, the value of the intangible assets, like skillful workers and the sophisticated supporting management that Landa has is difficult to estimate. At present, the annual output of Landa's compressors is about 1.4 million units, and the demand of Gree Electric Appliances is about more than 7 million units. Therefore to Landa Company, it does not have to worry about the selling of its products and it will be very easy the make profits, for Gree Electric Appliances will buy all its products. But the key problem is that how Landa makes efforts to become a bigger and stronger company so as to contribute more profits to Gree Electric Appliances. It is just the same situation with Greewire and Xinyuan Electronics. What's more, Zhu Jianghong added that, another goal for Gree Electric Appliances' purchasing the small appliance companies is that this purchase can realize the unified use, supervising and maintenance of Gree brand and can better help Gree Electric Appliances to build and manage the Gree brand.

Dong Mingzhu said that Gree Electric Appliance only makes air conditioning products; if the Gree brand wants to expand its business, it will only expand its business in air conditioner related area. The market itself does not need every enterprise to have a comprehensive development in the products. Only when the every product of an enterprise is of competitive and best quality can this enterprise be the winner in a real sense. In the accumulation of a certain brand, the first important thing is the quality of its products and the quantity of its product is the second important factor. With the quality and quantity of the products as the guarantee, an enterprise can build a good brand and with the accumulation of the product's quality and quantity, there will be a qualitative leap in the development of the brand. Since Gree air conditioner already has more than 35 million air conditioner users around the world, Dong Mingzhu said that Gree Electric Appliances has the confidence and boldness to aspire to be the world champion in this industry.

3) Independent Innovation Making the World Famous Brand

Every year, Gree will take 3% of the sales revenues to invest in its technology research and development, which makes Gree become the only enterprise to spend the most money on research and development in technology in Chinese air conditioning industry. It is the input in technology innovation that completely ended the situation that the air conditioner market in China once was monopolized by the brands of developed countries.

Once some people asked the leaders of the famous enterprises in China: what is the objective of business operations? The answer is: the market occupancy rate of the brand. It shows that most leaders in many famous enterprises have already come to realize the importance of brand. Especially in the current situation of the surplus production capacity in the international markets, all the countries with open market economy have entered into the buyer's market in varying degrees. Compared with those in the past, there are enormous changes in the environment and means of the market competition. Under the new circumstance, the primary means for the enterprises to win the market share cannot only depend on the product itself; it also includes the brand competition as well. It can be said that, the main form of the future international markets will be the competition between brands. By that time, the good or bad brand strategy will become the magic tool for many enterprises to win the victory with their unexpected moves in the market competition.

In reality, many world famous enterprises always consider the brand development as the priority strategy for exploring the international markets. For instance, Coca-Cola, Pesi-Cola and McDonald's all make great efforts in building its brand strategy, i.e. to create their own famous brands. Many multinational corporations regard their brand as a tool of exploring the overseas markets and they all try to capture the market share with their branding strategy. Because the comprehensive driving effect of the famous brand is powerful and its economic extrovert degree is also very high, it seems that when a brand is established and the development of related supporting industries also has been promoted. It is probably no exaggeration to say that a brand is the sharp weapon for enterprises to enter the markets and occupy the markets. As today's market competition is becoming increasingly fiercer, an enterprise's own brand strategy and its own brand and how the image of the brand looks like all become very crucial factors for an enterprise.

Moreover, in the process of an enterprise's development, there is a close relation between the brand and the price of the enterprise's products: the price of the products tends to affect the sales revenues and profits of an enterprise. Besides that the performance of products, technical content and use range will also decide the price of the products, usually there is an intangible factor existing in deciding the price; that is the brand name of the products. In the same kinds of commodities, there are great differences in the price between the popular brand products and the common brand products. For example, the shirts of the same texture, the price of world famous brand of "Lacoste" is several times higher than the price of Chinese brand "Kaikai". Therefore, it is not hard to see that the brand as the intangible asset of the enterprises is the great fortune for enterprises. In the international trade, as long as the products of a certain brand are of good quality and won the trust from the consumers, the traders will tend to choose this brand and the brand is becoming valuable. Even though the price of the brand is much higher than its peers, the consumers are still willing to buy the products of it and regard its high price as a symbol of noble identity. Such as the brands: "Pierre Cardin" and "Adidas" in clothes, "Rolls Royce" and "Mercedes Benz" in cars, all the value of these brands can bring the enterprises immense wealth.

Therefore, Gree always commits itself to building its own brand. Dong Mingzhu says, Gree Electric Appliances will continue to increase its investment in independent technology research and development in the future and dedicate to make the Gree brand the international first class brand as well as forge the famous brand which really belongs to Chinese people. While Gree Electric Appliances is making more researches in the core technology and improving the performance of the products, it will intend to design more energy saving and environment friendly products and make its own contributions to building a harmonious society.

In recent years, Gree Electric Appliances has frequently launched forceful strikes one after another in its independent technology innovation, which helped it to foster "Gree" to be the world class brand.

On August 24th, 2005, with Gree's intellectual property rights, the water-cooled centrifugal chiller developed by Gree Electric Appliances itself officially left the production line. Its emergence signified that Gree broke American central air conditioning enterprises' technological monopoly and filled up the gap for Chinese home appliance enterprises in the large central air conditioning field.

On November 7th, 2005, the world first ultra-low temperature multi-connected central air conditioner also successfully left the production line, which indicated that the technology of Chinese central air conditioners' heating and energy saving in the winter ultra-low temperature environment reached the top class level in the world.

"Our country's air conditioning industry is a late starter in the world and our technical level is lagging behind those established businesses in those advanced countries. Under the circumstance that the world air conditioning and refrigeration industry is monopolized by those American and Japanese enterprises, if we want to catch up with them and surpass the technology of the developed countries, we must have our own technological innovations. As a professional air conditioning enterprise, we should not only get ahead of our opponents in sales volume and sales revenues, but also should pull ahead of our opponents in research and development of technology. Only have our own independent core technology, can we take the initiative in the market competition." The Chairman of Gree Electric Appliances, Zhu Jianghong said. It is because of Gree's own autonomous core technology that makes today's "Gree" brand.

3. There Is a Long Way Ahead

The *Bible* tells us, "Enter through the narrow gate; for the gate is wide and the road is easy that leads to destruction, and there are many to take. For the gate is narrow and the road is hard that leads to life, and there are few who find it." Usually, many people tend to pick the road to the wide gate, for they think that it is easy and comfortable there, even it leads to destruction. Only few people will enter the narrow gate to get into the heaven, though the way leading to the narrow gate is very hard and difficult. Not like many people, Gree Electric Appliances has chosen a special way which looks easy; in fact, it is quite bumpy and hard—to do what an enterprise with a history of 100 years should do.

1) The Multi-channel Strategy Is the New Focus

The marketing channel system which is regarded as the lifeblood by all the air conditioning enterprises is becoming the high ground in the fierce battle of this industry. According to the statistical data analysis, at present, the growth rate of air conditioning sales is gradually slowing down in the first and second tier city markets, but in the vast third and fourth tier city markets, the sales of air conditioning products enjoys a rapid growth. In the broad market space of third and fourth tier cities, the large army of home appliance chain stores has not pressed on to the border of the markets yet. At the same time, the statistics show that in Chinese home appliance markets, the market share of chain stores and the marketplace in supermarkets is only accounting for 37% of the whole home appliance markets, and the rest 63% market share is distributed through the marketing channels built by the manufacturers, department stores and specialized stores.

The analysts in the industry think that the self-built channels are just the "supplement" to the "diversification of multi-marketing channels". The self-built channels are not the strong rival for those large appliances stores in the markets. The reasons for Gree Electric Appliance's taking the sales company model is out of the consideration for "three wins": to the consumers, the channel will be more flattening so that Gree can give the money once spent in circulation expenses back to the consumers; to the manufacturers, it helps to reduce the circulation links so that the manufacturers can quickly to meet the different market demands; to the distributors, they will have more support from the manufacturer and have a faster response to the changes in the markets. "The self-built sales channels built by the home appliance enterprises and the super terminals are the business model complementary to each other, which is a channel model bringing about the situation of mutual benefits and multilateral wins to the home appliance industry."

In the future channel-construction, according to some experts, Gree Electric Appliances will choose the multi-channel strategy as the new focus in its plan. The following are the reasons for it:

Firstly, to the expand production scale and form the scale economy. The first advantage of scale economy is that the manufacturer can get the volume discount from the upstream suppliers with the large order of raw material purchase. The second is that the cost shared by the depreciation, marketing and management will be lowered. The controllable production scale will make Gree's products have the absolute cost advantage! The reduction in costs can guarantee the enterprise to survive very well in the marginal profit era of home appliance industry, which also caters to GOME, etc, the large home appliance stores' preference for ultra lower price products.

The second important point is to promote the reform of the channel flattening. To cut the layers in the distribution channels, and change the sales companies into the organization providing logistics, marketing and management services for large dealers and second, third tier distributors as soon as possible. Let the "GOME stores" dependent on the high efficiency of logistics and services provided by Gree's sales companies. At the same time, to own a considerable number of specialized stores as well as the retail outlets. On one hand, Gree can sell and promote Gree's own high end air conditioning products through those retail outlets; on the other hand, those retail outlets can perform the functions of the brand monitoring, collecting the consumers' information and mastering the market dynamics, etc. And those outlets also can monitor and restrain the "GOME stores".

The third reason for Gree to choose multi-channel strateg is that Gree needs to nurture "the third party force". "The third party force" mainly signifies electronic commerce, especially the newly sprout up 3C (3C stands for China Compulsory Certification) stores in China nowadays. Those newly emerged marketing channels might grab parts of large home appliance retail stores' market share to prevent the "GOME stores" from dominating the market. Gree Electric Appliances also should help some regional chain stores to enter the national markets from its local markets so that there will be more giants like Daizhong, Yongle, and Suning checking and balancing each other.

The fourth reason is the multi-channel strategy can help Gree reinforce the customers' loyalty towards the brand of Gree. To retain the customers and let them have high customer loyalty to the brand name and depend on the customer's needs for the products of this brand to force the retailers to sell the manufacturer's products, which is definitely better than the manufacturer requesting the retailers to sell their products. At the meantime, the users' very high loyalty towards the brand "Gree" can help Gree Electric Appliances to enjoy the perferential right in the promotion of the new products, cooperative advertising and point of sale presentation, etc.

Fifthly, the multi-channel strategy can help Gree to intensify the efforts in making innovations in its products. If Gree Electric Appliances could constantly launch new products that can lead the trend in air conditioning industry and have the absolute predominance in the research and development of the air conditioning products, to the retailers, Gree will enjoy the "expert status". And Gree can complete its product line by keeping weeding through the old products and bringing forth the new products; in this way,

Gree can meet the promise of "one-stop shopping" services that "GOME stores" made to customers. The powerful innovation ability in products allows Gree to have the sales initiative to decide which retailer has the right to sell its new products, just like Intel has the initiative to sell its chips.

Moreover, if Gree has a team of outstanding salespersons and forms its remarkable advertisements and promotional capabilities, all the elements also can be very attractive and deterrent to those big retailers.

As a matter of fact, for any enterprise, as long as it has the absolute superiority in scale economy, customer brand loyalty, research and development, marketing capabilities and high market occupancy, it will not subject to the super terminal and certainly will win through in the game between the manufacturers and the intermediaries in the future.

The industry experts think that the implementation of multi-channel strategy is the manifestation that enterprises have returned from enlarging its production scale blindly to focusing profit making in the context that the whole home appliances industry is getting shrinking. But home appliance enterprises may suffer the pain brought by the "double-edged sword" of the multi-channel strategy when they are stepping into the retail industry from purely manufacturing industry, because it needs a relatively long "nurturing process", in which probably this strategy may not help enterprises to save expenses or enhance efficiency. In the meantime, the scattering markets of the third, fourth tier cities are also testing the remote control capability of the home appliance manufacturers.

2) Technology Breakthrough Dominates The Future

In 2006, the Chinese air conditioning industry suffered an unprecedented a "severe cold winter": affected by the combined effects of those factors, such as the increase in the cost of raw materials, etc, as a result, there was a general decline of 10% in the sales of the whole industry. The analysts in the industry believed that the Chinese air conditioning industry would fully enter into an era of the multi-channel competition with independent innovations in 2007 and the systematic and comprehensive game will be the key point in the competition between those air conditioning enterprises. The air-con makers' weakness in their independent innovation is the principal cause that triggers the crisis in the whole air conditioning industry; therefore, the technology breakthrough will dominate the future of Chinese air conditioning industry.

In spite of the fact that China is the largest manufacturing country around the world so far, as far as the Chinese air conditioning industry is concerned, this industry is still in the transition period of from the low end of the industrial chain to the mid and high-end markets. It is still in its growing period of catching up with others, so independent innovation is one of the important ways for Chinese air conditioning industry to catch up with and surpass those multinational enterprises. Under this circumstance, Chinese air conditioning industry should proceed as quickly as possible with constructing an independent innovation system when coping with the global competition and set the goal of having breakthroughs in the independent innovation as the main direction for the future development of this industry. In the meantime, Chinese air conditioning enterprises should promote its technology standardization strategy in an orderly fashion. Furthermore, Chinese airconditioning businesses should both implement the patent technology and achieve the patent standardization and international standards at the same time. Only in this way, can the quality of Chinese air conditioning products and the brand value can be enhanced in an overall manner.

The experts from the state sectors, namely, "Development Research Center of The State Council", "National Development and Reform Commission" and "General Administration of Quality Supervision, Inspection and Quarantine of the People' Republic of China" all think that, the rise in the cost of the raw materials and the suffering of the international trade barriers are not the main reason for causing this "severe cold winter" in the industry. "They are just surface phenomenon; the real cause for the crisis of the whole air conditioning industry is that the added value brought by the new products is too low and the product homogeneity of domestic air conditioning market is prevalent and serious!" Having started in imitating and drawing on the experience of other countries and industries, so far, Chinese air conditioning industry has the largest productivity after about more than ten years' great-leap-forward development, but the awkward situation of "large but not strong" in the whole Chinese air conditioning industry is still obvious. Especially, after the price wars in recently years and with the appreciation of Renminbi, the rise in the price of raw materials as well as the increasingly highlighted obstacles posed by the WEEE Directive (Waste Electrical and Electronic Equipment Directive) and the RoHS (Restriction of Hazardous Substances) of the European Union and other environmental barriers, the survival of Chinese air conditioning enterprises will under even greater pressure.

Li Xinghao, the board chairman of Guangdong Chigao Air Conditioning, said, in recent dozens of years, the domestic air conditioning enterprises have been persistently engaged in introducing series of new technology and making attempts in innovation; through making the full use of the advantages: localization marketing, cheap labor and scale expansion, finally they are gradually narrowing the gap between Chinese brands and the foreign brands in manufacturing, marketing and services, etc, but there is still a great gap in the brand value and core technology, etc, between the domestic air conditioning enterprises and foreign enterprises. He made a further analysis that the many years' price war has made that Chinese air conditioning enterprises have no funds and energy to put in technology research and development, which leads up to the crisis in the lacking of core technology faced by Chinese air conditioning industry. And because domestic air conditioning enterprises' lack of differentiation competitive advantages, codes and standards causes the product homogeneity, they have to continue their price wars and scale wars. This vicious circle is becoming standing out especially under the pressure of the rise in raw materials and European Union's green trade barriers. "In the technology reform of Chinese air conditioning products, the breakthrough lies in the key parts of compressors and refrigeration agents, but all the related technology is mastered by the foreign enterprises without exception. Therefore, it was not an accident that the plight of the industry appeared in 2006, which just was the outburst of the accumulation of contradictions in the industry in China. " Li Xinghao said.

The President of Gree Electric Appliances, Dong Mingzhu pointed out that the independent innovation is not a hot term; especially in the past one year, the independent innovation appeared in the development of the enterprises with highest frequency. More and more enterprises put the independent innovation at the first important place in their corporate development. However, quite a few enterprises have formed two misunderstandings about the word "innovation": one is "simply take in"; the other is "simply focus on innovation". The "simply take in" is just to focus on the introduction and improvement of the existed foreign technologies and management methods, which causes the enterprise to be lacking of its own competitive strength; the "simply focus on innovation" is to simply pursue the innovation in technology and ignore other aspects of the enterprises. Therefore, the result of the innovation is that the enterprise only made progress in a very short term, but the enterprise itself still lacks the competitive strength and motive power. "When the enterprises are engaging in their independent innovation, they should adhere to their self-improvement, autonomy and self-support. The independent innovation is not just innovation in technology but the innovation in a comprehensive way. It must proceed with innovation in personnel training, technology, management and marketing; the four aspects must be synchronized with each other and none is dispensable." Gree Electric Appliances itself is the best example to illustrate this point. If an enterprise wants to build its driving force, the innovation in talent training will be the fundamental factor, the innovation in management system will be the lifeblood and the innovation in technology development will be the core and cornerstone.

As to the concept of independent innovation, Dong Mingzhu believes that the technical innovation is the core for the development of China's manufacturing industry, because the development of Chinese manufacturing industry always constantly relies on the introduction of foreign technology and lacks the innovations in technology. Therefore, China perhaps is called as the "factory of the world" by other countires, but actually it is just a small "workshop" like a big bubble supported by cheap labor and raw materials. Once it loses the two supports, it will burst all of a sudden. So, we should revitalize our national industries and the key point for us to do so lies in the independent innovation in technology. In order to save the production costs, enhance the efficiency in work, expand the production scale, realize the large scale operation and have a health development of the enterprise, the domestic enterprises of different trades like Geely (a private automobile manufacture), Haier (home appliances company), Gree, Huawei(a multinational networking and telecommunications equipment company) and Nuctech(the world's top provider of security scanning equipment) all have achieved impressive results in their independent innovations. Among them, Gree Electric Appliances as the largest air conditioning manufacturer has invested heavily in its technical innovation and established a set of complete research and development system. In 2002, Gree had successfully accomplished its independent researches in developing the multi-connected air conditioner, which broke the Japanese enterprises' technological monopoly in the core technology of this field. And in 2006, following in the success launch in the field of manufacturing multi-connected air conditioners in the year 2002, the magnetic suspension centrifugal chiller designed and manufactured by Gree Electric Appliances has been officially off the assembly line, which changed the situation that the Chinese market of magnetic suspension centrifugal chillers was entirely monopolized by the United States. Then Gree Electric Appliances has become the world fourth home for magnetic suspension centrifugal chillers, the domestic first truly mastering the technology and the first manufacturer in China which can achieve volume production of this air conditioner.

Facing the powerful technical innovations from foreign home appliance giants, Gree Electric Appliances must continue its adherence to the idea of its independent innovation and break the monopoly of the foreign enterprises in the core technology and develop more core technologies with independent intellectual property rights. We have the faith that along with the persistent pursuit and efforts made by the Chinese air conditioning enterprises, like Gree, the pace of technical innovation in our air conditioning enterprises will be quickened. It can be predicted that China's air conditioning industry will be ushering into a brand new future development of the independent innovation.

Review: The Strategic Choice after Winning the Championship

Gree Electric Appliances has become the champion in the world air conditioning industry in the year 2005, which signifies that another Chinese enterprise winning global championship was born. It is a really big event worth of celebrating. But while we are celebrating it, we must be fully aware that this champion is just the champion in sales volume, not in the value of the products; this championship only has two years' history, not a "time honored and long-tested" one. We still don't know for sure whether Gree's status of champion is stable or not.

Under this situation, the author thinks that the strategic choice for Gree Electric Appliances after winning the championship should be: setting up "to be the global value champion of air conditioning industry" as its goal. Then all the corresponding activities and measures taken in integrating resources should be center around the realization of this goal. From the content of this chapter, Gree Electric Appliances is choosing the vertical integration and the diversification strategy through purchasing the four subsidiary factories of Gree Group and trying to enter the field of compressor and small home appliances, etc, which is obviously the strategic initiative dominated by the Gree Group and might not be the most favorable strategy for Gree Electric Appliances.

However, from the perspective of the market competition, the champion enterprise in the No.1 place should adopt the marketing strategy for the "defensive marketing warfare". As Al Ries and Jack Trout point out that there are three guidelines to remember concerning the "defensive marketing strategy" in their book *Marketing Warfare*:

1. Defensive strategies only should be pursued by the market leader.

The status of the market leader is not self-defining but based on the market facts. The firm itself cannot make itself the market leader. The market leader is the firm which has attained that position in the mind of the consumers.

There is only one leader in a certain market, not many leaders at the same time. If people see that there are many market leaders in a certain field, it means that the real leader has not been born yet.

Is Gree Electric Appliances the leader of the global air conditioning market? I am afraid that it is not the real leader yet. Therefore, to set the goal of being the market leader in the global air conditioning market as the strategic target is the perfect choice for Gree Electric Appliances at present. In China's home appliance enterprises, only Gree Electric Appliances is qualified to choose this goal for itself.

2. The best defensive strategy is the courage to attack yourself.

Since the market leader is in the dominant position and it has held the mountains in the consumers' mind, the best defensive strategy is the courage to attack its own self. In other words, the market leader should introduce products and services better than the existing ones that it already has so that it can preempt similar moves by competition and consolidate the leader status.

We can see that, Intel in the markets of central processing unit and Microsoft in the operating system markets are all the leaders in their own field. Thus, they all adopt the defensive marketing strategy of the market leaders by constantly introducing new products in the markets and eliminating their old products.

In consideration of introducing new products to replace the old ones, Gree Electric Appliance lays much stress on its innovation, which is the beginning of its self-attack.

However, it is much easier said than done for an enterprise in the leading position to really attack itself. Judging from the history of many enterprises, the loss of the market leader's status was not caused by the competitors but resulted by the leaders' mistakes of those enterprises.

    3.   Strong competitive moves should always be blocked.

For most enterprises, there is only one chance to win, but for the market leader, there are two chances. If the market leader misses the opportunity to attack itself, usually, it can copy the strategies of its competitors to launch the counterattack. And then, the market leader must have swift actions and moves before the attackers gain a foothold in the markets.

Before this article comes to an end, I give all my sincere wishes for Gree Electric Appliances to be the champion of the global air conditioning market soon and fully prepared itself for the future development with a perfect strategic scheme.

Afterword

In the field of home appliance industry, the development of many brands is stagnating in the markets, but Gree Eclectic Appliance is always making great progress by overcoming many adversities in the market competition. In its development, Gree not only has realized the great growth rate in the sales volume, but also has widened the distance between itself and other first tier brands. Thus, many enterprises or the media and the press are all looking for the explanation for Gree's success and most of the enterprises and the media attribute the success of Gree to the success of Gree business model.

In the development process of Chinese enterprises, there were too many ups and downs as well as too much birth and death of excellent enterprises, but Gree Electric Appliances is an exception. The miracle of Gree's rapid growth in the age of traditional industry can be described as an unprecedented case. It has built a brand new image for Chinese enterprises in the world as well as created a brand new history for the development of the national enterprises and an unbelievable economic myth.

Why Gree could make such a remarkable achievement? Why many Chinese enterprises could not become bigger and stronger when they reach a certain stage? If we try to trace the deep-seated reasons, we can find that the reasons lie in whether they could construct a unique business model and build a management team which can make a breakthrough in the status quo of its business conditions. The reason for Gree's remarkable achievement is that it is relying on the management team's business intelligence and thinking outside the box to create a unique business model in China.

In the past few years, Gree Electric Appliances has kept an unimaginably high growth rate and become the champion in the stiff market competition as well as the industry leader. Behind the high growth rate of Gree, its outstanding marketing strategy plays a significant role in its success. Thanks to the brilliant marketing strategy, the development of Gree's marketing network is transferring from the sales oriented phrase to the brand building oriented phrase. Gree also created its unique marketing ideas and model based on its own characteristics and the market environment, which offers the example and reference for other enterprises. According to the writer of this article, there are three vital factors in the success of Gree's business model: Firstly, offer distributors rebates and discounts in the off-season, at the end of every year or aperiodically, which could help Gree Electric Appliances keep a steady relationship with those distributors. Secondly, it is Gree's "stockholding system regional sales company", which perfectly solved the problems of the making and sharing of profits through a relatively clear join-stock property right relation. Thirdly, the corporate culture guided by Zhu Jianghong and Dong Mingzhu including the attitude of honesty and integrity in dealing with distributors and customers, the rigorous management system and the concept of executing an action to its best has pulled in a big group of large distributors to work together with Gree Electric Appliances in developing the markets.

It has been proved that the growth of an enterprise cannot go without a successful marketing strategy. In every "break point" of the changes in Chinese marketing environment, there will be one or several enterprises influencing the progress of Chinese marketing with its classic or advanced marketing model. They are the most talented ones in their time. They all will be written into the history of marketing for their outstanding contributions to Chinese marketing despite the fact that they became pioneers for their success or they became "martyrs" for their loss in their field. Gree's marketing model is a great marketing model. Gree as a shining star in Chinese business world, its development not only will influence the management model of Chinese enterprises, but also will provide a successful example for other Chinese enterprises in the following aspects, namely, strategic choice, marketing strategy, brand building and globalization, etc.

During the process of writing this book, we referred to some relevant materials, including TV programs, books, network information, newspapers and magazines, etc. Owning to limited space, we regret for being unable to list all the references here and we feel most grateful to those writers of all the materials. Without the help of the distinguished professors, the presidents of enterprises and the management experts who pay close attention to Gree Electric Appliances as well as the support and kindness from the people working in the industry and the editors from the publishing houses, this book would not have been successfully published. Here, I'd like to express my deep appreciation to all of them.

----Zhou Xibing
October, 2007

Bibliography

1. Dong, Mingzhu. *Check around the World.* Guangzhou: Huacheng Publishing House, 2000.

2. Zhou, Xibing. *Life Gate: the Survey on the Failure of Chinese Family Businesses.* Beijing: Oriental Publishing House, 2006.

3. Lu, Taihong, and Li Shiding. "The 'Remarkable Advertisement' of Gree Created Good Sales" *China Marketing,* 2006. Vol.8.

4. Qi, Xin. "Gree--'The Singles Champion' to Win the Market with Its Unique Channels" V*marketing China,* 2005. Vol.1

5. Xun, Xundong. "Gree Electric Appliances: Why It Is Different from Others?" *Securities Market Weekly*, 2006.

6. Tan, Jianglong and Zou Xilan. "Will Gree Become the King of Central Air Conditioner?" *China Economic Weekly*, 2005. Vol.46

7. Chen, Junjun. "Gree Was 'Badly Hurt'; TCL Entered the Market with Strong Force: The Reshuffling of Air Conditioning Industry Broke out". *China Economic Times*, 2004.

8. Zhan, Yanbing. "What Can We Learn From Gree?" China Enterprise News, 2006.

9. Lang, Lang "the Net Profit of Gree Electric Appliances Was RMB420,000 Million Last Year". *NFDaily*, 2005.

10. Huang, Hanying and Dong Mingzhu. "Last Year vying with LG for the Marketshare, This Year Leading the Whole World". NDDaily, 2005.

11. Jang, Rui. "Industrial Spirit Is Indispensable: Interview with Dong Mingzhu—the Deputy to the NPC and President of Gree Electric Appliance" *Shanghai Securities News*, 2006.

12. Zhao, Jingan. "Gree's Specialization Enhancing Its Competitive Strength" *People's Daily*, 2006.

13. Dong, Mingzhu. "The New Business World Is Full of 'Industrial Spirit'". *China Business Journal*, 2006.

14. He, Qing. "Gree Electric Appliances Made Unexpected Achievement In the Slump of Air Conditioning Market". *Shenzhen Economic Daily*, 2006.

15. Pan, XiangHai. "Chunlan and Gree Call For End to the Air Conditioning Price War and Shift the Focus from Price to Value". *Jiangnan Times*, 2004.

16. Sun, Zhuo and Zhang Sanwei "Gree Air Conditioner 'Produces' Its Brand Effect Unexpectedly to be a Best Seller in the Off Season" *NFDaily*, 2006.

17. Zhu, Jianghong. "The Big Home Appliances Chain Stores Are Not Able to Occupy all the Market Share". NDDaily, 2005.

18. Wang, Qi, "Gree Increased Issues in Stocks and Firmly Bound Itself to Distributors". *China Business Post*, 2006.

19. Dong, Mingzhu "Gree: To Create a Brand Recognized by the World". *China Business Times*, 2005.

20. Zhang Xingming. "Gree Denied Entering the Small Home Appliance Market". *Hong Kong Commercial Daily*, 2003.

21. Chen Yongzhi. "Gree: Use the Clumsiest Method to Make the Best Air Conditioners". *China Consumer Journal*, 2006.

22. Hu, Liyun and Chen Jun. "Quality Is the Life of Enterprises—the Scale Profit of Gree Enjoys Steady Growth". *Market Daily (People's Daily)*, 2003.

23. Liu, Yong. "The Third Anniversary of Gree's Implementation of Six Sigma: The Struggle in Groping". *First Financial Daily*, 2004.

24. Zhou, Yuwu. "Dong Mingzhu (the President of Gree Electric Appliance): What You Are Doing Should Be Responsible for Gree's Future". *Guangzhou Daily*, 2004.

25. Zhang Qingyao. "Gree Advocates: The Excellent Product Is the Best Service". *China Consumer Journal*, 2004.

26. Jiang, Rui. "Gree Electric Appliance: To Build Air Conditioner Highest After-sale Service Standard" *Shanghai Securities News*, 2005.

27. Deng, Huachao. "Gree's Technology in Central Air Conditioner Has Reached the World Advanced Level." *Shenzhen Economic Daily*, 2005.

28. Zhu, Jian. "Gree's Own Brand Products Sell Well Globally in over 60 Countries and Regions" *NFDaily*, 2005.

29. Tang Xuelai. "Gree Has Identified Two Major Development Priorities". *China Securities Journal*, 2003.

30. Yuan, Xiaoke. "Gree Expects to Increase Sales Revenues of $20 Million by Exporting Air Conditioner Spare Parts to Brazil" *Shanghai Securities News*, 2005.

31. Zhang, Xin "17 Air Conditioner Brands Didn't Survive 'The Severe Winter' of 2006" *China Times*, 2006.

32. Zhao, Yanping and Xu Xiaoqing "The Local Brands of Haier and Gree Are Marching into the Field of Central Air Conditioner" *Beijing News*, 2006.

33. Luo, Qingqi. "Japanese Air Conditioner Brands Were Kicked Out of Chinese Market after Experiencing a 'Cold Spell' in China". *Economic Information Daily*, 2006.

34. Duan, Zhiming. "Gree loses Billions of Contract and Faces a 30% Market Loss". *Beijing Times*, 2005.

35. Hua, Guang "Occupying the High-end Market: The Oligopoly in Chinese Air Conditioning Market is becoming Obvious". *Shenzhen Special Zone Daily*, 2007.

36. Lu, Defu. "No Regrets in Breaking with GOME". *Guangzhou Daily*, 2006.

About the Reviewers

Ke Yinbin, the research specialist of case studies on Chinese champion enterprises. Currently, he is the deputy director of World Chinese Businessman Research Centre of China Academy of Social Sciences, the visiting research fellow of Center for studies of World Modernization Process, Peking University and the editor of *Yearbook of the World Chinese Entrepreneurs*. Now, Mr. Ke is engaged in the research, development and consulting service of the applicable strategy for Chinese enterprises. He is also the author of the series books *the Way of the Champion*.

Jin Feng, the specialist in channel operation and marketing management. He has successively held the posts of the business director of the Distribution Center, executive deputy director and general manager assistant of *Beijing Times*. Now, Mr. Jin is the president of *Beijing Times* and the general manager of the Distribution Center of *Beijing Times* as well as the founder of well-known online shopping services –Yijia360.com. Beside, Mr. Jin is also the author of many books, e.g. *the Management Model of the Professional Logistic and Distribution System (Xiao Nanmao management model) of Beijing Times*.

This book is the result of a co-publication agreement between Guangdong Economy Publishing House (China) and Paths International Ltd.

A Chinese Firm Goes Global: The Gree Story
Author: Chen Zonglin, Zhou Xibing
ISBN: 978-1-84464-113-0

Paths International Ltd
PO Box 4083,
Reading, RG8 8ZN,
United Kingdom

www.pathsinternational.com

Published in the United Kingdom

Lightning Source UK Ltd.
Milton Keynes UK
UKOW06f0239090115

244199UK00005B/98/P